THE PARANORMAL

MORE TRUE STORIES OF THE STRANGE AND UNUSUAL IN THE CHRISTIAN LIFE

Copyright © 2022 Richard Lewis

All rights reserved. No part of this publication may be reproduced, distributed, or transmitted in any form or by any means, including photocopying, recording, or other electronic or mechanical methods, without the prior written permission of the publisher, except in the case of brief quotations embodied in critical reviews and certain other noncommercial uses permitted by copyright law. For permission requests, write to the publisher, addressed "Attention: Permissions Coordinator," at the address below.

www.zoranpress.com

ISBN: 978-1-7356264-1-3 (print)
ISBN: 978-1-7356264-2-0 (ebook)

Author Photo: John Bohon

Ordering Information:
Special discounts are available on quantity purchases by corporations, associations, and others.
For details, contact:
Zoran Press
1465 West 184th Street, Gardena, CA 90248
To find out more about The Paranormal Christian please visit www.theparanormalchristian.com.

Scripture quotations are from The ESV® Bible (The Holy Bible, English Standard Version®), copyright © 2001 by Crossway, a publishing ministry of Good News Publishers. Used by permission. All rights reserved.
Scripture quotations marked HCSB are taken from the Holman Christian Standard Bible®, Used by Permission HCSB ©1999,2000,2002,2003,2009 Holman Bible Publishers. Holman Christian Standard Bible®, Holman CSB®, and HCSB® are federally registered trademarks of Holman Bible Publishers.
Scripture taken from the Holy Bible: International Standard Version® Release 2.0. Copyright © 1996-2013 by the ISV Foundation. Used by permission of Davidson Press, LLC. ALL RIGHTS RESERVED INTERNATIONALLY.
Scripture quotations from The Authorized (King James) Version. Rights in the Authorized Version in the United Kingdom are vested in the Crown. Reproduced by permission of the Crown's patentee, Cambridge University Press
Scripture texts in this work are taken from the New American Bible, revised edition© 2010, 1991, 1986, 1970 Confraternity of Christian Doctrine, Washington, D.C. and are used by permission of the copyright owner. All Rights Reserved. No part of the New American Bible may be reproduced in any form without permission in writing from the copyright owner.
Scripture quotations taken from the (NASB®) New American Standard Bible®, Copyright © 1960, 1971, 1977, 1995, 2020 by The Lockman Foundation. Used by permission. All rights reserved. www.lockman.org.
Scripture taken from the New Century Version®. Copyright © 2005 by Thomas Nelson. Used by permission. All rights reserved.
Zondervan is granting permission for the latest edition of the NIV text only (currently 2011.) We are not granting permission for use of the earlier editions or version of the NIV text. For more information, please visit https://www.thenivbible.com/about-the-niv/about-the-2011-edition/.
Scripture taken from the New King James Version®. Copyright © 1982 by Thomas Nelson. Used by permission. All rights reserved.
Scripture quotations are taken from the Holy Bible, New Living Translation, copyright ©1996, 2004, 2015 by Tyndale House Foundation. Used by permission of Tyndale House Publishers, Carol Stream, Illinois 60188. All rights reserved.
Scripture quotations are from New Revised Standard Version Bible, copyright © 1989 National Council of the Churches of Christ in the United States of America. Used by permission. All rights reserved worldwide.
Scripture quotations marked (YLT) are taken from the 1898 YOUNG'S LITERAL TRANSLATION OF THE HOLY BIBLE by J.N. Young, (Author of the Young's Analytical Concordance), public domain.

Strange things are happening.
You can't deny it –
Mysterious hauntings, past-life memories.
Can your dead relatives visit you?
Angeles, demons…light ships?
Things really do go bump in the night.
Are ghosts real? Do aliens exist? How about UFOs?
These are questions many Christians are asking, but the Church is reticent to answer.

As a Christian and open-minded seeker, I have set out to find those answers for you –
Through the lens of our precious faith as revealed in the Bible.
And the answers found within these pages may surprise you.
What began in Book I, will reach the culmination here in Book II.
In the pages to follow, we will examine the unusual and enigmatic, not content to simply write it all off as demons, as so many of our belief are apt to do.

The mystical goings-on in the world today simply point us to our supernatural heritage. It's time we return to the Biblical worldview of our ancestors.

In this second book, the gap between the paranormal and the Biblical is again bridged—without denying the faith, or the reality of the unknown, the strange. The paranormal.

This work will challenge you to dig deeper, with new insight.
There is much more to the story.
And in the telling, a new picture is revealed.
This is the story of you and me,
The Paranormal Christians.

BOOK II
THE QUICKENING

THE PARANORMAL

MORE TRUE STORIES OF THE STRANGE AND UNUSUAL IN THE CHRISTIAN LIFE

RICHARD D. LEWIS

This book is dedicated to Mom.
You are still the center of my universe.

And to every little child, whoever opened up a book,
or looked up into the sky,
And wondered…

And finally, to my Father and the other honored dead,
Both known and unknown.
Who come to visit in these pages.

Contents

Prologue xiii

Introduction xxiii

Chapter 1: Out-of-Body Experiences 1

Chapter 2: Spirit, Soul, Body 13

Chapter 3: The Body Temporal 19

Chapter 4: Near-Death Experiences 27

Chapter 5: On the Other Side 39

Interlude—You Can Watch Anything But Football 49

Chapter 6: After-Death Communications 61

Chapter 7: Gone Too Soon. 75

Chapter 8: 1977 83

Chapter 9: The Easter Boys 91

Chapter 10: Born Again 107

Chapter 11: The Argument for Reincarnation 121

Chapter 12: Ghosts 141

Chapter 13: Strange Encounters 155

Chapter 14: Other Hauntings 167

Chapter 15: The Ghostly Adventures of Uncle Ron and Friends . . . 183

Chapter 16: Christ the Conqueror 193

Chapter 17: UFOs: The Cosmic Conundrum 205

Chapter 18: Intelligent Design 217

Chapter 19: Air Force, NASA, and the Pentagon 227

Chapter 20: The Great Endeavor 245

Chapter 21: Nocturnal Lights and Area 51 259

Chapter 22: Classic and Ancient Encounters 283

Chapter 23: UFOs and Religion 297

Chapter 24: Disclosure 311

Chapter 25: The Fourth Kind 317

Afterword—40 Days of Testing: A Reflection 329

List of Bible Versions and Acronyms 337

Endnotes 339

"There are more things in heaven and earth, Horatio,
Than are dreamt of in your philosophy."
– Hamlet

Prologue

The Confession

The light in Pastor Michael Abram's office was growing dim, as the coming dusk slowly replaced the yellow-orange sunset outside, transforming the sky into a dark blue and soon-to-be-black nightfall.

It was October 2017, and even in the dimly lit office, I could see Pastor's eyes staring intently, piercing to my soul. Those eyes were alight with the flames of God, full of concern and compassion.

In previous meetings, we discussed my future—the possibility of my becoming a pastor like him someday. We even interviewed together with the program director of the Lutheran Church's Cross-Cultural Ministry program at Concordia, Irvine. I thought it was going to be a slam-dunk.

Pastor Michael and I had thoughtfully planned an outreach ministry program that would benefit the culturally diverse, mostly unchurched, members of the local community. The initiative would help them, my church, and me as well. I would simultaneously fulfill my graduate studies, and upon successful completion of my cross-cultural outreach, become an ordained minister in the Lutheran Church Missouri Synod.

I spent months filling out tedious application materials, written questionnaires, some of them fairly intrusive, and other documentation—not to mention all the meetings and the formal interview—but it all came crashing down. The Lord seemed to have shut the door.

Pastor Michael knew the circumstances surrounding my divorce. I had told him all the facts. But now, here I was back in his office re-telling him everything—only this time, I was confessing. This time, I placed the blame squarely where it belonged—right on me.

Michael listened, eyes blazing—but patient, waiting. Finally, I stopped talking and took a deep breath.

"You have a great Sin," Pastor Michael said flatly. "It is a sin that will haunt you the rest of your life. There are just some sins that change everything. They follow you forever."

Guilt washed over me for a moment, a feeling of hopelessness, until Michael leaned forward.

"I have sins like that in my life too," he said softly. "It's just something you live with."

"Like Paul's Thorn in the Flesh?" I asked.

"Yes!" Pastor said. But then he recited the rest of the scriptural quote, saying, "My grace is sufficient for you."

"Now," Pastor Michael continued, "I have a Word from the Lord. I am going to speak prophesy over you." He paused for a moment. Gathered his thoughts. Closed his eyes.

"I feel that…God is telling me…He wants you to spend more time with Him, time alone with Him. He wants you to get closer to Him. Over time He will reveal His Will to you. And after a time, yes…I think…He *will* use you to minister to others. But right now… You have your own demons."

Then we prayed.

November 27, 2017, around 2:00 a.m. I stare up at a starry, North Carolina sky, alone with my thoughts, alone with God. It was 31 degrees Fahrenheit, a chilly departure from the record 90-degree heat I experienced just days earlier in Los Angeles.

Prologue

I pulled the hood of my winter jacket over my head and blew out cigar smoke, which wafted magically up into the pre-dawn air, intermingled with the steam of my own breath.

My thoughts were swirling like the smoke—manic, alternating between prayers for my cousin Kelly, only 52 and dying of cancer, and unbelief at having just attended the funeral for his 49-year-old brother, Marty, who had recently died in an unfortunate accident.

My thoughts were jumping all around. Such unrest is what can happen when you finally spend time alone following tumultuous events, especially once you completely get away from it all.

Things emerge that you previously repressed: thoughts of family, regrets, that crazy Rage Against the Machine's song stuck in my head. Oh! And that problem employee at the office. Should I write him up? Anger flashes over me… Then repentance. Forgiveness.

God…help me, I thought.

Stargazing now…puffs of cigar smoke cleared away to reveal the constellation Orion. The night sky over Kernersville is not great, but it's definitely better than L.A.'s.

I look over, far to the right and see Cygnus the Swan. Turning back and above, I catch a glimpse of Auriga, his shape looking suspiciously more to me like a scorpion's tail than a charioteer—standing above and to the right of Orion—threatening even? Perhaps he is in cahoots with Scorpius in the conspiracy against Orion. Of course, the mighty scorpion will have to wait until summer to take over the night sky.

To the right, I see the Pleiades star cluster, the Seven Sisters—celestial hotties. Squinting, I can barely make out the red-orange tint of the giant star Aldebaran in the constellation Taurus—the bull's blazing eye, not unlike Pastor Michael's before.

My thoughts turn to another Taurus—my first wife, Susan.

Susan…

You should have listened to your parents' warning about me, I thought.

Just then, I hear a small boom as a meteor streaks across the night sky, right through the constellation Orion. A sign, perhaps. But what does it mean?

Then I thought about those silly little cousins. I just met them that afternoon during lunch at my Aunt Rita and Uncle Maynard's house following Marty's funeral—second cousins, daughters and son of my and Marty's cousin, Amber. The kids dragged me outside where we were enjoying the last of a cool, autumn day.

There was nine-year-old Ivey, leader of the pack—skinny and blonde and outspoken—her bendy frame growing just as her namesake suggests.

"The other kids make fun of us because we live in a trailer park," she said.

"Don't you let them get to you," I replied. "I grew up in trailer parks too, and now I have a big house in California."

Then seven-year-old Austin urged me to get back to the game of whiffle-ball scoop we had been playing. He looked irresistibly cute in his newsboy hat, formerly mine, currently his, now framing rounded cheeks, ruddy from the cool, dusk air. I could smell the Carolina pine trees all around us. Madison, North Carolina, is one of those places where nature speaks through the wind in the trees.

Later, I would learn that Cousin Kelly had been watching us through the living room window, smiling that big smile he always had, even at the end. I wonder if Kelly was pondering how much time he had left to play with the kids—or perhaps he was thinking of the times when he, I, and Cousin Marty were playing outside when we were kids, along with Cousin Kim and Uncle Bru. Or maybe he was just grinning at the site of me trying to keep up with the little balls of energy, the next generation of cousins.

"Will you buy me an iPhone?" Little Austin asked. The kids had been taking selfies with my mobile.

The littlest of them all, tiny six-year-old Hope, pulled on my hand.

"Let's go to the trail," she urged. She had Austin's chubby cheeks, but was not blonde and blue-eyed like her brother and sister. Hope was also slightly tanner than they were, perhaps inheriting less of her dad's pale Irish skin in favor of the Cherokee hue from her mother's side.

Hope's auburn hair tousled about as her big brown eyes begged for attention.

"Pick me up," she said.

I lifted her up. Her arms were short but stout. I could feel a slight choke as she squeezed my neck and kissed my cheek. Hope was my favorite sprite of them all.

"Austin and me are gettin' baptized in January," Ivey said, a slight southern drawl coming through as she stared up at us.

"What about Hope?" I asked.

"No, she's not saved yet."

Somehow we had gotten onto the topic of heaven.

"They have everything in heaven," said Ivey. "Except sin."

"Close your eyes!" yelled Hope, giggling, hopping back down and pulling me along. Austin grabbed my other hand, and Ivey led the way as they guided me toward the woods.

"He's cheating!" said Hope. "Close your eyes, Rich!"

I closed them.

The chilly autumn breeze now kissed my cheeks and started whistling in my half-frozen ears as I was whisked off toward the woods, trusting my fate to three children who had no idea what an arthritic knee felt like.

Nonetheless, I surrendered my fate to those laughing, giggling kids—and I did not so much as stub a toe or even crackle a branch. They were like three fairies buzzing around my ears, leaves crunching beneath our feet. I must say it felt like flying as we zoomed along.

"We're here!" announced Hope. The trail led us to a creek. Fall leaves were scattered everywhere as day was turning to night, and it was time to head home.

On our way back to Aunt Rita's house, Hope asked me to pick her up again.

"Look, there's the moon!" she shouted. It was a big half-crescent. "Do you have the same color moon as ours (California versus Carolina)?

Is yours blue?"

"Our moon," I answered, "looks the same as yours. So, when you look up at your moon, know that I will be looking up at the same moon."

Ivey and Hope both sent me off that night with drawings. Ivey's was of a large tree perched by a tiny cardinal, the North Carolina state bird. Hope's was a picture of her and me, with the caption, "I love you."

Looking up at the stars now, I thought about the pure love that came so easily from those children.

"Truly I tell you," Jesus said in Matthew 18, "unless you change and become like little children, you will never enter the kingdom of heaven. Therefore, whoever takes the lowly position of this child is the greatest in the kingdom of heaven."

"God, help me to love like that," I prayed. "Help me to love more."

Suddenly, I feared the energy drain that comes from loving others.

"But help me not to give out too much love."

To my surprise, God *answered* me. I heard His voice so clearly. It was powerful, a masculine voice, full of resonance and energy, yet calm and soothing.

"You can never give out too much love, my son," He said.

BOOK II

The Quickening

The following work represents the author's personal views and are not necessarily those of the DoD, the U.S. Air Force, or the U.S. Space Force.

Introduction

Some forty years before that afternoon in Pastor Michael's office, I had watched Steven Spielberg's *Close Encounters of the Third Kind* from the backseat of my stepdad's Ford Thunderbird, eagerly peering between James' and Mom's silhouetted heads. Spilling the buttered popcorn bucket and ruining James' white pants was a mistake that would soon be forgiven. How could I not be distracted? The images of mysterious alien figures, the ominous Devil's Tower, and the giant mothership with flashing colored lights, and eerie, synthesized-symphonic tones all would leave an indelible mark on our collective memories, long after the popcorn spill.

I was interested in UFOs and the mysteries of the universe long before that night, but even more so, after watching the film. I would go on to eagerly read the mass-market paperback *Situation Red: The UFO siege* released in 1978. The well-researched book, written by the now departed Leonard H. Stringfield, was captivating.

I kept my nose buried in that book, barely coming up for air, while reading it from a front booth at the Steak and Egg diner on Summit Avenue, in Greensboro, North Carolina, where my mom worked third shift as a waitress. She would bring me coffee with extra cream and sugar plus steak and egg Jr. platters, as I passed the time waiting on her to get off work.

My step-dad James would join me in the booth as I sipped my

warm, beige beverage. He nodded at the book. "What does he say about it, Richard?" He suspected the government knew more about the phenomena than we were being told.

That same year, I read Jay Anson's chilling *Amityville Horror* on the balcony walkway outside the Travelodge Motel in downtown Greensboro, my childhood home. By 1978, when I was nine, I had absorbed probably hundreds of books and TV shows on astronomy, science fiction, and the paranormal.

I spent summer nights staring up at a starry sky, in rural Summerfield, North Carolina, my other childhood home, staying with my dad and stepmom, Shirley. I spent hours observing the moon and stars with my dad's binoculars. I learned to spot planets and constellations, but I didn't see a UFO until many years later. And that only truly unexplainable, unmistakable, cosmic-level encounter occurred only once, many decades later, starwatching under a desert sky, thousands of miles away.

In my first book, *The Paranormal Christian*, I discussed contact with strange beings such as angels and demons. I described paranormal encounters and examined various psychic phenomena. Now, here in Book II, we will journey even further beyond to find out what happens to us outside the body, looking at the near-death experience and after-death communications. We will also examine ghosts, consider other mysterious hauntings, and finally, analyze UFOs and the abduction phenomena.

The universe, both seen and unseen, may be a lot more diverse than many realize. But that should come as no surprise. Just take a look at the vast diversity in the natural world: from the macro to the micro to the subatomic. I propose this cornucopia of complexity demonstrates the creative majesty and glory of our God and the Lord Jesus Christ, "the firstborn over all creation." Through whom "all things were created: things in heaven and on earth, visible and invisible" (Colossians 1:15-16, NIV).

All of it is a testament to the amazing wonder that is His creation.

As you embark on this journey with me, I trust you will come to a greater understanding that we really do live in a wondrous universe, orchestrated by divine intention—an almost indescribably vast aggregate of cosmic forces, laws, and nature, with amazing galactic wonder and beauty—that seamlessly blends with the mysterious forces of an unseen universe. And it all somehow emanates from a great, cosmic, infinite being, of power and love, and personal intent and concern, that resonates all the way down to you and me, and to every living creature on Earth.

Throughout this book, you will find many references to the Holy Scriptures. I am no theologian. I am simply a Christian seeker and lifelong student of the Bible. I believe everything the Bible says is true. I hold to the centrality of Christ and honor the traditional confessions of the Church. But some of my conclusions may not be in accordance with the opinions of many in mainstream Christianity. Some of the things I have to say may even stir up controversy in the Church, and that is okay. The truth of the Scripture never changes, but our understanding of the Bible does evolve and expand as our awareness grows. And sometimes, we find our current thinking is actually not in accord with the ancient writers, even though modern theologians tell us differently. The writers of the Bible had a supernatural worldview. That context of their testimony should not only be understood but adopted by modern readers as well, especially those of us who call ourselves Christians.

Do you have questions without answers? Do you wonder what happens when we die? Can our dead relatives visit us? Are UFOs real? These are questions many Christians are asking.

The church is oft ready to eschew such questions. Shut them down. Theologians speak against such things in absolutes—but maybe the answers aren't always so clear cut. Maybe there is more room in the Bible and our faith for the unexplained than they dare to admit. Maybe it all correlates, rather than contradicts, the witness of Scripture.

Let me ask you a question: Are you willing to consider new possibilities? If you are open to the idea that many of our beliefs and traditions are simply constructs—a 'Matrix' if you will, holding the mind captive—then keep reading.

It's time to take the red pill, Neo.
You have questions? I did too.
Keep reading.
The answers are coming.

I know a man in Christ who fourteen years ago was caught up to the third heaven—whether in the body or out of the body I do not know.
2 Corinthians 12:2
Holy Bible, English Standard Version (ESV)

Chapter 1

Out-of-Body Experiences

Many Christians shy away from the topic of out-of-body experiences, or OBEs, and I can understand why. Although OBEs point to the existence of an afterlife, some researchers in the field and experiencers challenge the Christian worldview, making assertions that question the very foundations of our beliefs. Don't let them scare you.

I find the subject very compelling, and in the final analysis, encouraging. The mounting evidence suggests out-of-body experiences do happen. This supports the non-materialistic worldview, which correlates to the Biblical concept of life after death.

Studies have revealed most Americans, even those who are not religious, believe in life after death. "Americans' belief in an afterlife is very stable across the decades, showing little variability since 1944."[1]

Most Americans believe in the hereafter, especially heaven—but many believe in hell too. Belief in the afterlife is widely seen regardless of religious preference and among those with no preference at all, even those who don't believe in God.[2]

As to the near-death experience, evidence is mounting, with scores of people coming forward claiming to have experienced and returned from a journey outside their physical form. Such people report seeing and hearing things while outside the body, things that would have been impossible for them to know in an unresponsive, lifeless state. Here are some of the more compelling examples.

Pam Reynolds

Perhaps the most remarkable example of a near-death experience with strong evidentiary support is the 1991 case of singer-songwriter Pam Reynolds. According to numerous sources, Reynolds had a dangerous aneurysm, which was threatening her life.[3] The size and location of the anomaly meant it was not treatable with standard brain surgery.

Reynolds' only hope was a daring medical procedure that would drop her body temperature to 60 degrees, stop the heart, drain all the blood from her head, and render the woman brain dead, where all brain wave activity would cease.[4]

This pioneering surgery was the only way to remove the aneurysm without permanently killing Reynolds; but, in order to pull off the procedure, the doctors had to temporarily kill her, then bring her back. Indeed, Pam Reynolds was rendered clinically dead then brought back to life by doctors following the operation, which successfully removed the aneurysm.

Following the procedure performed by Dr. Robert Spetzler at the Barrow Neurological Institute in Phoenix, Arizona, Reynolds reported a very descriptive near-death experience. She experienced the classically reported occurrence of floating above her body. She was also able to accurately report details of the surgery and things that were said in the room while she was clinically dead: sights and sounds that her body was physically incapable of receiving at the time.

Not only was she unconscious during the procedure, Reynolds' eyes were taped shut and her ears were plugged with speakers, which emitted clicking sounds to confirm her brain was in flatline. She correctly reported the surgery room chatter, for example, as well as discussion concerning her small veins and arteries, which had apparently complicated the procedure. Reynolds even described the tools used during the operation!

Shoe on a Ledge

Another widely reported case is that of a woman named Maria, a migrant worker who was visiting friends in Seattle, Washington, when she suffered a heart attack and was admitted to Harborview Hospital.[5]

Maria suffered cardiac arrest a few days after being admitted to Harborview, but was quickly resuscitated by hospital staff. Maria experienced a vividly lucid near-death experience (NDE), where she reported seeing a shoe on a third-story ledge on the north side of the building.

Maria relayed this observation to Kimberly Clark, a critical care social worker, who retrieved the shoe. Incredibly, Maria described detailed features such as the shoelace being underneath the heel and the little toe area being worn. Clark documented this incident, noting the only way for Maria to have seen the shoe was to have been floating outside at eye level with the shoe, hovering right next to it.[6]

Still, amazing as those stories are, not all out of body experiences involve near-death. Sometimes the spirit will travel during sleep. I remember very clearly having an OBE when I was about six years old.

The Ambulance Drove Through Me

I was standing in the middle of East Market Street, in Greensboro, North Carolina. It was night. As I looked around, I could see the buildings and homes in the surrounding neighborhood. To my left was my Grandma Clara's house. Then, off in the distance, I heard the scream of a siren. I looked ahead and saw an ambulance barreling toward me. The vehicle grew in size, its flashing red lights reflecting off the surrounding buildings. Before I could move, the ambulance *drove right through me* and kept on going west, screaming down the road toward downtown Greensboro. I awoke and sat straight up in bed in my darkened room on Pine Street not far from where my Grandma lived, the faint sound of the siren trailing off in the distance.

I believe OBEs happen more often than people think, usually while we are sleeping. You know that feeling you get as you are drifting off to sleep, when you feel as though you are falling suddenly and you jerk awake? That is the feeling of the spirit body disengaging as you are dozing off, then suddenly re-entering the physical body, startling you awake.

In other cases, you might experience moments of lucidity during sleep in which you find yourself visiting different communities and the people seem far too real. You might even feel and experience their thoughts about you. Then there are those moments where you find yourself flying, and you are conscious it is happening, even though you are sleeping. One must give such ideas and experiences some thought.

Apostle Paul's Experience

Consider for a moment these concepts in the light of Scripture. Paul, for one, records experiencing what sounds like it must have been an OBE, although the Apostle said he was not sure whether he was in the body or not.

> I was caught up to the third heaven fourteen years ago. Whether I was in my body or out of my body, I don't know—only God knows. Yes, only God knows whether I was in my body or outside my body. But I do know that I was caught up to paradise and heard things so astounding that they cannot be expressed in words, things no human is allowed to tell. (2 Corinthians 12:2-4, NLT)

"That part really interests me," says Luis Minero, author of the 2012 book *Demystifying the Out-of-Body Experience: A Practical Manual for Exploration and Personal Evolution*.

"The part about sounds that cannot be expressed. That is what we find when we return from an OBE."

Minero states the information received out of body is too vast to be stored in the physical brain. "It doesn't fit into the hard disc," he says, smiling and pointing to his head.

Is it so hard to believe? Imagine visiting heaven and returning. The human mind is incapable of downloading the information from that dimension—we don't have the hardware. "I declare to you, brothers and sisters, that flesh and blood cannot inherit the kingdom of God…" (1 Corinthians 15:50, NIV).

This is why those who have had a vision of heaven can only describe it in terms such as "pearly gates" and "streets of gold."

"And the twelve gates were twelve pearls, each of the gates made of a single pearl, and the street of the city was pure gold, like transparent glass" (Revelation 21:21, ESV).

Luis Minero, OBE Researcher

Luis Minero is a tall, handsome man—charismatic, intelligent and well-spoken—with an absorbing dialect, not unlike the great Mexican actor and inseparable voice of my childhood, Ricardo Montalbán. Alert but relaxed, Minero radiates poise, confidence, and charm.

Although thin, he is a solid gent, athletic even, in his dark slacks and salmon-colored dress shirt neatly tucked in, implying that here is a man who takes care of his physical body as well as the spiritual one.

Mr. Minero accepted my request for an interview without hesitation, which took place in August 2014, at the International Academy of Consciousness (IAC), Los Angeles center, in Culver City, California. Minero was very calm and composed during the interview; so, it was clear from the outset that this sort of thing was nothing new to one of the world's leading researchers into the OBE phenomenon.

Minero is the former director of IAC's California Office, where he served as the president of IAC globally until 2018. A worldwide organization, IAC seeks to study the out of body experience from a scientific, rather than religious, perspective.

Minero does not profess any religious affiliation. Although raised a Catholic, he considers himself to be a spiritual humanist. So, I asked him about the cases of near-death experiences where people report seeing Jesus.

"I think in most cases they are not [seeing Jesus]," says Minero. It might be. Some could be; but really, most of the time, they saw energy and they say, 'I saw Jesus.' Maybe it was a guide."

In his book, *Demystifying the Out-of-Body Experience*, Minero talks about guides, spiritual beings that he says occupy the astral plane of existence. "They help us," he says. The guides Minero describes sound a lot like what we Christians call angels.

"What do these guides look like?" I asked.

"A silhouette of light. Sometimes a ball of energy," he answered. "They appear in different dimensions. Sometimes they appear more clear than others, depending on how many dimensions are in between." Minero says the closer you are to the dimension of the being whom you encounter, good or bad, the more clear they will be.

"It is a real person," Minero insists, but says it may or may not be the actual Jesus.

Wixon's Life Review

Tom Wixon was the chief video engineer at the television production center at Los Angeles Air Force Base between 2010 and 2016. Wixon had an impressive career in television. He performed engineering design around the Los Angeles area for decades, having worked on classic TV shows like *The Twilight Zone* and *Star Trek*. He is also the inventor of several product innovations in the film and television industry and holds various patents in TV engineering design.

An enigmatic yet affable man, Wixon caught me in my office at the Air Force base after hours on many occasions where I worked as the chief of multimedia services.

A Vietnam vet, Tom was injured by a land mine while deployed as an Army airborne radio technician during the war. His family is gifted with good genetics. His mother lived to age 103, and his father passed away in 2014 at the incredible age of 108. Tom is now in his 80s and has cheated death more than once. He injured his eye in a private airplane crash and smashed his foot in a parachute jump accident a few years back, finally forcing the wily rascal to slow down.

Tom cornered me in my office late one night, and told me the story of how he was involved in a horrific car crash years ago where he went through a near-death experience.

"I don't tell many people about this," he started. "Because they would think I'm crazy."

"Go ahead," I replied. "No judgment here. My office is a 'free speech' zone."

Tom chuckled. Then looked up at me. His eyes were squinting, now serious.

"I met this…being," Tom said. He described the entity as a being of light. "I do not know who this being was, but to me, it was Jesus." Tom's describing a being of light sounded a lot like what Minero spoke about.

Tom says the being he took as Jesus showed him a review of his life. The main thing Tom said he realized during the interaction is the importance of how we treat other people. I am sure it would be a painful realization to us—when the veil of this earthly life with all its many distractions is lifted—if we cross over with regrets in how we treated others, especially if our life were truly over and we could not return. At least the near-death experiencers get to come back and change things.

Embraced by the Light

This revelation on the importance of how we treat others is echoed by Betty J. Eadie, author of the bestselling 1992 book, *Embraced by the Light*. Eadie reported a near-death experience following surgery November 19, 1973 in which she also says she met Jesus.

When in the presence of the Savior, I felt his unending love, and I will never forget the sincerity and affection in his loving voice… "Above all else, love one another…" were his parting words…[7]

Tom said he felt guilty for things he had done, but the being of light would tell him, "Many people make that mistake."

Tom also said the being had a loving disposition, which does sound a lot like Jesus. Tom said this Jesus showed him his wrongs, but did so in a positive, encouraging way.

Visitation by Three Beings

Author Mark Rickert had a childhood filled with trauma. He burned down his family's house when he was only 14. No one died—even the family dog made it out alive—but there was no insurance, so the Rickerts' lost everything. Mark's mom and dad divorced, and the boy even contemplated suicide.

Mark relayed this story to me on November 16, 2018 when we were lingering in the hallways after class at the Defense Information School. But you can also read about it in the intro to his 2014 supernatural horror/thriller, *The Tone Poet*. One thing he does not mention in the book is this: when things seemed their darkest, Mark had an out-of-body experience one afternoon while he was meditating.

"I was approached by three beings," Mark said.

He describes them as beings of light. He says they each had a glowing head and silhouette form for a body. He says they helped him to regain focus. Following this experience, Mark started spending time at church and gave his life to Jesus Christ. I believe the beings Mark encountered were angels.

Mark went on to become a successful writer, journalist, and leader in the military public affairs community. The ghosts of the past still haunt Mark at times, but with Christ at the center, I know he will find peace.

A Higher Perspective

During his near-death experience, Tom Wixon says he got to experience his interactions with others during his lifetime from a higher perspective—outside of himself. Apparently in that state, you perceive the exchanges with others as you lived them, but also as a third party—observing and understanding, sensing and grasping the thoughts and feelings of both parties. This theme is a common one in the literature, where people in an NDE are removed from the limitations of their ego-self, to see their interactions differently, understanding fully the internal turmoil experienced from the other person's point of view. It can be a troubling realization.

In Book I, I detailed how I studied under Dr. Doreen Virtue in 2003. Dr. Virtue teaches that you actually *feel* the pain you have caused others during your life review, as you experience *everything* you ever did to them from their perspective. Imagine the implications for those who have lived a life of mistreating others. The thought should cause any rational person to shudder, or at the very least, pause and reflect upon how they treat other people.

As the Scriptures say, "So then, each of us will give an account of ourselves to God" (Romans 14:12, NIV). That includes even our idle words. As Jesus said, "I tell you that on the day of judgment, people will have to account for every careless word they speak" (Matthew 12:36, HCSB). "For we must all appear before the judgment seat of Christ, so that each of us may receive what is due us for the things done while in the body, whether good or bad" (2 Corinthians 5:10, NIV).

Still, it was comforting to hear that although the being Tom Wixon described as Jesus showed Tom where he had gone astray, the being did so in a positive way. As Tom apologized for his wrongs, the being encouraged him, "Many people make that mistake."

The quiet in my office was calm and peaceful. A moment of serenity in what, during the day, was often filled with frenetic goings on and Tom fretting over this technical issue or that. But this silence was something different. Tom just looked me in the eyes and smiled.

Whether or not the being Tom encountered really was Jesus is hard to say. And whether or not this is how our final judgment will be rendered, we really don't know. After all, the near-death experiencer does return to life. The NDE may or may not correlate with the actual death experience. We don't know. But I have no doubt that Tom really believes in the experience he described, and no matter how many years the Lord continues to bless him with, Tom has a comfort in knowing what to expect on the other side.

Traditional Christianity teaches there will be a final judgement, the so-called "Great White Throne Judgement" of Revelation 20 which occurs at the end of the age. This decisive event is where all people will be judged by God for our works, both good and bad. Many Christians believe only the reprobate, or those who reject Jesus Christ will be judged—but the Scriptures are clear—*all* people will be judged.

> And I saw the dead, great and small, standing before the throne, and books were opened. Then another book was opened, which is the Book of Life. And the dead were judged by what was written in the books, according to what they had done. And the sea gave up the dead who were in it, Death and Hades gave up the dead who were in them, and they were judged, each one of them, according to what they had done. (Revelation 20:12-13, ESV)

The difference though, for the believer is our misdeeds will be considered as forgiven sins—covered by the blood of our savior Jesus Christ.

"Whoever believes in him is not condemned, but whoever does not believe stands condemned already because they have not believed in the name of God's one and only Son" (John 3:18, NIV).

As to Luis Minero, he does not agree with the traditional Christian view of the judgment day as a separation of the righteous from the unrighteous (Matthew 25:31-46). He says there *is* a life review, but it is constructive, not a negative thing.

"Take, for example, being in school and learning math," offers Minero. "Let's say we learn long division. They don't punish you if you don't learn it."

"You don't know the math teachers I had," I replied.

Minero laughs at my joke.

Still, the judgement does not sound like a negative thing for those who believe in Jesus. And only those who reject God will be spurned. "For the grace of God has appeared that offers salvation to all people" (Titus 2:11).

Soteriology aside, having someone in front of me who regularly travels outside the body, I could not help but indulge a few other curiosities with Mr. Minero.

"When does the spirit attach to the body?" I asked.

"At conception," Minero replies. In that, he aligns with mainstream Christianity.

The researcher goes on to compare our existence in this world to the James Cameron movie *Avatar* (2009). Our spirits apparently somehow activate and operate this machine, our avatar, called the human body.

That view is surprisingly congruous with the Bible teaching on the three parts of man: spirit, soul, body (1 Thessalonians 5:23).

Chapter 2

Spirit, Soul, Body

Before we delve into the question of beginnings—concerning just when the immortal human spirit attaches to the body—let's take a moment to consider the difference between spirit and soul. First of all, the church has never made a clear delineation between spirit and soul, and the church fathers have often used the terms interchangeably. But the Bible does make a distinction.

The Apostle Paul spoke about it like this: "Now may the God of peace himself sanctify you completely, and may your whole spirit and soul and body be kept blameless at the coming of our Lord Jesus Christ" (1 Thessalonians 5:23, ESV). Some take this Scripture to imply a Trinitarian or tripartite view of humanity, correlated with God's triune nature as Father (soul), Son (body), Spirit (spirit).[8]

It stands to reason that man would be triune in nature, just like God. After all, humans are made in God's image. "Then God said, 'Let us make man in our image, after our likeness'" (Genesis 1:26, ESV).

I offer it can be understood like this: the spirit is the immortal essence of man when separated from the body. Soul is the consciousness incarnate in the physical joining of mind, body, and spirit. It is how we move in sentience through life's journey in the body. The body is simply the body, and when our life ebbs away, the body is no longer a body, but a corpse.

That is not to say the spirit does not have consciousness; indeed it does, as the OBE, NDE, and Biblical accounts indicate. The Apostle's words even illustrate the order of spiritual descent to the body—first spirit, then soul, then body. Although we shed this earthly body at death, at some point, God will re-join our spirit to a glorified body (1 Corinthians 15:35-44).

Many believe that God creates the spirit at conception. But could it really be true?

A woman who is of childbearing age expels many, if not most, of her fertilized eggs. They simply do not attach to the uterine wall. For example, a study published in the *New England Journal of Medicine* in 1999 gleaned very precise information about when pregnancy actually occurs.

The researchers say that as a natural protective mechanism, the uterus tends to reject fertilized eggs that take too long to adhere to the lining because they may be less fit. On day 11, more than 50 percent of pregnancies fail and on day 12, that number jumps to over 80 percent![9]

Also, an online University of California San Francisco article titled, "Conception: How it Works" says, "In nature, 50 percent of all fertilized eggs are lost before a woman's missed menses."[10]

A Stanford University Medical Center Study went even further to state, "Two-thirds of all human embryos fail to develop successfully."[11] This study is also cited in the *Science Daily* article titled, "Which fertilized eggs will become healthy human fetuses? Researchers predict with 93% accuracy."[12]

Also, as noted in the cheekily titled but unmistakably astute Reason.com article by Ronald Bailey, "Is Heaven Populated Chiefly by the Souls of Embryos?"

> [B]etween 60 and 80 percent of all naturally conceived embryos are simply flushed out in women's normal menstrual

flows unnoticed. This is not miscarriage we're talking about. The women and their husbands or partners never even know that conception has taken place.[13]

As most fertilized eggs never get the chance to develop, is it not strange to think of all those millions—even billions—of conceptions ending up as discarnate spirits in heaven?

Trying to correlate the research with the traditional Christian viewpoint here is very hard to do. These scientifically verified statistics would mean that most humans, up to two-thirds, never get the chance to live as they will be expelled from their mothers before ever getting a shot at life. This rigidity is even more troublesome if you hold to the traditional Christian viewpoint that reincarnation is not valid. At least with reincarnation, if human life truly does begin at conception, but something happens and the embryo does not attach to the uterus, then perhaps the spirit would get another try at a physical life later on. But for that human life to simply be over—that just does not make sense.

What about abortion?

Abortion is an uncomfortable topic in almost any context, but in a discussion of consciousness outside the body, and life after death, I think it only pertinent to discuss life before birth.

Whether or not triune human life—body, soul, and spirit—begins at conception, or sometime after conception, please do not take this discussion as an argument or justification for abortion, which involves deliberately removing a baby that has implanted in its mother's uterus. I do not understand how anyone who holds to Christian ideals or even the ideals of our nation can remain silent about abortion. A cursory view of our Declaration of Independence makes the point clear "that all men [people] are created equal, that they are endowed by their Creator with certain unalienable Rights, that among these are Life…"[14]

And the Bible is far from silent on the sanctity of life in the womb. "Thus says the Lord who made you, who formed you from the womb and will help you…" (Isaiah 44:2, ESV).

Although I think abortion is wrong, I do not presume to judge any woman who has ever made such a difficult decision. Only God can judge us for our sins, and the Scriptures teach us there is no sin so great that God cannot forgive it. He is a God of love and forgiveness.

"If we confess our sins, he is faithful and just to forgive us our sins and to cleanse us from all unrighteousness" (1 John 1:9, ESV).

Of course, that does not mean we should sin willfully knowing God will forgive us after the fact. To the future mom contemplating abortion, I would say this: please don't do it. Trust in God. He will make a way for you and your child in this difficult time.

To the woman who took the other route, I say this: God still loves you and He will forgive you. "If we confess our sins, he is faithful and just and will forgive us our sins and purify us from all unrighteousness" (1 John 1:9, NIV). Just look at how lovingly Jesus treated the woman caught in adultery.

The religious leaders brought the woman to Jesus, claiming that by the Law of Moses she should be stoned—the death penalty. They said this trying to trap Jesus. If He agreed they should stone her, He would seem cruel. If He showed mercy, they could accuse him of violating the religious laws. But Jesus knew their hearts and so He told them, "Let him who is without sin among you be the first to throw a stone at her" (John 8:7, ESV). One by one the men were shamed into leaving, beginning with the older ones first, until the woman was left alone with the Lord.

> He said to her, "Woman, where are those accusers of yours? Has no one condemned you?" She said, "No one, Lord." And Jesus said to her, "Neither do I condemn you; go and sin no more." (John 8:10-11, NKJV)

So the Lord forgives, but He also asks us to repent and turn from our sins.

The Old Testament Scripture actually addresses the matter of harming a pregnant woman and her unborn child.

> If men fight, and hurt a woman with child, so that she gives birth prematurely, yet no harm follows, he shall surely be punished accordingly as the woman's husband imposes on him; and he shall pay as the judges *determine*. But if *any* harm follows, then you shall give life for life… (Exodus 21:22-23, NKJV)

The NIV says it like this:

> If people are fighting and hit a pregnant woman and she gives birth prematurely but there is no serious injury, the offender must be fined whatever the woman's husband demands and the court allows. But if there is serious injury, you are to take life for life… (Exodus 21:22-23)

I read this to mean the harm or loss of life could apply to either mother *or* child (or both).

Personally, I believe sentience starts in the womb, long before that first breath. But does it really matter exactly when the soul is formed?

No matter what your views on abortion are, it cannot be denied that the unborn is a living being, which abortion kills; a being that, if left uninterrupted, will go on to have a future life. As King David said:

> For you formed my inward parts;
> You knitted me together in my mother's womb.
> I praise you, for I am fearfully and wonderfully made.
> Wonderful are your works;
> My soul knows it very well.
> My frame was not hidden from you,
> When I was being made in secret,
> Intricately woven in the depths of the earth.
> Your eyes saw my unformed substance;
> In your book were written, every one of them,
> The days that were formed for me,

> When as yet there was none of them.
> - Psalm 139:13-16, ESV

And as the Lord told Jeremiah, "Before I formed you in the womb I knew you, and before you were born I consecrated you; I appointed you a prophet to the nations" (Jeremiah 1:5, ESV).

We don't really know for sure when the spirit forms or joins the body. Some say the spirit starts forming or attaches at conception. I would propose that once the fertilized egg attaches to the uterine wall, that is a huge demarcation line for human life. The embryo has implanted in the uterus. The journey of life has begun in earnest.

Chapter 3

The Body Temporal

The Apostle Paul compared the physical body to a tent. It will eventually be taken down when we die and our spirit leaves the body (2 Corinthians 5). This understanding first became real to me as I gazed down at my Grandpa Noah's body at his wake in 2005. It was like I was staring at an artificial reproduction that looked like my grandpa, but Grandpa Noah was not there. He was long gone.

I remember sharing this observation later with my Stepdad James. James was quick to offer how a corpse looks like wax figure. I compared it to a mannequin. The body houses the spirit, but only for a time.

The body is us when we are alive—or rather, it is a part of us. We are fused to it as one (body, soul, spirit). We animate the body, like an incredibly sophisticated marionette.

A crude but apt comparison comes to us in the way of certain animals, reptiles for example, like snakes. When snakes molt and shed their outgrown skin, what is left behind looks like a snake, but the snake is obviously gone. The same happens when we outgrow or outlive our worn-out bodies. What is left behind resembles the person, but as in the example of the snake above, you can instinctively tell is just a shell—the person is long gone.

One might think of the human body as a life-support system for the spirit to dwell physically in this earthly realm. Our spirit operates in the physical body and through it, interfaces with this physical reality. The body is our "earth suit," as my Christian friend Juan Hinojosa once said to me.

Juan's example of the body having the relationship to our spirit, in the same way a spacesuit is related to a man on the moon, is easy to visualize. Just imagine the human being inside the spacesuit as the spirit inside a man—but I think Minero's comparison to *Avatar* is probably even closer to reality.

Here is an example from Scripture that provides a metaphor on how the spirit is tethered to the body until death by the "silver cord."

> Remember him—before the silver cord is severed,
> And the golden bowl is broken;
> Before the pitcher is shattered at the spring,
> And the wheel broken at the well,
> And the dust returns to the ground it came from,
> And the spirit returns to God who gave it.
> - Ecclesiastes 12:6-7, NIV

In relation to the heavenly or spiritual realms, the spirit must be a linked projection, as in the film *The Matrix* (1999), which is a great allegory not only for our spirit indwelling this earthly plain or "matrix," but also in describing our struggle against the negative entities or "agents" while we fight for the lives of our fellow humans who are not yet unplugged (a metaphor of the unsaved).[15]

The Matrix even has a Satan, "Agent Smith"; a Mary Magdalene, "Trinity"; a John the Baptist, "Morpheus"; a Judas, "Cypher"; and a Christ figure, "Neo," or as they say in the film, "The One." Neo is even resurrected from the dead to be the savior of mankind!

So clear is the gospel message ingrained in this and other popular cinema, I have begun to think maybe God implants His messages in these films to reach people, perhaps without the filmmakers even realizing it!

Desert of the Real

But in the world we inhabit, this "desert of the real," maybe it is more like the physical body that is actually the projection.

As Morpheus said to Neo, "Your mind makes it real."

"If you're killed in the matrix, you die here?" asked Neo.

"The body cannot live without the mind," Morpheus replies. And who could forget his trippy line, "Do you think that's air you're breathing now?"

Of course, the physical has substance. Matter is real. Or is it? In his classic 1991 work, *The Holographic Universe*, Michael Talbot reveals how physicists marvel at the strange nature of reality at the subatomic level.

Although an electron can sometimes behave as if it were a compact little particle, physicists have found that *it literally possesses no dimension… Perhaps most astonishing of all is that there is compelling evidence that the only time quanta ever manifest as particles is when we are looking at them.*[16]

So this physical existence, this construct, is apparently a dimensional reality in which our higher self, our spirit, is projected to and linked to the material body, for a time. Perhaps life then is a very real but also virtual reality.

But the physical *is* real. So, perhaps as some among us have said, the spiritual is *more* real than the physical. Paul alludes to this. "So we fix our eyes not on what is seen, but on what is unseen, since what is seen is temporary, but what is unseen is eternal" (2 Corinthians 4:18, NIV). Even if the universe is found to be a simulation, complete with error-correcting codes as some have argued, that just proves it was designed—which points right back to God.

The Ticking Clock

You and I and everyone alive is on a timer. Our body is programmed to function a number of years, then shut down. How long do you have? I believe we all have an appointed time to die and God knows when that is (Ecclesiastes 3:2). My mom always said you could cut your time short though, through folly, and I believe that too (Psalm 102:23-24). There is an appointed time for each of us (Hebrews 9:27) which means there is a specific number of days. Some say you can ask God when your time will come, and He might even tell you (Psalm 39:4-5). But He already gave us a good estimate of what to expect.

> Our days may come to seventy years,
> or eighty, if our strength endures;
> yet the best of them are but trouble and sorrow,
> for they quickly pass, and we fly away.
> - Psalm 90:10, NIV

Psalm 90 is amazingly profound. Written by none other than Moses, it is the oldest Psalm, from about 1440 BC, and incredibly relevant today, over 3,400 years later![17] So, you can expect to live up to 70 years—perhaps even 80 if you are strong and healthy. Or your life may be cut shorter than 70 due to poor health choices, illness, injury, etc. In extraordinary cases, a person may live past 100, but even that is apparently capped by the Lord.

"My Spirit shall not abide in man forever, for he is flesh: his days shall be 120 years" (Genesis 6:3, ESV). Now, there are different interpretations on just what that means. I take it to mean 120 years is about as long as a person can possibly live. If you think about it, even with modern medicine, people do not usually live past 120. Interestingly, Moses, the author of Psalm 90, was 120 when he died (Deuteronomy 34:7).

This theory of a 120-year limit on lifespan is bolstered by the fact that in the Genesis account, God was becoming exasperated with people, due to the wickedness and increasing corruption on the earth. Then came the Flood (Genesis 6-9). Prior to that, the Bible records humans living for hundreds of years. After the flood, human lifespans decreased steadily.

Perhaps the deluge had a devastating effect on the favorable conditions of Earth that forever altered our lifespans. Add to that, genetic defects, compromised DNA, mutations, etc., and we end up in our present state.

I worked with a brilliant computer engineer once, who was an early Microsoft employee and co-invented the mini-laptop track ball. He became an editing client of mine. As a scientist, he said the Genesis account of people living hundreds of years is actually very tenable.

"If our DNA were pure, uncorrupted from years of pestilence, famine and corruption, we would live for hundreds of years," he said. "We are built to last." But alas, whether we live for hundreds of years or only dozens, this mortal life is short.

"Man who is born of a woman is few of days and full of trouble" (Job 14:1, ESV).

Our time passes quickly.

Dust to Dust

The physical body, although perfectly suited to life on earth, must be left behind when we depart, since "flesh and blood cannot inherit the kingdom of God, nor does the perishable inherit the imperishable" (1 Corinthians 15:50, NIV).

So, it seems likely Paul's physical body remained on earth, while his spirit journeyed to encounter what must have truly been a profound, out-of-body experience. Remember Paul reported being caught up to "the third heaven" where the apostle experienced things that he said "cannot be expressed in words" (2 Corinthians 12, NLT).

Perhaps the spirit then exists in a lower level of heaven and roams in the heavenlies, while linked to our physical form. As mentioned in Chapter 1, there are those who speculate on the levels of heaven. "The third heaven" or paradise is described by Paul, as well as by Jesus while on the cross to the criminal who hung beside Him, saying, "This day you will be with me in paradise" (Luke 23:43). Paradise is likened to the place of rest described as Abraham's bosom (Luke 16:22-23), and many scholars believe they are one and the same.

Paradise is thought by some not to be the highest level or "heaven of heavens," but believe it is a lower level of heaven. Some also reason that if there are multiple levels of heaven, there must be multiple levels of hell as well. Still others say the third level of heaven simply aligns with an ancient Jewish belief that the sky and clouds, the air we breathe, our atmosphere, makes up the first heaven; the stars and planets, outer space, is the second heaven; and the third heaven is another dimension altogether, the highest heaven, where God and His angels roam.[18]

Whether one believes in multiple levels of the extra-dimensional heaven or not, it is clear our spirits continue on after death—for believers, it is into a place of comfort and rest.

What Paul described does sound like an OBE. Perhaps we will experience something similar at death.

Death, then, is not the end. So, we need not mourn our physical body when we die. It is a part of us for sure, but it is a part we leave behind, for now.

We will discuss the subject of reincarnation later on, and it is a rich matter for debate, concerning if our spirits return to inhabit future bodies in this earthly plane. Whether or not you believe in reincarnation, one thing mainstream Christianity agrees on is we will have our earthly bodies restored one day, in a glorified form.

> The body that is sown is perishable, it is raised imperishable; it is sown in dishonor, it is raised in glory; it is sown in weakness, it is raised in power; it is sown a natural body, it is raised a spiritual body. Listen, I tell you a mystery: We will not all sleep, but we will all be changed—in a flash, in the twinkling of an eye, at the last trumpet. For the trumpet will sound, the dead will be raised imperishable, and we will be changed. For the perishable must clothe itself with the im-

> perishable, and the mortal with immortality. (1 Corinthians 15:42-44, 51-53, NIV)

Even the manner of decomposition of the human form shows God's wisdom of design. The skin, which decays slower than the internal organs, gives our loved ones the chance to see us as we appeared in life, so that they can say goodbye. Also the process of rigor mortis, or stiffening of the body, indicates God's design. The stiffness sets in shortly after death but only lasts about 24 hours. Why does the stiffness come and go? Well, of course, there is the chemical explanation, but there is also a practical one: God made it such so it would be easier for us to carry away our dead loved ones.

Eventually our bodies melt away and return to the Earth, while the spirit returns to God (Ecclesiastes 12:7). But we can take heart in that someday He will reunify our spirit to a glorified body, which will not perish (1 Corinthians 15:42-54). Some say we receive the resurrection body when we die; but most Christians believe we will receive it at the end of the age.

But what of the mystical experiences reported by those who are near death?

Chapter 4

Near-Death Experiences

Paul's vision from 2 Corinthians sounds a lot like what Christian minister Don Piper described concerning his NDE, which he wrote about in his 2004 book, *90 Minutes in Heaven*. Piper was in a horrific car accident back in 1989. He was traveling along Texas Highway 19 and crossing the Trinity River Bridge when an 18 wheeler going about 60 mph smashed into and obliterated his '89 Ford Escort. *Near* death does not do the experience justice, because Don Piper died that day.

When paramedics found his mutilated form, there was no pulse, and they covered his body with a tarp. Later, Baptist minister Dick Onerecker happened upon the scene, asking if there was anyone he could pray for. The police officer on site advised Onerecker against going to the car for Piper, who was dead and his body mangled. It was a grizzly scene.

The minister, a former Vietnam medic, was unafraid of blood and felt led by God to go and pray for the man. Onerecker felt for a pulse. There was none. He began praying for Don Piper and even singing hymns. Incredibly, Piper revived and *began singing with him!* Rescue workers could not believe Piper was alive. They had to use the

Jaws of Life hydraulic rescue tools to extract his broken body from the wreckage.

Doctors still felt there was no way the man would live; but after enduring many months of tortuous medical treatments and therapy, Don Piper made a full recovery, with a testimony to share about his time in heaven.

> I get frustrated describing what heaven was like, because I can't begin to put into words what it looked like, sounded like, and felt like... For me, just to reach the gates was amazing... My words are too feeble to describe what took place.[19]

But Mr. Piper did go on to describe the gates of heaven to be iridescent, glowing, and shimmering, and he says he saw the streets as being paved with gold, which sounds a lot like the description of the "new heaven" in Revelation 21. He also described celestial music, heavenly praise that was never-ending, and says that sound is the single most vivid memory he has of the experience. Piper said heaven was perfect.

Other people have reported similar near-death experiences, hearing constant heavenly music with choirs of angels praising God.

My Grandpa Noah, for example, had an amazing vision of heaven before he died.

Noah Bill

My grandfather on my dad's side of the family was a man named Noah Wilson "Bill" Lewis. Grandpa Noah grew up on a farm in rural Wilkes County, North Carolina. The 1920 census record shows baby Grandpa Noah, just under 2 years old, living with his eight other brothers and sisters in the town of North Wilkesboro, across the muddy Yadkin River. At the time, the tiny town and future "Key to the Blue Ridge" Mountains provided a wholesome, if not humble, beginning for the future patriarch.

Faith and dirt were the only birthrights for my family growing up in the depression era. Farming was an honest living, way more so than running moonshine as Noah's dad, my Great-Grandpa Oscar Lewis, was occasioned to do. NASCAR racing got started in North Wilkesboro, thanks to rebels like Great-Grandpa Oscar running 'shine back in the day when Junior Johnson's family was rising to prominence in Wilkes County.[20]

Perhaps it was a bit of the Lewis's scoundrel reputation that earned the scorn of Mr. Elzie St. John, Grandma Joyce's dad—my other Great-Grandpa.

Mr. St. John was firmly against the match between Noah and his daughter Joyce. No matter—thankfully to me and all his progeny—Grandpa Noah stole away with Grandma Joyce and they eloped in secret. After about a half-dozen or so children, I understand, old man Elzie finally began to accept Noah Bill.

Figure 4.1: Left to right: *Grandma Joyce Blanche St. John Lewis, Grandpa Noah Wilson Lewis, Great-Grandma Mary Elizabeth Money St. John, and Great-Grandpa Elzie Emanuel St. John,* circa 1950. Family photo.

Grandma Joyce had a softening effect on Grandpa, and the two became faith leaders in their North Carolina communities. They were instrumental in starting Reidsville Family Church and Andrews Memorial Baptist Church in Graham and Bethel Baptist Church in Greensboro. Grandpa and Grandma literally built those churches and have their names on the scroll in the cornerstone at Bethel, where many in my family continue to worship today.

Grandpa Noah was a deacon in the church and an ordained minister. Together with Grandma, they toured with the *Victory Quartet* in the 1940s and '50s and sang on WPET radio. There is something unique and charming in the wonderfully incongruous nature of mountain people—with their folk music, deep faith, moonshine, and ass-kicking ways.

The Boxing Grandpa

Grandpa Noah had a big, beautiful smile and a warm voice. He was full of love and patience, especially toward his grandchildren. I remember one time I mowed down his entire crop of tomato plants, thinking they were weeds. I was mortified to learn what I had done, but all Grandpa did was laugh.

But he had a quick temper for rascals who crossed the line. At times taken to drink, and especially as a younger man, quick to fight, Grandpa ended up in fisticuffs many times with the rough men at Cone Mills where he worked to support his family of nine children. Perhaps those troublemakers underestimated him.

Grandpa was a man of medium height with a slim build, but his biceps were like baseballs, even in old age. Perhaps it was his thin build and average size that gave the burly men at the mill the idea they could shove him around—and probably why Grandpa had to stand up for himself so many times.

By the way, Grandpa Noah may not have been a large man, but along with his swollen biceps, he had big hands. When he made a fist, those mitts turned into mini-wrecking balls, perfect for whacking faces.

Grandpa mastered the art of bare-knuckle boxing in those days, as rugged workers would gather round, shouting and spitting, to watch the fights. Whether they bet against old Noah Bill Lewis or not, I do not know. If they did, they lost their money.

Grandpa retired undefeated.

Figure 4.2: *Grandma Joyce Blanche St. John Lewis and Grandpa Noah Wilson Lewis,* circa 1945. Photo taken by the author May 21, 2016 from an original print. Family photo.

By the time I was an adolescent, Grandpa Noah had quit drinking hard liquor—praise God—so, I only saw his softer side. But even as an old man, Grandpa was still ready to scuffle.

I remember as a teenager having to escort Grandpa Noah out of the old curb market on Franklin Boulevard near Eastland Avenue where Grandpa had built his home. Franklin Market became a dangerous place over time. The kindly Vietnamese owner I knew as a teen, Mr. Kim, was murdered there in an armed robbery.

I was standing in Franklin Market with my cousin Ronald Harris, who could not stop laughing at Grandpa Noah as he was ready to go fisticuffs with a young man in the market who Grandpa felt had disrespected him. Even as an old man, Grandpa was like John Wayne toilet paper—*he wouldn't take crap off no one.* Thankfully, we got Grandpa out of there and back home without incident.

Grandpa was a skilled boxer. He taught me the fundamental basics, the left jab and the right cross, the ol' one-two, from the living room in the old home place—3945 Eastland Avenue in the blue-collar Hope Valley area of Greensboro, N.C.—a house I watched Grandpa build from the ground up with those two big hands back in 1972. A three-year-old then, I was in awe, thinking the frame looked like a birdcage. Then it magically became a house, transformed by those arms banging away at the work of constructing a home. I was just as in awe years later as a teenager, when I saw those strong biceps and big fists, as the scrappy old brawler punched in the air with speed and power. Grandma just watched from the kitchen—and chuckled.

Grandpa showed me how to throw my entire shoulder into the right cross for maximum effect, as he grunted with the effort. I remember laughing, a little scared just imagining how devastating such a blow would be to the hapless face of a nemesis. Finally, Grandma Joyce had enough. She scolded Grandpa from the kitchen, worried that all that boxing talk would encourage me to fight. Grandpa just laughed, "Okay, Momma."

Several witnesses in my family recounted the story of how Grandpa once confronted two trespassers on his land. When he questioned them, they told him in no uncertain terms to mind his own business. Grandpa Noah quickly dispatched both those individuals and dragged their unconscious bodies into the ditch just outside his property line, with my family members looking on in amazement from the front porch.

Grandpa Noah lived a long life. I remember my dad ruefully joked that Grandpa was "too mean to die."

The Old Home Place

Grandpa may have been rough and rowdy as a young man, and still scrappy in old age, but he had a big heart. Oh, how he laughed at me when I accidentally mowed down his tomato plants. I thought I would be in trouble for sure! I will never forget how he lovingly taught me and Cousin Ron how to shave, and how he never let any of us grandkids come or go from his house without a big hug. I remember Grandpa Noah baking fresh, sweet potato pies at Thanksgiving, and playing baseball with his grown children in the large field on the south side of Eastland Avenue (which is now lined with little houses built in the early 1990s). It was directly across from the front porch of the house he built—that old home place—which would become a focal point for the entire family.

Family gatherings at Grandpa Noah's house always involved mountain music, with my dad singing and playing guitar or mandolin, and his brothers playing guitars and harmonizing. In later years, my Cousin Jeff would play along on guitar and banjo, and, if you were lucky, every now and then Grandpa Noah would pull out his old harmonica from the end-table drawer that sat between his and Grandma's chairs in the living room, and join in. Those music sessions would go on until late in the evenings and end with everyone singing along to old country hymns. My Grandma Joyce's favorite of all was that classic southern gospel song, "I'll Fly Away."

Beautiful Water

Years later, as Grandpa Noah lay dying in his hospital bed, he began to call out, "Water, water." My Uncle Jerry, Grandpa's youngest boy and Cousin Jeff's father, came close to listen. "Water," Grandpa whispered. Jerry went to offer his dad some water, but Grandpa brushed it away.

The old fella went on like that for a few days, saying, "Water... water," but he did not seem to want a drink. Finally, on the last day of his life, Grandpa Noah started saying, "I *see* water." He kept saying, "I see water."

Grandpa's last words, as his eldest son, my Uncle Roy, held his hand were this:

"I see beautiful water."

So inspired by those last words from Grandpa, my brother Devin wrote a gospel song about it called "Beautiful Water."

One cannot help but imagine Grandpa Noah had a vision of the crystal sea in heaven, as he was transitioning to the afterlife. Apostle John talks about that celestial body of water in the Book of Revelation.

> After this I looked, and there before me was a door standing open in heaven. And the voice I had first heard speaking to me like a trumpet said, "Come up here…and there before me was a throne in heaven with someone sitting on it…Also in front of the throne there was what looked like a sea of glass, clear as crystal." (Revelation 4:1, 2, 6)

Deathbed Visions

Deathbed visions have been observed by cultures around the world since ancient times. Departed loved ones are commonly seen, and dying children have even reported expressing surprise at seeing angles without wings.[21] This was noted by Sir William Barrett, a Professor of Physics at the Royal College of Science in Dublin. Barrett was a pivotal mover, founding member, and former president of the Society for Psychical Research, established in 1882. In his classic book on the subject published in 1926, *Death Bed Visions*, he found people had visions of departed loved ones they were not even aware had died. And visions even occurred in people who did not believe in the afterlife.[22]

These visions have certainly occurred in my family. Grandpa Noah Lewis saw beautiful water just before he died, and my mother reported seeing a figure in her hospital room. "Who's that over there?" Mom said, pointing to empty space across the room, past the foot of her bed, just hours before she passed away.

Many have reported seeing loved ones before they die. This has led to a common belief by many that our departed loved ones come to welcome us and guide us to the other side. Some even claim to see their departed pets![23]

The idea that we will be met by beings on the other side and escorted into paradise is biblical. Jesus gave us a glimpse of this, when He told the story of a poor man named Lazarus. When Lazarus died, the angels carried him to heaven (Luke 16:22). Who is to say God would not allow our departed loved ones to act as angels, welcoming us into the hereafter?

Mr. Richard P. Notch

My Father-in-Law, Mr. Richard Notch, was another man of faith I greatly admired. A devout Catholic and devoted family man of stout and sturdy German ancestry, he grew up tough as a boy, enduring harsh Minnesota winters during World War II.

"A war was on," Dick told me. "There was rationing. People did what they had to do. Being German didn't help much."

Mr. Notch served in the U.S. Navy as an electrician in the years following the Great War. Later, the young man carried over those skills and eventually established his own business, Notch Electric. In the years to follow, Dick and his family became valued members of the community in the charming town of Long Prairie, Minnesota.

Figure 4.3a: *Central Avenue in w Long Prairie, Minnesota* by Tim Kiser. Photo taken May 29, 2007 (public domain), Wikimedia Commons.

I remember this view walking back toward the Notch business and home many times. The residence would appear on the left side of the frame were you to keep going straight ahead up the street.[24]

Dick was a private pilot who flew his own plane and was also an avid outdoorsman. He enjoyed golfing and clearing trails for hiking and cross-country skiing on the large tract of wooded land he owned. He was even a self-taught accordion player, who would entertain family and guests in his music room downstairs in the Notch Electric building, which also housed the family quarters.

A cerebral, logical man and deep thinker, Dick was always looking for a project that we could work on together, first with me, then years later with my boys and me. I think problem-solving appealed to his inquisitive nature, and teaching life skills was something he wanted to impart to the people he cared about—whether it was helping me assemble Miranda's toy ironing board for her second birthday or driving me crazy as we worked together finishing my basement laundry room—there was always a practical goal achieved. But I think the main thing Mr. Notch sought was an opportunity to bond. For out of all his many interests, the most important thing to Richard Notch was his family.

I was only 19 when I first met Mr. Notch, shortly after getting engaged to his baby daughter, Susan. He always treated me like a son, even after she and I were amicably divorced many years later. It was a painful experience nonetheless, which haunts me to this day.

Mr. Notch and I shared many private moments together, which I hold close to my heart. We used to spend hours alone driving through the Minnesota backwoods, talking about what life was like for him growing up during the war years.

He took me along on numerous excursions, such as when he made electrician calls on the local businesses; and he chuckled at my fear of heights, which I was unable to disguise as I tried to keep up with him. Mr. Notch was surprisingly nimble despite his stout frame as he easily and quickly scaled rooftop ladders during those cold, Minnesota winters.

From skinning a deer together, to de-icing his storefront sidewalk, to sipping Canadian whiskey in the hot tub while lamenting the latest Vikings game, Dick always had a kind word of encouragement and was quick to share a laugh.

A rugged individual, Mr. Notch balmed the long days spent outside in the bitter cold as an electrician, with cozy nights indoors soaking in the warm hot tub, a whiskey-coke to comfort his frozen, aching body. He was a giant of a man in my eyes and a true hero to me.

Dick had a gruff, raspy voice with that distinctive Minnesota accent *Fargo* actors try to imitate. Despite his masculine demeanor, Dick had kind eyes and a soft heart, leading his family in prayers over the evening meal. He once told me people from Minnesota had the true American accent, which produced a big laugh from my southern-dialected self at the irony, and a surprised look from him as to what I could possibly be laughing about.

"Well, it's true," he said.

Silly anecdotes aside, Mr. Notch was not one given to fanciful tales, not even during the private moments we shared. Although he was a member of St. Mary of Mt. Carmel Catholic Church in Long Prairie and later the Church of Mary of the Visitation in Big Lake, where he attended church faithfully, I never once heard him talk about mystical things or the paranormal. Yet, in the moments before he passed away on May 19, 2013, surrounded by his children and grandchildren, Dick said he could see his mother in the room, and other departed loved ones appeared also, gathering around, smiling, welcoming—waiting to take him home.

Figure 4.3b: *Mr. Richard Notch, my father-in-law,* circa 1970 with his plane. Family photo.

For the believer, there is no doubt we will see our loved ones again. King David, upon losing his son, took comfort in this knowledge.

> "While the child was still alive, I fasted and wept, for I said, 'Who knows whether the Lord will be gracious to me, that the child may live?' But now he is dead. Why should I fast? Can I bring him back again? I shall go to him." (2 Samuel 12:22-23, ESV)

Chapter 5

On the Other Side

A common report among people who experience NDEs is seeing deceased friends and relatives. Although the departed loved ones are easily recognizable, they no longer appear old or weary. They appear vibrant and youthful, perhaps the best representation of themselves. Again, we turn to Don Piper.

> Age expresses time passing, and there is no time there. All of the people I encountered were the same age they had been the last time I had seen them—except that all the ravages of living on earth had vanished.[25]

Fear of death is very natural; however, death is just about the most natural thing in life—and not something to fear for those who know the Lord. "Precious in the sight of the Lord is the death of his faithful servants" (Psalm 116:15, NIV).

The great truth that should help alleviate your fear is the assurance that life goes on after death. I know this because of the many after-death communications I have personally received, not to mention the many written accounts out there—which, of course—includes what the Holy Bible has to say. The Bible, in no uncertain terms, declares that your spirit, the essence that is you, does continue on after your earthly body dies.

As Jesus hung, dying on the cross—two thieves were hanging with him, one on His right and the other on His left. These men also were sentenced to the slow, cruel, painful, and suffocating death of crucifixion. Although the Bible records at one point both thieves were hurling insults at the Lord (Mark 15:32), one of the men clearly had a change of heart (Luke 23:40-41). This penitent man asked Jesus to remember him when He comes into His kingdom. The Lord assured the man, who was justified by his faith, there would be no wait—indeed, that day he would join the Lord in glory!

> Then one of the criminals who were hanged blasphemed Him, saying, "If You are the Christ, save Yourself and us."
>
> But the other, answering, rebuked him, saying, "Do you not even fear God, seeing you are under the same condemnation? And we indeed justly, for we receive the due reward of our deeds; but this Man has done nothing wrong." Then he said to Jesus, "Lord, remember me when You come into Your kingdom."
>
> And Jesus said to him, "Assuredly, I say to you, today you will be with Me in Paradise." (Luke 23:39-43, NKJV)

There are many famous NDE accounts. Dannion Brinkley, a lightning-strike survivor, reported multiple near-death experiences, documenting heavenly journeys in books like his 1994 bestseller, the intriguing *Saved by the Light*. But the one that really blew my mind was the aforementioned 1992 classic, *Embraced by the Light*, by Betty J. Eadie. I first encountered *Embraced* at the bookstore on Incirlik Air Base, Turkey, where I was stationed in the early 1990s. A real page-turner, I was both inspired and a bit spooked by the account, which I started reading right there in my car just after leaving the bookstore. I finished the entire story, cover to cover, in only a couple of days.

A commonality among Eadie, Brinkley, Piper, Wixon, and pretty much everyone who reports an NDE is a profound life change following the encounter, usually for the better. They become more spiritual, more appreciative of their life, and become less focused on superficial, worldly things.

Dr. P.M.H. Atwater is one of the original researchers of the near-death phenomenon, having begun her work in 1978. She allegedly survived three death events that produced three different near-death experiences in 1977. One of the more arcane things Atwater says that actually makes perfect sense is this—*not breathing is more natural than breathing*.

> There is no pain at the moment of death. Only peaceful silence... calm... quiet. But you still exist. It is easy not to breathe. In fact, it is easier, more comfortable, and infinitely more natural not to breathe than to breathe.[26]

That statement is enough to make one ponder long after hearing it. It is simple, yet profound, and ultimately comforting. Stop and think for a moment how much work your body is doing right now as you read these words. Your heart is pumping, your chest rising and falling with each breath, food digesting—poorly, perhaps, depending on what you ate and your constitution—mouth salivating, cells dividing, neurons firing, eyes blinking, perhaps a bit dry, as you follow along. That is a lot of work!

The human body is an amazing and beautiful mixture of form and function. From the classic sculptures of Michelangelo to Rodin, to the drawings of da Vinci, the human form has fascinated us from the beginning of time, with its perfect balance of beauty and function. Imagine Adam when he first saw Eve.

"At last!" the man exclaimed. "This one is bone from my bone, and flesh from my flesh! She will be called 'woman,' because she was taken from 'man'" (Gen 2:23-25, NLT).

We love our bodies. As the Scripture says, "No one hates his own body" (Ephesians 5:29, NLT). Indeed, the human body is a wonderful machine. The brain regulates so many functions, keeping most of them in a state of autopilot, outside of our consciousness.

Just think of the overwhelming complexity of tedium if you had to consciously tell your heart to beat, tell your stomach to digest food, or instruct your cells to divide.

Now, back to that bit about breathing verses not breathing. Breathing is interesting because it is one of those things, like blinking your eyes, that functions automatically, yet it can also be consciously controlled.

Stop for a moment to notice your breathing. Is it not amazing how your chest rises, expanding with each breath, then falling as the breath is exhaled, and on and on? Without causing a panic attack in the reader, I am content to make you mindful of the amount of work it takes for the body to keep itself alive!

Yet, at some point, we must shed this body. Indeed, one day our body will stop working. Perhaps instead of dreading our exit from the body, when the time comes for us to depart, we might instead find it liberating.

As Betty Eadie said, "I felt a surge of energy, and my spirit was suddenly drawn through my chest and pulled upward. My first impression is that I was free."[27]

Now, imagine at that moment being freed of the body. You are still you, you still have a body, but it is a spiritual body. Imagine how you would feel if you no longer had to toil in this dense physical form. Not breathing *would* seem more natural than breathing! It is good to think about these things. Remember the words of Moses: At some point this earthly tent must come down and we will fly away.

> Seventy years are given to us!
> Some even live to eighty.
> But even the best years are filled with pain and trouble;

> Soon they disappear, and we fly away.
> - Psalm 90:10, NLT

Paul gives hope in the spiritual body to come. "They are buried as natural human bodies, but they will be raised as spiritual bodies. For just as there are natural bodies, there are also spiritual bodies" (1 Corinthians 15:44, NLT).

Most theologians believe we do not receive the spiritual or resurrection body until Christ returns—that until that time, after death, we exist as discarnate spirits.[28]

Others, like the late Pastor Chuck Smith, founder of the Calvary Chapel movement, held that we are given the resurrection body at death—and Chuck's argument, while controversial, correlates well with the Scripture that says, "The dead in Christ will rise first" (1 Thessalonians 4:16).[29]

> For if we believe that Jesus died and rose again, even so God will bring with Him those who sleep in Jesus. For this we say to you by the word of the Lord, that we who are alive and remain until the coming of the Lord will by no means precede those who are asleep. For the Lord Himself will descend from heaven with a shout, with the voice of an archangel, and with the trumpet of God. And the dead in Christ will rise first. Then we who are alive and remain shall be caught up together with them in the clouds to meet the Lord in the air. And thus we shall always be with the Lord. (1 Thessalonians 4:14-17, NKJV)

I think Pastor Chuck makes an interesting point concerning when we are given the resurrection body. What if we naturally have our spiritual body at death? Maybe that is what Pastor Chuck was saying. If you look at the Scriptures in bold above, Paul tells us that 1) The dead in Christ will rise first (Verse 16), and 2) God will bring with Him those who sleep in Jesus (Verse 14), so rising after death and being clothed in the resurrection body could explain how the dead, those who "rise first" are brought back with Jesus. While this is not the viewpoint of mainstream Christianity, it might otherwise preclude the controversial idea of reincarnation, if true.

How do we reincarnate, if we are given the resurrection body at death? Then again, who can say? The nature of the resurrection body is a mystery. Based on the example from Jesus, the "firstborn from the dead" (Colossians 1:18, NKJV), the resurrection body portrays both physical and mystical characteristics.

In His resurrection body, Jesus could appear and disappear (Luke 24:36-37, 24:31, John 20:26), prepare and eat food (Luke 24:30, 24:41-43, John 21:9-13) and be touched (Luke 24:39, John 20:27). Also, in that state, Christ was ultimately able to ascend into heaven to be at the right hand of God the Father (Acts 1:9-10).

Pastor Chuck's idea that we receive the resurrection body at death may or may not be true. Again, the orthodox view is the resurrection body is given at the Second Advent of Christ; so the dead in Christ who rise first, receive their new body at that point.

Side note: don't be thrown by the part about "those who 'sleep' in Jesus," which simply means the departed believers at rest in Paradise with the Lord. It does not imply, as some have wrongly interpreted, that we exist in an unconscious state of "soul sleep" until Jesus returns. No, that is not what the Bible teaches at all. This error emerges so frequently among Christians when the topic of ghosts and after-death communication comes up that I will take a few moments to dispel it now.

God of the Living

In 2 Corinthians 5:8, the Scripture teaches that to be absent from the body is to be present with the Lord. In Mark 12:26 and 27, the Bible reiterates our Lord is the God of Abraham, the God of Isaac, and the God of Jacob. He is "God of the living, not the dead." If you recall, Samuel returned to speak with Saul (1 Samuel 28:13-19), and God allowed it. Samuel was not sleeping.

On and on through Scripture, we see that those who have died are alive and conscious, from the transfiguration where Moses and Elijah appeared and spoke with Jesus (Luke 9:30), to Lazarus being awake in Paradise (Luke 16:22-24). Jesus even told the thief on the cross he would join Christ in Paradise the same day they died! (Luke 23:43).

"Have you not read in the book of Moses, in the burning bush passage, how God spoke to him, saying, 'I am the God of Abraham, the God of Isaac, and the God of Jacob'? He is not the God of the dead, but the God of the living" (Mark 12:26-27).

If you think about it, the idea of dead people climbing out of graves at the Lord's return, commonly held among many Christians, is more like something out of a Romero flick than a reasoned understanding of Scripture.

The Spirit Body

When I interviewed Luis Minero in 2014, he said during an OBE you are in the spirit, but you have a spiritual body. You look down and there are arms and legs, hands and feet. Perhaps this is the very resurrection body Paul was talking about, but Minero seemed to believe it was more of an effect of the conscious mind-force projecting a self-image.

To follow that logic for a moment—if you think about it—you have arms and legs in your dreams. Most people do not even know they are dreaming. When you use those twilight appendages, you see them, you feel them. But real as they might seem while dreaming, are they not projections of the mind?

Then there is the phenomenon where many people who have lost a limb, in a war-related injury or other amputation, will report sometimes still feeling that missing appendage, as if it were still there.

> Although not all phantom limbs are painful, people will sometimes feel as if they are gesturing, feel itches, twitch, or even try to pick things up. The missing limb often feels shorter and may feel as if it is in a distorted and painful position.[30]

Whether by pain, perception, or electric tingles, is this troubling condition evidence of a spirit body or simply a function of the central nervous system firing signals as if the missing limb were still attached?

Whether the spirit body is a conscious projection from our own sentience, a projected spirit form that correlates to the body, or the true resurrection body remains to be seen. It is also possible the resurrection body is something else altogether—a new form of physical body we must wait for in order to inhabit the "new earth" of Revelation 21.

> Then I saw "a new heaven and a new earth," for the first heaven and the first earth had passed away, and there was no longer any sea. I saw the Holy City, the new Jerusalem, coming down out of heaven from God, prepared as a bride beautifully dressed for her husband. And I heard a loud voice from the throne saying, "Look! God's dwelling place is now among the people, and he will dwell with them. They will be his people, and God himself will be with them and be their God. 'He will wipe every tear from their eyes. There will be no more death' or mourning or crying or pain, for the old order of things has passed away." (Revelation 21:1-4, NIV)

For the trumpet will sound, the dead will be raised imperishable,
and we will be changed. For the perishable must clothe itself
with the imperishable, and the mortal with immortality.
When the perishable has been clothed with the imperishable, and the
mortal with immortality, then the saying that is written will come true:
"Death has been swallowed up in victory."
1 Corinthians 15:52-54
Holy Bible, New International Version (NIV)

Interlude

You Can Watch Anything But Football

Westly-Long Hospital, Greensboro, N.C., October 10, 2010 –

The Cancer Ward

Mom was moaning in pain, almost incoherent. She had been like that for most of the four days since I arrived from Los Angeles to be at her side. I hardly left her now. No bathing. Barely sleeping. It is the most important thing I have ever done.

"You've got to eat, Rich," Mom said softly, between agonizing waves of pain.

"I will, Mom." I replied. "I'm fine."

"You're doing so good, Rich," Mom smiled.

She was in and out a lot. Most people are comforted when you hold their hand. Mom was in too much pain to tolerate her hand being held. The one thing she could tolerate was tiny little kisses on her pretty head, bald from the poisonous chemotherapy.

The nurses would turn her over to take care of soiled diapers. Mother would scream out in extreme agony at the torture of being moved, no matter how careful they were—but she never had a harsh word for anyone.

I spilled water on her once, trying to quench her constant thirst.

"You about drowned me," she joked, choking a bit. Mom was still there, all right.

When I was a kid we used to laugh so much—Mom, James, and I. I remember one time around 1981 when we were living at the Travel Lodge in downtown Greensboro. Mom had come in late one night after her shift at work. I would always get an excited feeling when I would hear her return from work. I met her in the kitchen area and we began figuring out something to eat. So, I picked up a large, kitchen knife. Something like Michael Myers would carry. Suddenly, I started stabbing it in the air, mimicking the scary screeching music sounds from *Psycho* (1960).[31] It must have looked strange and spooky to see a 12-year-old kid acting that way. But Mom just laughed.

"Rich, knock it off."

"Why Mom?"

"You better put that thing down before a demon jumps in your ass," she said, still laughing. I was laughing too.

"Ain't no demon gonna jump in me, Momma."

"You don't know that, Rich."

"Well, I would never hurt you. Besides, I'm just a kid. I couldn't hurt you."

"With that thing you could." She was serious. "Now put it down."

"Yes, Momma." I gently placed it on the counter.

"Good," she chuckled. "I don't want to die tonight."

Westly-Long Hospital, Oct. 10, 2010 –

It was a Sunday afternoon during the ordeal, and Mother seemed to be dozing. Mom had told me to watch some television. I had not watched TV for days. She seemed to be sleeping now so I thought I would see what was going on with the NFL. She said I could watch some TV, so I put it on the game.

You Can Watch Anything But Football

✝

719 Pine Street, Greensboro, NC, November 24, 1974 –

My Dad, George Lewis, and his good friend Rodney Herd were whooping it up in the den.

"Go 'Skins, let's go Jurgensen," yelled Dad. "Come, babe!"

Rodney was laughing, especially when he saw the cross look on Mom's face as she stood in the hallway peering into the den. Mom always hated football.

"Uh-oh, George, Vivian's here," Rodney snickered. He knew that Sunday was "fight day," as he called it, at the Lewis household.

"Hey, sugar-babe," Dad cooed.

"George, do you have to watch those awful games all day long?" Mom asked.

"But honeybun, it's the Redskins."

"Hey Daddy," little five-year-old me chimed in, pointing at the visiting Philadelphia Eagles, all clad in that unmistakable 1970's emerald Irish-like, Kelly Green color.

"Are those the 'Greenskins'?" I asked.

Both Dad and Rodney laughed at my silly but astute question.

"Greenskins!" squealed Rodney.

"But I wanna go somewhere," Mom pouted. "Let's go see your mom."

"Now sugar-babe," Dad scolded. "You got your chores. I told you—when you get all your chores done, then I'll take you over to see Momma. Then the two'a you can go shoppin'."

Mom stormed off, furious. Then whipped around and came back.

"George, I'll cut your heart out and watch it bleed."

Dad and Rodney just laughed.

Then Mom's expression stopped Rodney.

"Oops, Oh. Uh-oh, George," Rodney sniffled. "Uh, Vivian?"

"Shut up, Rodney," Mom said, crying now. But off she went to finish her chores.

Mom hated football. Maybe it wasn't so much the game itself, but how it represented the neglect she felt from her husband.

I was ashamed because I had been laughing at her too. I left the noise of the game and Dad and Rodney behind in the den. The sounds faded as I made my way down the hall to the kitchen, where I could hear the purr of water running. Mom's back was turned away from me. She was facing the sink and looking out the window as I approached her from behind.

Her shoulders were shaking. She was sobbing, while slowly scrubbing away at the dishes. As I came to her side, looking up at her, the sun from the afternoon light made her tears sparkle like diamonds. Mom's pale face was pink and puffy, pretty, despite the tears, her eyes as blue and forever as the ocean.

"I'm sorry, Momma," I said, patting my tiny, five-year-old hand on her back.

She smiled down at me through her tears. "It's okay, baby."

And she kissed me.

The Redskins dominated the Eagles at Washington that day, 26-7. I don't suppose it made Mom feel any better when the 'Skins lost the following Thursday, Thanksgiving Day, at Texas Stadium to the reviled Dallas Cowboys.

Dad and Mom's "fight days" were numbered it seems, and it really was no laughing matter at all. They split up less than a year after that game. Not over football, of course.

Football was just a metaphor.

Later, Mom would marry my Stepdad James, who never once watched a football game. James would tolerate my watching a game, from time to time, if Mom wasn't around, of course. But as soon as Mother walked through the door, she would make us change the channel.

Westly-Long Hospital, Greensboro, NC, October 10, 2010 –

It's 2010, I am in my 40s now and right by Momma's side. It's Sunday. Game day. Mom's sleeping now, or so I thought. She said I could watch TV. I thought maybe I'd just check in on the game, just for a moment...

CLICK. The silence in the hospital room was broken by the little speaker on the nurse-alarmed bed remote, squawking out play-by-play of the NFL football game.

"Not that," Mom sighed, eyes closed.

How did she know?

Mom always hated football.

Westly-Long Hospital, Greensboro, NC, October 10, 2010 –
The Night Before

Her agony was all-consuming—excruciating.

She softly moaned in pain throughout the night, her suffering cries, piercing to my soul—startling me awake if I momentarily drifted off to sleep.

It was nearly overwhelming for me, but somehow it was also inspiring to witness the dignity through which Mom bore it all. My pain was nothing: hunger, tiredness, the slight throbbing of a headache over my eyebrow. But I was suffering too—a very different but real discomfort.

I had never felt it before, this unmistakable burning, like a piece of coal in my sternum. I have since come to know that pain as the feeling of hopelessness. It is the pain of standing by, watching helplessly, as you slowly lose someone you love.

It is the feeling of your heart breaking.

It is what you feel when you want so desperately for your loved one to get up out of that bed and go home; but you understand that will never happen. You are powerless. All you can do is wait for the inevitable. I felt it again just two years later when my Stepdad James would lie upon his own deathbed.

But now, thankfully, Mom really was sleeping, peaceful for a moment. Her form, skeletal.

Those blessed moments in the middle of the night when Mom finally dozed off were a godsend, for both her and me. I waved at the nurses as I passed by to go outside, cigar in hand. I must have looked a fright, but their sleepy eyes smiled back in kindness.

I had found a walking trail outside the hospital. There sat a lone park bench. It was a brief but welcome respite from my bedside vigil. I puffed away at my cigar and reflected—alone in the darkness. It was not food or drink; but it was refreshment.

Sitting in the darkness at Mom's bedside, the smell of stale coffee wafted into the hospital room from outside in the hallway. I could hear the voices of the nurses, laughing and chatting at their station as Mom lay there, moaning in pain. It would be daybreak soon.

"Oh Jesus," she said, writhing in torment. "Please help me."

Mom requested very few drugs during her ordeal because she wanted to remain as coherent as possible. The attending staff did try to control her pain, but as one of the doctors explained to me, "The cancer is everywhere." Pain medication could only do so much.

"Please God..." then she paused.

It was the pre-dawn hours of October 10, 2010.

Then Mom whispered something I will never forget.

"Let me die."

Mom wasn't talking to me. She was talking to the Lord.

The searing pain burned like a lump of coal flaming in my chest.

"Help me, Jesus!" Mom called out. She had been talking to the Lord like that for days. When would it end? Only He knew. But she only asked the Lord once, "Let me die."

He would answer that prayer very soon.

You Can Watch Anything But Football

†

Blackness. What happened? I had dozed off for a moment.

Out of the blue, Mom started talking to me like there was nothing wrong anymore. She had completely cleared up. I leaned closer to her bed. Mom was speaking in complete, articulate sentences now. I perked up, and we started talking. We talked about everything. It was like she wasn't even sick anymore! It was like being a teenager again talking to my Mom with our whole lives left to live.

"Hey, something changed!" I told a lady at the nurses' station. Mom's doing a lot better! I think she may be getting well!"

"Yes…" the nurse replied hesitantly. "It could be that…*or*…" She paused. "It could mean…something else."

Early that morning, James came by to visit as he did every day. He brought with him juices and Boost drink and just about anything he could think of to try and feed my mom.

He wanted her to get up out of that bed too. He wanted her to live, just like I did.

Mom tried to please him and sup off a little of the liquids he brought. You could tell she was happy to see him. He smiled at her, pure love in his eyes.

Two soulmates they were, having a last dance.

"Who's that?" Mom asked, pointing across the room, toward the foot of the bed.

James was sitting beside her head, on the side nearest the window. I was standing by her head on the side nearest the door, exiting out to the nurse's station.

"Who, Mom?" I asked.

"Over there," Mom mumbled, then closed her eyes.

I looked but saw nothing there.

"It's that Death spirit, Richard." James said softly.

We visited together with Mom for a little while more. Not very long.

The night before, as James was leaving us for the evening, he turned back to me from the doorway and said, "I love you." My stepfather had raised me since I was a five-year-old. Now, here I am in my 40s, and he tells me he loves me for the first time in my life.

Something about Mom changed again.

"Richard....Richard..." James said, near panic in his voice. "Richard, she's in pain. She's in PAIN!"

I went to the doorway to find our attending nurse. What was his name again? Justin, I think. I yelled down the hallway for him, "Justin!" JUSSS-TINNNN!"

Why were there tears in my throat?

"Richard, your mother wants you," said James, his voice gripped with urgency.

I turned and Mom was motioning for me to draw near. She grabbed my right hand and took James's hand on the other side. Mom stared into my eyes. Although she had been too weak to sit up before, she now *sat straight up in bed*, all the while still staring into my eyes.

Then...

Mother pushed out her spirit.

It was like watching a woman give birth.

I saw her spirit fly by my head. It zoomed by like a phoenix in flight. It was a shadow.

Mom's body collapsed, and she gently fell into my arms.

Out of my body came a sound I had never heard before. It was something of a howl, ancient and mournful. Perhaps it is a sound common to man? I have heard something similar in movies and TV, but those were false, empty replications. I did not consciously produce the sound—it just came up out of the pit of me. The wail was long and deep, and it must have been heard, for now there was the nurse Justin and a blonde lady doctor standing over me. The doc was patting my back, her voice cooing, attempting to soothe.

"There, there..."

Almost as if I were a baby.

"There you go, now. Look at her."

The doc was gazing at something beautiful.

"Doesn't your mom look peaceful now?"
No. She looked dead.

Hours later, I was riding home with my cousin Tracy and her boyfriend Phil. I sat in the backseat of the car. Daylight was blinding, coming through the windows as I bounced along on that stiff, leather backseat.

Suddenly, I felt electricity encircle my neck. My neck was being gently squeezed by this enveloping electrical field.

It was a hug.

Then I felt gentle electrical pecks on the top of my head. The location and pressure were unmistakable—they were *kisses*, identical to the kisses I had been placing on Mom's pretty, bald head the night before.

Then I heard *her voice*!

"I'm free, Rich!" Mom said. "I'm free!"

My cousin Tracy and Phil did not hear the voice.

As evening approached, I sat on the concrete driveway in front of Phil and Tracy's garage. I was taking notes and reflecting on all that had happened.

Suddenly, a cricket dropped on my head.

Mom always told me crickets were good luck. But that was the first and only time one ever landed on my head.

10/10/10—the day Mom passed. Some believe that number signifies good luck.

101010—Binary converts to 42 in decimal. My actual age that day, 42 years from the moment I began growing in my mother's belly.

In Japanese culture they are wary of 42, because the numerals sound like the word "death" when pronounced out loud.[32]

42 degrees is the critical angle for which a rainbow appears.[33]

42 reduces to 21, the age my mother was when I was conceived.

Of course I wasn't thinking about any of that at the time.

All I knew, in that split-second was—I had a cricket on my head.

I gently brushed the creature off. Caught it. Then let it go. The cricket hopped away.

Mom's voice echoed again *one last time*. The sound was in the blue sky and clouds.

"I'm free, Rich! I'm free!"

Figure l.1: *Vivian Lee Spence Brandon,* my beloved mother, circa 1974. Photo taken by the author June 9, 2021 from an original print. Family photo.

For in the resurrection they neither marry
nor are given in marriage,
but are like angels in heaven.
Matthew 22:30
Holy Bible, English Standard Version (ESV)

Chapter 6

After-Death Communications

I was contacted by both Mom and Dad after they passed away. With my Father George Allen Lewis, it happened at the viewing in 2008. I had just sat down after seeing his body for the first time. Tears streamed down my cheeks as both my Stepmom Barbara "Bobbi" and Dad's sister, Aunt Beverly, sat on either side of me, sobbing mightily.

My arm was squeezing my stepmother as she cried on my left shoulder. Then I felt a hand land on and gently grasp my other shoulder. I looked to the right thinking it was Aunt Bee, but Beverly had her head bowed in her hands now, quietly weeping to herself.

As I turned to Beverly, I saw someone had appeared in front of me. This person was the one with his hand on my shoulder.

I looked up to see who it was. It was Dad, smiling, comforting me with his countenance.

My father appeared 10 feet tall and looked almost like a projection—flat, wider at the bottom than the top. His image was glowing slightly, luminous, black and white—again, something like a projection. No one else could see him. He was there to console and reassure me, which seemed odd to me, as he was the one who was dead.

Figure 6.1: *George Allen Lewis,* my handsome father, circa 1969. Family photo.

This all happened in an instant, but none of it seemed strange at all.
It was my Dad. I could feel his presence.
Just as real as when he was alive.
I spoke to Pops telepathically.
"I'm worried about *you*, man," I said, still crying in my thoughts.
"I'm fine," Dad replied. "I'm fine."
That's all he said. Then he disappeared.

Both Dad and Mom have visited me many times in my dreams since they passed away, but they never talk. The only words I ever heard them speak were those times when they said, "I'm fine" or "I'm free!" Even then, I am sure they must have been speaking telepathically.

With Mom, I clearly heard her voice and even felt her spirit, but I did not see her when I heard her voice.

With Dad, I saw his image—his spirit, or perhaps a projection beamed over from somewhere else—but only received his voice in my mind. Imagine watching a movie with the volume turned down, but you hear the sound in your head. The projected image did not mouth the words. It stands to reason that we talk with our mouths because we need air, teeth, tongue, throat, and vocal cords to physically speak. With the spirit, there is no such requirement.

I have had other after-death communication experiences with my parents. An amazing visitation from Mom happened one night in 2013 in a strange motel, as I feared I might be going blind.

The Beatific Vision

Mother always fretted about my eyesight. I started going dramatically near-sighted at an early age. In 1st grade, I brought home a report from school showing I had badly failed the vision exam. It was 1975. I remember Mom talking to me about it as we walked out onto the tiny front porch of our little house on 719 Pine Street in Greensboro. She stood, staring at the test results.

"Oh Lord, Rich, you need glasses." Mom looked at me. "I don't know how we're gonna pay for it."

Figure 6.2: *Happy Days*. This Polaroid of Mom and Dad and me was captured during Christmas 1970 at our home on Pine Street in Greensboro, North Carolina. Although my parents had been together since Mom was 12 and Dad was 15, their marriage would be over by 1975, only a few years after this photo was taken.

Later, doctors would determine my left eye cornea had been scarred by the forceps that the M.D. used to turn me as I was being born. As I related in Book I, Chapter 14, that injury was a small price to pay considering the procedure saved my life from choking on the umbilical cord.

Still, the scarring had a permanent effect on my worsening eyesight. In every exchange in life where there is a gain, it seems there is always a loss, and with every loss, comes a gain.

I lost vision capability in my left eye. The right eye was much better, but also progressively growing more near-sighted with an ever-increasing myopia. Mom even feared I might go blind.

But we were very poor, so I had to wait to get glasses. With Dad gone, it was all a single mom could do juggling multiple minimum-wage jobs just to make ends meet. Even after my Stepdad James showed up, it was hard for a Black man to find good work in those days.

By 7th grade I had to sit in the front of the class and pull my right eyelid into a squint with my left index finger to bring the chalkboard into focus, while taking notes with my right hand. Luckily, that was also the year I finally got my first pair of glasses—they were my birthday present that year!

Both sets of parents split the cost, with Mom and James taking care of the exam, while Dad and Shirley, my first stepmom, paid for the glasses. Shirley dropped the gold-framed wonders off with James and me as we were standing outside the Travel Lodge Motel in downtown Greensboro, where I grew up. "There's your birthday," Shirley said, smiling and waving as she drove off.

I felt like a comic-book hero. Like I had super-vision, as now the buildings in downtown Greensboro came to life in sharp relief! James and I jumped into his green, four-door, 1974 Chevy Impala, and he drove me around town, testing me to see if I could read the lettering on buildings and on the signs around town. "Richard, can you read that?" he would say, laughing. "What does that one say?" And on and on we went.

Mom always worried I would go blind because it took so many years for my eyes to stabilize, which they eventually did—thank you, Lord—as the myopia finally settled down.

We prayed about it a lot, and once the myopia stopped getting worse, my eyes have stayed about the same to this day. Praise God!

Now doing much better financially in 1986, Mom bought me my first set of contact lenses when I was 17. My newfound freedom from glasses made me feel like a superhero again. But the ultimate goal would be to have no need for corrective lenses at all.

Back when I was fitted for glasses in 1981, I remember the doc talking about radial keratotomy, a terrifying procedure where they made scalpel incisions in the cornea to correct near-sightedness. Later, less barbaric procedures would follow, and become perfected, such as laser eye surgery, a state-of-the-art procedure to permanently fix my vision.

LASIK

I was evaluated and turned down for LASIK in the early 2000s. Doctors felt the scaring on my left cornea from childbirth was too deep and problematic to risk having the procedure.

That all changed in 2013 when I went on a whim to Saddleback Eye Center in Laguna Hills, California. There I met Dr. Charles Manger, a crusty old military veteran who graduated from the Naval Academy majoring in math and nuclear science and later worked as an engineer on a nuclear submarine.

Manger had about as much bedside manner as a Marine drill-instructor; but with nearly 80,000 procedures to his credit and rating in the top 1% of all LASIK surgeons in the country, he was my pick.

Dr. Manger approved me for LASIK the same day of my initial screening. He saw the scarring on my cornea and was not intimidated at all, as the other doctors were.

The next thing I knew, I was processed in for a same-day procedure. It was all run with the curt, military efficiency I would expect from a former submarine officer.

The procedure itself was something akin to an alien abduction, medical torture scenario. I soon found myself on my back staring ahead at multicolored lights.

I reminded Manger of the scarring on my eye.

"Yeah, I see it," he growled softly. "I'll work around it."

The doctor blasted a laser, cutting across my cornea. Sparkles of light flashed all around. Then blackness.

The eye was numbed so I did not feel any pain, but there was a strange pressure as my vision returned. I stared ahead as small, flicking wiping motions went across the surface of my eye. The whole thing was over rather quickly.

Before the surgery, the nurse was supposed to give me a Valium pill to take before the procedure, but she forgot and I did not request it. I decided to tough it out—probably a mistake on my part.

I did not experience the instant, miracle vision restoration many LASIK patients claim. Yes, I could see a little better, but my vision was still very blurred, and it was not long before I was feeling uncomfortable. Perhaps it was due to my extreme myopia that I would experience more significant side effects than others.

Eyes on Fire

Saddleback put surgery patients up in a nearby hotel so we could be seen for follow-up by the doctor the next morning. We were instructed to take a nap, after which we should start feeling a lot better. We were also sent away with two 500-mg Tylenol pills and instructions on applying eye drops, which would become a complicated regimen of medication and moisturizing maintenance for the next several days.

I do not even remember what hotel I stayed in, because I honestly could not even see the signage at the hotel check-in. But, somehow, I managed to sign in and stumble down the hall to find my room. If only I had taken that valium I likely would have dozed off, but that never happened.

Over time, I began to suffer severe burning in my eyes with rivers of tears streaming down my face. I never took that nap, and now the pain had become almost unbearable. I had also developed an extreme light sensitivity; so I had to turn off all the room lights and the TV. The condition became so acute I could not see to use my cell phone, or even bear to look at its illumination.

Waves of burning pain passed over my eyes, sending streams of salty tears down my face. It was all I could do not to squeeze my eyes tightly in response. The issue was if you blink your eyelids too hard it could disturb the corneal flap, which would mean another surgery.

It was a vigil of torment. I would lay in bed for a moment, then jump up and pace around the darkened room. I was in too much pain to sit still, and I could not get comfortable on the bed.

I fumbled around in the darkness with the coffee maker in the room. Somehow I got it going, spilling water and coffee grounds and reeling from the blinding light-switch on the machine. Something approximating coffee was brewed, as the burner sizzled from spilled liquid. Little grounds of coffee crunched in my teeth as I sipped at it.

I sat there, shivering in pain, supping off small, warm sips of brownish water. It was a momentary comfort as the burning tremors continued passing through my eyes in waves.

I found out later what I was going through was the corneal cell wall rebuilding. I was supposed to be sleeping through this, which is probably part what the Valium was all about. Now, I was in too much pain to sleep.

Laguna Hills is a good, hour and a half drive from where I lived in Redondo Beach at the time. I was in a strange town, an unknown hotel, and could not even see to dial the phone. Was this pain a normal reaction or had something gone horribly wrong with the LASIK procedure? Was I finally going blind as Mom had always feared? I was beginning to think I should call 911.

Vision of Mother

But then, right there in the darkness, as I lay staring up at the ceiling, a familiar face materialized, hovering between the ceiling and me as I lay in bed…it was Mom!

Her face appeared youthful and happy. It was drawn in a silvery outline, which approximated the way Mother looked in her 20s, back in the 1970s when my vision problems were first diagnosed.

Mom was her young self, but instead of the concern furrowing her brow back when she first read that eye exam report, her face was smiling now, full of reassurance.

She said not a word but simply blew me a kiss, then vanished.

I knew right then and there I was going to be okay.

Figure 6.3: *Christmas 1970*. Although my parents divorced, they remained friends and united in their love for me and for the Lord. The vision of Mom I saw hovering over me that night in the agony after eye surgery was almost identical to this image of her here. Although she did not say anything, her spirit sent a kiss my way, letting me know I was going to be okay.

I fumbled around in the dark until I managed to get the clock radio turned on. The light from the LED display was blinding, so I had to look away while turning the dial. I found a jazz station, fine-tuned the reception a bit, stopping once the signal was clear. I closed my eyes and focused on the soothing sound of the DJ's smooth baritone voice and eventually fell asleep.

Later, Dr. Manger would invite me back to speak at his free LASIK seminars. Although Manger appeared nonplussed during the procedure, I apparently was something of an unusual case, with the level of myopia, astigmatism, and corneal scarring. A noticeable gasp was heard in the room as the doctor revealed my former 20/1000 myopia on a chart.

It is great to be free of contacts and glasses!

Happy Day! RD!!

One way I believe you can tell that your departed loved ones are reaching out to you is if you start thinking about them a lot. Such was the case recently with my dad. Pops passed away suddenly on September 5, 2008. We think it was a heart attack, my primary care doctor suspects it might have even been sleep apnea, as Dad snored heavily, but we don't really know. He simply laid back in his recliner for a nap and never woke up. My Stepmom Barbara briefly left the basement den where Dad was sleeping, and went upstairs to do the dishes. When she returned, Bobbi said my father was as "cold as ice."

Dad has returned to me both in my dreams and the vision at his wake, to let me know he was okay. At other times, I have felt his presence around me.

The week he passed, I was staying with my Cousin Ron at his mobile home in Oakwood Forest in Greensboro. I was between the living room and kitchen all alone one night. Ron and his wife Debbie had gone out. Suddenly, I felt Dad's presence in the room. Even though I knew it was Pops, all alone now in the silence, it felt a little spooky.

I spoke out loud. "Dad, I love you, but you are scaring me a little." His familiar presence then drifted away.

More recently, I was thinking about Pops around my birthday in 2018. For some reason, I was mindful of the crisp $50 bill he gave me on June 20, 1986, standing in my bedroom, still wearing the uniform and work boots from his day at the Carolina Steel mill industrial plant. "Happy Birthday, Son," he said. "I love you." It was the most money anyone had ever given me. It may not sound like much now, but $50 was a lot of money to me back then—more than a day's wage in my job as a bagger at the Food Lion grocery store in rural Summerfield, NC.

When I was born, I am told my dad fretted over me a lot. My face was bruised and disfigured from the forceps procedure at birth, so he was very concerned. As I grew into a toddler, Dad was careful to watch every step I took, to make sure I would not get hurt.

I loved my dad's record collection. I enjoyed hearing the music and was fascinated watching the little 45s spin. I could name them all by seeing the label only, even before I could read. One of my favorites back then was a hit song from the year I was born, "Oh, Happy Day," by the Edwin Hawkins Singers. I also sat at my dad's feet and watched him play guitar, and he would sing to me.

My dad recorded my stomping around the house soon after I started walking. He played the recordings over and over again for guests when they would come by. You could hear my feet clomping on the old wood floor at the house on Wooddale Lane, the place Mom and Dad lived when I was born. I was running around, barely speaking yet, but you could clearly hear me merrily screaming, "Happy day, happy day, happy day!" after my favorite song back then.

The most common term of address my dad used with me was "Son," but he also called me "Richard" or "Rich." When he wanted to feign playful annoyance, he called me "Richard Donald," or "RD" for short, especially when calling out to me from another room. My Aunt Beverly used to playfully call me "Richard Donald" too, but Dad is the only person on earth who ever called me "RD." He would yell from the kitchen, "RD, get in here, boy." Or "RD, your mother's on the phone." If I said something he did not approve and he wanted to mildly scold me, he would use a drawn out, "RD..."

For my birthday in 2018, my wife Janet and stepdaughter Yuni put up a big sign in the living room made up of giant computer print offs of one letter per page, which were combined to read, "happy birthday! Richard!!" It was a big surprise to me when I walked in the door.

Figure 6.4: *Happy Birthday! Richard!!* The author stands in front of the sign shortly after coming home. Photo "selfie" taken June 21, 2018.

I loved the sign so much I left it up for several days. On June 26, 2018, we were in for another surprise.

The three of us were sitting around in the living room when, out of nowhere, the sign partially came down. This kind of thing would probably have seemed normal, were it not for the new message revealed now that some of the letters were covered up.

Before it read, "happy birthday! Richard!!"

Now it said, "happy day! rd!!

As far as I was concerned, the message was clear. The feeling I had been getting about Dad reaching out to me was confirmed. Janet was amazed as I had been talking about Dad lately. Very few people would ever know "Happy Day" was my favorite song as a child. But Dad did—he even took the time to record me singing it as a toddler, "Happy day, happy day, happy day…" And he is definitely the only person to ever call me RD. It was validating to know those feelings I had been getting recently about Dad meant something. As far as I

Figure 6.5: *Happy Day! RD!!* This picture was taken by the author June 26, 2018 at 11:39 p. m. shortly after the message appeared. It was close to the same time of evening as 6.4 above, taken five days earlier.

was concerned, the message was clear. The feeling I had been getting about Dad reaching out to me was confirmed. Janet was amazed as I had been talking about Dad lately. Very few people would ever know "Happy Day" was my favorite song as a child. But Dad did—he even took the time to record me singing it as a toddler, "Happy day, happy day, happy day…" And he is definitely the only person to ever call me RD. It was validating to know those feelings I had been getting recently about Dad meant something.

Even as I was working on this section of the book manuscript, my fire alarm in the hallway outside my den tweeted for no apparent reason, then my television in the den made a cracking sound as if its internal electronics popped, or its weight just settled into the wooden TV stand in front of me. It had the feeling of movement, as if an entity passed from the hallway into the den to join me.

Getting a sign from a loved one is not something that can be proven. Skeptics will say it is just coincidence, but when your loved one reaches out to you from the beyond, you just know it.

Figure 6.6: *Shirley Fay Williams Lewis and George Allen Lewis (my stepmom and dad)*, circa 1982, playing and singing at the "old home place," Grandpa and Grandma Lewis's house on Eastland Avenue, in Greensboro, NC. Photo taken by the author May 25, 2016 from an original print. Family photo.

Chapter 7

Gone Too Soon

Roy Harper

Roy Rogers Harper was my good friend, coworker and Air Force videographer. He made an indelible mark on everyone he touched, from teammates, to customers, to anyone he came in contact with. His was a bright spirit who always seemed to light up any room. Everyone who ever met Roy loved him. He was a keen judge of character and one of the wisest people I have ever known. His family and friends were crushed at the shocking news of Roy's illness diagnosed soon after retirement, and his untimely passing shortly thereafter on September 29, 2014. But Roy's spirit seems to have made contact with me and other people at work numerous times and in various ways since he passed away.

On October 8, 2014, I gave the eulogy at his memorial service at Los Angeles Air Force Base, but it was the evening before when I truly felt Roy's presence, reaching out to me.

I found myself alone in the office on October 7. It was night, and I was exhausted by a long couple of days, but grateful to have a few moments to myself. Mainly, I was tired after having finished writing Roy's eulogy. The next morning I would deliver the tribute at his memorial scheduled for 10:00 a.m. in the Daedalian Room at the base. Everyone in attendance would be looking to me to lead them through the emotional event. I really wanted the memorial to be a success and to truly honor my friend's memory.

So, now it was late. The sky outside through my office windows was pitch black, the only light in my office being the yellow-orange glow of a desk lamp off to the side and the bluish light emanating from the computer screen with Roy's eulogy on it. My eyes were tired. I had been working alone there in my office for hours and got the script as good as I could. But as it turned out, I was apparently not really alone after all.

Something told me to look at the 'It's a Boy' sample gift bottle of vodka celebrating the baby shower for Roy's new grandson, the shower being one of the last events Roy was blessed to experience. Less than 48 hours after the baby shower, Roy died, following a brief but brave battle with pancreatic cancer. Roy had asked the people from work who were visiting at his deathbed in Macon, Georgia to make sure to give the gift bottle to me when they returned to Los Angeles. And the bottle had sat there in my office, right exactly as they had left it.

Something drew my hand to the bottle, now nudging my fingers to turn it around.

So, I slowly spun the bottle around for the first time, instantly stunned by the message on the reverse side. The tag on the back of the bottle read 'Thank You,' a note from Roy Harper—received after I had just finished writing his eulogy.

Figure 7.1a: *Mr. Roy Rogers Harper, former Air Force Videographer,* at the Fanfest event in Pasadena, California, December 31, 2010. Roy was filming on location as the parade floats were being rolled out for the 122nd annual Tournament of Roses Parade taking place the following day. Photo by the author.

Angel Roy

Other people mentioned to me they have sensed Roy's presence at work, especially during after-hours when they were alone in the building at night. Mr. Rod Jones, who worked down the hall from us in the contracting office, said he would get the feeling Roy was there—then the lights in his cubicle would flicker. He also said he would turn and see a shadow fly by the corner of his eyes, and he knew it was Roy.

Another coworker and friend, Krista Knaus, told me she could sense Roy around her, especially when she was feeling troubled at work. Krista feels as though Roy is like an angel now, watching over her. I am not surprised. Roy told his wife, Christine, his position as videographer at Los Angeles Air Force Base was the best job he ever had. He loved the work and he especially loved the people he worked with. Following the ceremony, our Inspector General at the time, Mr.

Todd Trabue, shared that he felt the event was like "reconnecting with an old friend."

Yellow was Roy's favorite color, and I will never forget his smiling face, wearing his Porta Brace videographer vest, yellow or orange polo shirt and ball cap, happily filming on location so many times.

In addition to delivering his eulogy, I was honored to preside over the scattering of Roy's ashes at the Manhattan Beach pier June 15, 2015, as his wife, Chris, returned to California to carry out the event, which was one of Roy's last wishes. After prayers, the dropping of yellow flowers by coworkers and friends, and tearful, final goodbyes, I turned away to power up my iPhone to capture some memorial photos of those in attendance. Just then, as I looked at the blank screen, I saw the reflection of a man wearing a yellow polo shirt and ball cap pass behind me. So, I turned around to see who it was. *But there was no one there.*

Figure 7.1b: *Starbucks Run*. Left to Right: Roy Harper, Krista Knaus, and the author, returning from a walk to the Starbucks at work Aug. 28, 2012. Ms. Knaus and others have said they sense Roy's presence in the office following his passing. Photo taken by Joe Juarez.

To 'Bee' Continued

Although bees and wasps had made a habit of visiting me on various special days on my balcony in Redondo Beach, I had not experienced the phenomena at my new house in Gardena until the morning of July 23, 2018, nearly 10 months living at the new place.

It was a yellow-jacket wasp. Could it be Roy?

July 16th was Roy's birthday, but something told me this flying envoy was from Mom, whose birthday was less than a week away.

That night Mother came to me in my dreams. I have enjoyed visitations from both Mom and Dad in my dreams occasionally. It is a rare and unforgettable experience. Those who have had their loved ones visit them in their dreams will understand what I mean. When it happens, you know it is real.

They never say much, if anything at all. It is more like your spirit is mingling with theirs, content to be fellowshipping once again. After we had visited for a while, Mom spoke these words to me.

"I have to go back now."

"I love you so much," I replied, kissing her neck and cheek.

"I love you too," she said.

Then I woke up in my bed. I grabbed my iPhone off of the nightstand to take a note about the dream so I would not forget. I then dozed back off to sleep.

The next morning on my way to work, the dream was still lingering in my mind. Much to my surprise, soon after merging onto the 405 freeway heading north, a car in front of me appeared with a license plate that read "MOM" on the back. That is the first and only time I ever recall seeing the word "MOM" in a license plate. I took a picture of the license plate, but decided not to share it out of respect to the privacy of the driver.

Then, on Sunday afternoon, July 29, 2018, we were relaxing at home after church. I was sitting in the living room watching one of my favorite shows, *Ancient Aliens* on A&E while Janet was organizing in the kitchen. I reminded her it was Mother's birthday.

"Yay," she said. "Happy Birthday, Mommy!"

Just then, on the screen, a shot appeared from the remains of the ancient city of Tiahuanaco, Bolivia, showing the megalithic ruins of Puma Punku. At that moment, the picture on screen showed ruins, which looked just like they were spelling the word "MOM."

Figure 7.2a: *"MOM" image on TV* (view one), taken on July 29, 2018. This picture came on right after I reminded Janet that it was Mom's birthday. Photo by the author.

Figure 7.2b: *"MOM" image on TV* (detail), taken on July 29, 2018. This picture came on right after I reminded Janet that it was Mom's birthday. Photo and zoom/crop by the author.

Chapter 8

1977

Uncle Tony

My Uncle Tony Martin Myers passed away on May 30, 2017 after a long battle with COPD and emphysema. Uncle Tony was a light-hearted guy who smiled a lot, joked around constantly and enjoyed fishing, music, and the beach. Uncle Tony was also a baptized believer in Jesus Christ, but much like Mr. Notch (Chapter 4), Tony never seemed much interested in talking about religious things. He just believed in the Lord, and that was that.

When I heard of the sudden loss of my Uncle Tony, I immediately started having a flood of memories. It would be impossible to capture in words what my Uncle Tony meant to me, but here are a few brief thoughts that come to mind.

Uncle Tony treated me more like a son than a nephew. Nearly every Friday night when I was in junior high and high school, Uncle Tony would make the drive from Greensboro, North Carolina to Summerfield to pick me up, so I could spend the weekend with him, Aunt Beverly, and my Cousin Ron and Cousin Krystal. I would also spend large amounts of spring, winter, and summer breaks with Uncle Tony and Aunt Bee.

We used to watch things like those awful *Captain America* made-for-TV movies in 1979 and much better *Knight Rider* show in the 1980s. When I was only eight years old, Tony took care of me when I got such a horrible stomach flu that I still cannot eat Funyuns to this day!

Uncle Tony would take me and Cousin Ron, who is like a brother to me, fishing nearly every weekend, and Tony encouraged me in my writing and drawing. We watched wrestling together every Saturday night, and he would get mad at me because I would pull for Ric Flair even though Flair would cheat. We went to see several matches live at the Greensboro Coliseum. I will never forget my Uncle Tony laughing and yelling down at the ring from our nosebleed seats as we watched Roddy Piper, Greg Valentine, Ric Flair, and all the greats chopping and slamming and throwing each other around the arena.

Uncle Tony taught me not to be ashamed to dance, although he never liked my singing voice. He used to get on stage during beach concerts with Alabama and ZZ Top before those groups were well-known and dance and sing along with them. He once broke his knee dancing in platform shoes at the Barrel Lounge in Greensboro back in the 1970s. I learned to appreciate popular country music like Kenny Rogers thanks to Uncle Tony, and he even took me to the local radio station where I met the DJ. The experience was a great inspiration toward my later becoming a broadcaster in the U.S. Air Force.

Uncle Tony loved the beach, and he loved music. He could not get enough of the Ray Parker tune from the movie *Ghostbusters*. He bought the 45 rpm record of that and also Hall & Oates's song "Maneater." He drove us crazy with both those records, which he would play for hours and dance and sing while Ron and I ran up the high-score on the Atari Pac Man.

We saw *Ghostbusters* together at the movies in 1984 as well as the *Karate Kid*. I think Tony cheered more for Daniel-san than any of us teens in the audience.

1977

Uncle Tony taught me the importance of standing up with your family, even if you got your butt kicked by a bully. I also learned a lot by the example of how much love he showed my dear Aunt Beverly and how much respect he showed to my Grandpa Noah Lewis and Grandma Joyce Lewis.

When I was a teenager, Uncle Tony taught me it was no big deal to flirt with girls, and he dropped me and Cousin Ron off for our first double-date meet-up with some young ladies at the Carolina Circle Mall in Greensboro. One night, while everyone was sleeping, Uncle Tony took me to the curb market for fresh fried chicken. We stayed up past midnight and ate 15 pieces of chicken between us!

Uncle Tony made a great morning breakfast, scrambling dozens of fluffy eggs and delicious fried liver pudding and crispy bacon. And he always kept a cheerful disposition; making jokes, trying to get 'chin' on me and Cousin Ron, and he made up strange words like "hun-gah-gah" and he would go around saying, "Beirut!" for some crazy reason.

I remember watching Uncle Tony wipe a tear from his eye one Christmas Day as Cousin Ron opened up his new boombox, so excited! Ronnie was not his natural-born child, but I know Tony loved him like his own son.

Then there was a Christmas Eve at the old home place on Eastland Avenue with Grandpa Noah and Grandma Joyce. While all my family was celebrating inside, and Dad and my uncles were busy playing Christmas music, Tony called me out on the front porch in the dark of night and slipped me a large sum of money. "Merry Christmas," he said. "I love you."

In later years, I really began to appreciate what a loving presence Uncle Tony had always been in my life. I surely miss him, but I know he is at a better place in heaven.

Prior to his passing, Uncle Tony reportedly saw both his mom and his son-in-law Michael, a young man who had died suddenly without warning a couple of years earlier.

I find it very comforting to know death is not a journey we take alone.

Figure 8.1: *Uncle Tony Martin Myers,* circa 2015 at Myrtle Beach, SC. Family photo.

But then, something strange happened shortly after Uncle Tony passed away. The wake was held at the stately old Fairview Baptist Church, on Yanceyville Street in Greensboro, June 1, a Thursday night. My cousin Ron was a deacon at the church.

Figure 8.2: *Fairview Baptist Church* on Yanceyville Street, Greensboro, NC. Photo taken by the author June 21, 2021.

Tony's body was kept in state at the church building overnight. Before he left, Fairview's pastor asked Cousin Ron to set the thermostat at the church to 68 degrees Fahrenheit, and keep it there until the funeral the next morning. Ron, the last person to leave the building that night, switched the A/C to 68 as the pastor had asked and locked the doors.

The next morning when he arrived at Fairview, Ron found the temperature had somehow changed to 77 degrees. So he re-set the temperature to 68. Ron was taken aback.

As I have said, Cousin Ron is like a brother to me. Ron and I know each other so well by now we can almost read the other's mind. Oh, about the strange thing with thermostat at Fairview Church changing temperature:

"I have no idea why it changed," Ron said.

"Come on, Ron, don't you know?" I replied.

My cousin squinted at me, a slight smile on his face.

"Seventy-Seven," I continued. "That's the year Uncle Tony met Aunt Beverly—1977!"

Ronnie's eyes grew big and wide.

He turned to Aunt Beverly, "Hey, Mom, did you hear that?"

Figure 8.3a: *Me and Cousin Ron at our joint birthday celebration in June 1978* at the Old Home Place on Eastland Avenue, Greensboro, NC. Photo taken by the author May 25, 2015 from an original print. Family photo.

1977

Figure 8.3b: *Cousin Ron and I,* December 12, 2009 at Oakwood Forest Mobile Home Park, 4100 U.S. 29 N., Greensboro, NC. Photo taken by Ron's wife, Debbie Harris. Family photo.

Chapter 9

The Easter Boys

Cousin Kelly

Kelly Easter was the star of my high school football team, the Northwest Guilford Vikings. I will never forget that Friday night in 1983 when I watched him catch the winning touchdown against our arch-rivals, Western Guilford. It was the first time we had defeated them in nearly 10 years! It was a sight to see his dad, my Uncle Maynard, and the rest of the crowd, whooping and hollering as Kelly caught that ball and ran like lightning into the end zone.

Kelly was a senior when I was in 8th grade. He used to tell me stories of waking up on Saturday mornings barely able to move, as he was so sore after those Friday night games—but he told me he loved it!

Kelly was tall and muscular, nimble and fast—with excellent hands—the perfect wide-receiver. I remember playing backyard football with Kelly and his brother Marty. With Kelly as the opposing QB, I would rush in and he would avoid my tackles like Neo in the Matrix.

And despite his rock-star good looks and superior athletic prowess, Kelly never looked down on me. He always treated me kindly and encouraged me. He was a great older cousin to look up to.

Kelly was the first to teach me how to bench press, and he would pull Cousin Marty off of me when we got to 'rasslin' too rough.

Kelly also instilled in me a life-long love of heavy metal, that "devil music," which people in our old country church would tell us kids.

Kelly had the looks of a teen idol, with a big smile and light heart—the picture of health and happiness his whole life. You can imagine my shock when I learned Cousin Kelly had been diagnosed with colorectal cancer in his mid-40s.

He had been fighting the disease for many years. The doctors said they never knew such a fighter as Kelly. So tragic, to be facing the possibility of having to say goodbye to children and young grandchildren, not to mention parents who will have to bury a son.

Visiting in June of 2017, I sat in Uncle Maynard and Aunt Rita's living room in rural Madison, North Carolina, listening to Kelly talk about the harsh chemo and radiation treatments. He was considering stopping those seemingly useless therapies because they were making him so sick. "How could they not be killing a human?" Kelly asked.

My mother had to take her chemo home, with taps plugged into her veins, so the poison could slowly ease its deathly touch throughout her entire body. My Aunt Cathy, who was assisting Mom at home, once spilled a single drop of that vile fluid onto her toe and watched in amazement as her toenail fell off the next day! So, I knew exactly where Kelly was coming from.

I got us talking about happier times—like how we used to lift weights together—and I showed Kelly recent pics of me and my son Preston on the squat rack.

"Looks like he's pushin' more than you, boy," Kelly smiled.

And I brought up Ozzy and all that "devil music" we used to listen to.

"That's what they called it at Northwest Baptist Church," Kelly laughed.

"That's what it is!" Uncle Maynard cut in.

"No, it's not," said Kelly. "It's what you make of it."

"Oh yes, it is!" Maynard insisted. "You better believe it, boys."

Kelly just chuckled and flashed that big smile. He seemed wistful, content.

I could still feel Kelly's strong muscles through his shirt as we hugged for what I feared might be the last time as we stood outside Uncle Maynard and Aunt Rita's house, a warm gem of Christian hope nestled in the woods of Madison, North Carolina. It seemed cold for a June night.

"I love you, Cuz," Kelly said.

"I love you too," I replied.

November 18, 2017 – I got a text from my brother, Devin Lewis, alerting me to the unfortunate news of a death in the family. I looked away from my cell phone, not wanting to read the message. I looked again—saw the name, "Easter." I squinted back at the screen.

To my complete surprise, I read that *Marty* Easter, Kelly's brother, had just died the night before.

Cousin Marty

Little Maynard "Marty" Easter was an athlete, like his older brother. But while Kelly was taller than me, Marty was shorter. I am sure being shorter, not to mention having an older brother like Kelly to push him, forged a stubborn determination in Marty.

That and the fact that he was born with a mean-streak.

When we were kids, it got to where his dad, my Uncle Maynard, had to whip him almost every day. One time, exasperated, Maynard turned to Marty mid-spanking.

"Son, I don't know what else to do," his father despaired.

"I guess you'll have to kill me," Marty replied.

I remember walking along in the fields and meadows of southwestern Summerfield with Marty one day and finding an old carburetor sitting in the tall grass. Marty explained to me all about how carburetors and car engines worked. I could have cared less, but I tried to understand because I wanted Marty to like me.

He would quiz me on what I knew about girls, and we would take turns shooting my BB-gun at cans we lined up on an old wooden fence that ran through the fields.

When we were kids, Marty always wanted to compete. We wrestled and raced and shot basketball; but Marty always seemed to have the edge. Late one fall afternoon, with the reddish pink sky of dusk all around, my Uncle Randy—"Bru" they called him, as he was Shirley and Rita's brother—hatched a scheme where I could finally best Marty once and for all.

We were playing football, Randy and me against Marty and Kelly—getting our butts whooped as usual.

"Richard," Randy whispered, pinching my shoulder, "when Marty comes over to block you, do this…" Uncle Randy showed me how to cross my arms together in front of me, using my forearms to catch my rowdy little cuz under his chin. Then, lifting my arms up in one smooth motion, I would run right through him. With the cool air flushing my cheeks, I crouched down in my stance and prepared to make my move.

Bru snapped the ball and I did just like he said. I bolted forward and caught Marty under the chin lifting him up with my crossed forearms. The move sent Marty flying through the air! Marty's feet went out from under him, and he landed hard. Poochie, a freckled-faced brunette girl from around those parts had been watching us play. She was pissed at our dirty trick.

"That shouldn't be legal," she scolded.

I don't think it was.

You would expect Cousin Marty would have been mad about the cheap shot too, but he just laughed it off. Marty sprang back to his feet. "Good one," he said, eyeing me.

Marty faced me off at the line of scrimmage once again and smiled.

"Let's go," he said.

We lost the game that night, as usual.

The Christmas of 1982 was unusually warm in Summerfield, so the old gang—Uncle Randy, Mary, Kelly, myself, and Cousin Kim, another regular from the country neighborhood—were outside in short-sleeves, shooting basketball on the makeshift dirt court that Randy created for us. He mounted a basketball goal to an old telephone pole in the backyard, where we spent many an afternoon laughing and playing and smack-talking. On that Christmas afternoon we were playing H-O-R-S-E. My dad came out with his Betacam to film the action.

"Let's go, Granny Swish!" Dad said, encouraging skinny little Kim, her go-to shot explaining the name. This time her two-handed granny fell short of the rim, skimming the net.

"Next up, it's the Jamaican left-hander!" That is what Dad called Uncle Randy, who had a wicked hook shot and a mean, left-handed lay-up. Dad called me "Dr. Arc" for the often exaggerated, arcing balls I would launch. Dad had taught me to arc it, to improve my accuracy and touch. Perhaps I overdid it at times.

I cannot remember my dad's pet name for Marty, but I will never forget the incredible, long-range shot the boy made that afternoon.

Marty climbed up on my brother's red Radio Flyer wagon, and leapt in the air, releasing the ball mid-air in an arcing, missile-like trajectory. I watched that ball in slow motion—we all watched it. Marty was way beyond three-point range, probably about half-court distance at least.

"Swoosh! The ball sank, blasting through the net. Marty turned right to my dad on camera, all excited, "Did you get that?!" He yelled, grinning ear-to-ear.

And son-of-a-bitch—I was up next.

Over the years, Marty and I grew up together and became

good friends.

It's funny the things you recall: the Halloween party at Penn National Insurance on Wendover, where our stepmoms worked; how they dressed us up like hobos for the festivities; the sleepovers; all those countless family dinners. So many good times going to services together at Northwest Baptist, our little country church in Summerfield. All the delicious homecoming potluck meals there. All the conversations about heavy metal and country music. All the movie nights in our living room.

Dad was the only person around with a Betamax machine; so we would rent the latest Chuck Norris or Schwarzenegger flick, or *Star Wars* or old Honeymooners episodes, and our families would watch those wonderful shows all cozy together at home.

But it was at the movie theatre where we saw *E.T. the Extra-Terrestrial* in 1982. Shirley, Aunt Rita, and Uncle Maynard were there, Kelly too. Marty and I sat together in the middle of our row. I was 13 at the time, and Marty was 14. Everyone enjoyed the show, but there is one little thing that stands out in my mind.

It is the scene where ET is dying as a medical team works furiously to save him, performing CPR, and even using a defibrillator on the little alien. Just then, as things on screen could not possibly get any more tense, Marty turns to me and whispers, "This is bullshit."

I busted out laughing. Then he tells it to Kelly who laughs in agreement too. Aunt Rita gave us a puzzled look of amusement until Kelly cupped his hand and shared the "bullshit" observation in her ear. Then she started laughing. This went on until finally everyone in our group, even Uncle Maynard, was laughing about it too. Marty just sat there smiling.

We shared many good times together. I remember standing in my room as older teenagers, talking about girls. Marty was telling me about Carol, a girl he had recently met, and showed me her picture. I nodded in approval of her good looks. She is the woman he would eventually marry so many years later.

"She says I look like John Cougar Mellencamp," Marty said.

"Yeah, you kinda do," I replied.

"I asked her, 'is that good?'" Marty continued. "She said, 'yeah—it's good.'"

Marty and I parted ways upon both of us joining the military. I went into the Air Force. Marty joined the Army, serving in the first Gulf War, and receiving several medals for bravery for his actions under enemy fire.

Years later, it was said of Marty that he would be seen in the aisles of Walmart, laying on hands and praying for strangers he had just met. Even if he did not always attend church services on Sundays, he still faithfully sent in his gifts and offerings to Northwest Baptist Church every week. He felt it was the right thing to do.

Marty stayed in the lives of his stepchildren, whether or not he was with their mother. Marty did not believe in "steps."

Common parlance he would share with his stepdaughter Natasha when he felt she required extra motivation was to ask her if she needed "a swift kick in the ass."

That was Marty.

November 18, 2017 – I find myself sitting on the concrete slab outside my house in Los Angeles, the chill of the night barely fended off by an old flannel. I am puffing a cigar, eyes glazing over, remembering the story my brother told me about how Marty, 49, died.

Marty's wife, Carol, his high school sweetheart—still newlyweds, married only eight months—found her husband face down in a small pool of water within a ravine.

No one knows what Marty was doing down there, but his truck was stuck in the muck, and his head was bleeding after apparently landing on a concrete slab near the water.

Carol attempted to provide life support as she waited for paramedics to arrive, but Marty never woke up.

Poor thing, I thought, imagining Marty's wife—all alone in the cold and dark—trying to bring her husband back to life.

Just then, my cell phone lit up.

Must be Devin texting me again, I thought.

So, I picked up the phone, but there was nobody there—no text, no call.

Thanksgiving Day, 2017 – I rushed to finish mowing the grass, as guests arrived early. My thoughts were torn between our hosting duties in California and the fact that I would be on a plane to North Carolina the next day—flying back for Marty's funeral.

Upon finishing the backyard, I turned to go inside. Looking back, I saw an orange basketball sitting in the yard, near my house. It was an outdoor ball, orange and faded, not unlike the ball we were shooting outside at the old place in Summerfield that Christmas of 1982.

How did it get into my yard? I wondered. It was like it appeared out of nowhere, not there one moment, sitting there the next. I never heard any sound of it landing. There are no children in the homes on either side of me, and the neighbors next door on the side where the ball landed are elderly. One minute the ball was not there, the next minute, there it was. And no one ever came to claim it (And no other strange ball has landed in my yard since then at the time of this writing).

"Did you get that?!" Marty had yelled.

"Yeah, Cuz," I whispered. "I get it." With a slight smile, I turned and entered my home, greeted by the sounds of loved ones laughing and the smell of warm turkey roasting in the oven.

November 25, 2017 – I sat in the very back of the chapel at Colonial Funeral Home in Madison, North Carolina, as services for Marty were beginning. From my vantage point, I could see friends and family all the way up to the front where the flag-draped coffin of my cousin sat in the center of the room.

The sounds of sobbing and crying formed a cacophony of mourning all around my ears as the ceremony began in earnest. Way up front in the aisle, there was Kelly, Marty's brother—now in a wheelchair—as the radiation treatments had broken his back. Kelly wiped away many tears from his eyes that afternoon. Tears for his brother.

Uncle Randy, "Bru," sat immediately in front of me, loudly shouting "Amen!" in agreement with the pastor's assurances of eternal life in God's Kingdom. A Southern Baptist funeral is an emotional mash-up, blending great sorrow on the one hand at the loss of a loved one, while at the same time functioning as a celebration of life, of this life and the life to come, both for the one who passed as well as for all of those in attendance.

As I sat there meditating on Marty and his many accomplishments in life, it was still so hard to believe that he was truly gone. And we still do not fully understand the circumstances of his passing. All we know is it appears to have been an unfortunate accident.

Several people entered the chapel after me, so it should come as no surprise that I felt a hand on my shoulder as an arm encircled my neck. But the next part was very astonishing…

A face appeared in front of mine. It was… *Marty*—leaning down to look at me!

His face was frozen in the familiar smile of the spirit departed, his arm still around my neck as he looked right at me. Marty's specter must have been at least seven or eight feet tall. He was no longer "little Marty."

My cousin spoke to me telepathically. "I'm good," he told me. It was almost nonchalant. I heard the voice in my head, as his face continued smiling. I was thinking about heaven. He knew my thoughts.

"It's not what you think," Marty answered. With that enigmatic statement, the large figure turned away from me and rose, walking down the aisle toward the flag-draped coffin at the front of the room and disappeared.

✝

I blew Cousin Kelly a kiss as they wheeled him past me after the service. I am not sure why I chose such a gesture, but Kelly nodded to me nonetheless as he passed by, still wiping away tears. My own tears began to flow once I saw the grief-stricken faces of Uncle Maynard and Aunt Rita, both of them coming over to hug me simultaneously.

I spoke to Kelly in the reception room outside the chapel, as he was surrounded by many comforting family members. He still managed to show that winning smile.

"I thought you would be coming back to see me," he said (meaning at his funeral).

"I am glad to see *you*," I replied.

Later on, back at the Easter house in Madison, as the afternoon turned to evening, Kelly hugged me from his seat at the end of the kitchen table. Even then his muscles still felt strong.

"How you holdin' up, boy?" Kelly whispered in my ear.

"I'm good," I answered softly. "How 'bout you?"

"I'm hangin' in there," Kelly answered.

"You keep hanging in there, Kelly," I said. "God bless you. I am praying for you, every day. I love you, Cuz."

"I love you too," Kelly replied, hugging me again.

I never told my family what I saw that day at the chapel. They were grieving so deeply, I was not sure if my vision would bring them comfort or make things worse—especially if I told them what Marty said to me about heaven—"it's not what you think." Most of all, I did not want to offend them.

An experience like this is not the kind of thing the Southern Baptist understanding can easily explain, nor my Lutheran belief system either, for that matter, where "we don't know" is the common response that you will hear from most any LCMS pastor when prodded to draw out speculation about things not directly spelled out in Scripture. Worse yet, they might think I had gone mad.

Perhaps the puzzling nature of Marty's statement was less about biblical eschatology and more about my own personal belief system. Perhaps I got something wrong along the way? Maybe that is what he was trying to tell me. Or maybe I am just making too much of it.

These are things I will be thinking about for a long time.

December 19, 2017 – Less than a month after Marty's funeral, I got the news that Cousin Kelly, 52, had also passed away. In the days before he died, he told Aunt Rita, "I already saw Marty." Apparently his loving brother was waiting to welcome Kelly into heaven.

Figure 9.1a: *Cousin Kelly and Marty,* circa 1974. This is how the Easter boys looked in childhood shortly before I met them. Image taken by the author from an original print on November 25, 2017. Family photo.

Figure 9.1b: *Cousin Kelly and Marty,* circa 2015. Image taken by the author from an original print on November 25, 2017. Family photo.

This mystery of the afterlife, of being told, "It's not what you think," was nagging at me. It made me think back to my 2014 interview with Luis Minero at the International Academy of Consciousness. Mr. Minero, you may recall from Chapter 1, started out as a Catholic in childhood, but now feels the sightings we have of Jesus or the saints are probably just a projection of our own expectations onto the beings we encounter out-of-body.

Minero believes in a non-corporeal existence outside the body, of course, and he acknowledges entities beyond the physical; but, he seems to have given up his traditional faith.

It is vexing to imagine our faith as simply a construct coming from shared history, experiences, beliefs, and expectations. Did Christianity get it wrong with our concepts about heaven and the afterlife? Could we be in for a big surprise on the other side?

No, I reject that. The Bible is true. Jesus is real. I have seen him. Felt His love. Experienced Him.

Minero admits we have spirit guides. He has encountered them in his OBE journeys. What else could those entities be if not what the Bible suggests?

I did enjoy my visit with Mr. Minero, and it is important to keep IAC's outlook in perspective. Their intention is not to study the out-of-body experience in a religious way. The group states "Our work is based on scientific precepts and aims to deepen human knowledge in a non-reductionist paradigm, centered on the consciousness... We value non-dogmatic learning and apply the highest level of integrity and ethics in our work."[34]

Although the IAC does not profess association with any particular religious belief system, I would say the work done by Mr. Minero and groups like the IAC is of particular interest to those of us who do believe; because it *does* lend credence to the non-materialistic, Biblical worldview—that the spirit continues on and exists outside of and independent of the physical form. In the end, this validates the Bible.

In addition to studying the Scriptures, interviewing people and hearing the stories of so many, not to mention the number of after-death communications I have personally received, I am convinced that we do *immediately* continue on after death.

My Uncle Coy "Maynard" Easter followed his sons into the afterlife on Saturday, January 15, 2022, after his own battle with cancer. In addition to Marty and Kelly, Maynard was preceded in death by his infant son, Derrick, who died the same day he was born, November 29, 1976–a cousin we never got to meet. Now the Easter boys are all together again.

As they were going along and talking, behold, *there appeared* a chariot of fire and horses of fire which separated the two of them. And Elijah went up by a whirlwind to heaven.
Elisha saw *it* and cried out, "My father, my father, the chariots of Israel and its horsemen!"
And he saw Elijah no more.
2 Kings 2:11-12
New American Standard Bible (NASB 1995)

Truly I say to you, among those born of women there has not arisen *anyone* greater than
John the Baptist! And if you are willing to accept *it*,
John himself is Elijah who was to come.
Matthew 11:11, 14
New American Standard Bible (NASB 1995)

Chapter 10

Born Again

Study of the out-of-body experience yields convincing evidence of the existence of consciousness outside the physical form. Taken further, perhaps the ultimate OBE is the idea of the spirit leaving the body at death, only to return to earth at a later point to occupy a new body and a new life—transmigration—or as it is better known, *reincarnation*.

The cycle of rebirth is a long-held belief in many religious systems; however, it is considered heresy to most in mainstream Christianity. The Catechism of the Catholic Church number 1013 states, quite simply, "There is no "reincarnation" after death."[35]

But many Christians do believe in reincarnation. A 2009 Pew Research Center study found that over 20% of American Christians believe in reincarnation.[36]

Early gnostic Christian sects professed the belief, and some say there were even those in the early church who believed in reincarnation as well.[37] It is easy to understand how a belief in transmigration could have arisen among the first Christians, many of whom were Greek converts. Greek philosophers discussed the concept as far back as the 6th century BC.[38]

The Enigma of Origen

The great church father Origen of Alexandria, who lived from about 184 to 253, was a towering intellect, prolific writer, and devoted believer in Christ. He was perhaps the greatest early theologian and biblical expositor since Paul, and was the father of systematic theology.[39]

Origen would eventually be martyred, succumbing to injuries sustained during brutal torture on the rack for his refusal to sacrifice to the Roman gods.[40]

Some say Origen's writings indicate the provocative church father believed in reincarnation. Without a doubt, he believed in the eternal nature of the soul, which was repeatedly referred to in his theological treatise, *On the First Principles* or *De Principiis,* which he wrote between AD 220 and 230.[41]

Origen said, "…we human beings are animals composed of a union of body and soul, and in this way (only) was it possible for us to live upon the earth."[42]

Spirit of the Matter

The idea of a dichotomy of body-soul, or soul (spirit) separate from the body, is found among many ancient peoples in different variations of concept. Most clearly informing our Western thinking were the Greeks, most notably Plato, who argued the number of souls must be finite because souls are indestructible.[43] That in itself is an argument for reincarnation!

This idea of spirit being independent of the body was not foreign to ancient Christianity, with thinkers like Saint Gregory and Saint Augustine understanding the spiritual nature of man apart from the natural, and the concept does not conflict with the biblical account at all. Why else would David say, "Bless the Lord, O my soul, and all that is within me" (Psalm 103:1, ESV), and Paul say, "The Spirit Himself bears witness with our spirit that we are children of God" (Romans 8:16, NKJV)? Also, James the brother of Jesus asked, "Do you suppose it is to no purpose that the Scripture says, 'He [God] yearns jealously over the spirit that He has made to dwell in us?'" (James 4:5, ESV).

Some writers say James is talking about the Holy Spirit, but that is unlikely, as the Apostle does not mention the Holy Spirit anywhere else in his book. Besides, why would God yearn jealously over His own spirit? No, He yearns to commune with you and me, the hidden treasure of His kingdom, buried in this field of the earth—yes, even hidden in these earthly bodies! (Matthew 13:44).

The idea of a human soul or spirit, apart from the body, and surviving the body after death is so well established in Scripture that I do not even need to argue it. Now, whether or not the spirit actually precedes the body as Origen believed, we simply do not know for sure. I would propose there is nothing in Scripture to expressly disprove it, certainly nothing decisive to prove spirit and body are created simultaneously, as many Christians believe.

Theologian and translator Tyrannius Rufinus, believing heretics deliberately altered Origen's Greek manuscript of *De Principiis*, may have ended up muddling Origen's writing to bring it in line with orthodox Christianity of the day. He was convinced that Origen's treatise had been interpolated in such a way that heretical teachings were introduced into the manuscript. So in 397 Rufinus heavily modified and paraphrased Origen's text when translating it into Latin.[44]

This action may have obscured whether Origen believed in and taught reincarnation or not. It is hard to say, as little of Origen's original Greek version of *De Principiis* survives today.[45]

Saint Jerome also translated Origen's *De Principiis* into Latin around AD 400, at the request of Pammachius, a Roman senator and Christian, to correct the previous Latin translation by Rufinus from 397 that Jerome called a "misrendering."[46]

CatholicAnswers.com has a tract on reincarnation that claims the church father did not believe in reincarnation and puts forth the following quotes supposedly taken from Origen.

> …One might say that John did not know that he was Elijah. This will be the explanation of those who find in our passage

a support for their doctrine of reincarnation, as if the soul clothed itself in a fresh body and did not quite remember its former lives… [H]owever, a churchman, who repudiates the doctrine of reincarnation as a false one and does not admit that the soul of John was ever Elijah, may appeal to the above-quoted words of the angel, and point out that it is not the soul of Elijah that is spoken of at John's birth, but the spirit and power of Elijah.[47]

In Origen's commentary on the Gospel of Matthew, it would seem he speaks against reincarnation.

In this place, it does not appear to me that by Elijah the soul is spoken of, lest I should fall into the dogma of transmigration, which is foreign to the church of God, and not handed down by the Apostles, nor anywhere set forth in the Scriptures.[48]

Here also, Origen seems to support the view that early Greek Christians were indeed trying to correlate reincarnation with the Christian faith.

But to one who has insight into the nature of things it is clear that each of these things is fitted to overturn the doctrine of transmigration. But if, of necessity, the Greeks who introduce the doctrine of transmigration, laying down things in harmony with it, do not acknowledge that the world is coming to corruption, it is fitting that when they have looked the Scriptures straight in the face which plainly declare that the world will perish, they should either disbelieve them, or invent a series of arguments in regard to the interpretation of the things concerning the consummation…[49]

Still, Origen's commentary on Matthew only survives in a Latin translation, which may be problematic. Again, some say when his works were translated into Latin, the references supporting reincarnation were concealed.[50]

As to Saint Jerome, he held that Origen did believe in reincarnation.

Saint Jerome

Eusebius Sophronius Hieronymus, or Saint Jerome, was a priest, theologian, and translator of great significance who lived from around 347 to 420. Jerome is responsible for producing a near entire translation of the Bible into Latin. Known as the Vulgate, this historic work was an important precursor to our modern English language Bible.[51] For over a thousand years, the Vulgate was the definitive edition of the Bible, the most influential text in Western Europe throughout the Middle Ages and Renaissance, and perhaps even eclipsing the later King James Version's influence in English.[52]

Although an admirer of Origen, Jerome wanted to faithfully translate the early church father's words, for good or for bad. If Origen's beliefs were heretical, it would be there for all to see. Here now are the words of Saint Jerome taken from his Letter 124 , Paragraph 15.

> The following passage is a convincing proof that he [Origen] holds the transmigration of souls and annihilation of bodies. "If it can be shown that an incorporeal and reasonable being has life in itself independently of the body and that it is worse off in the body than out of it; then beyond a doubt bodies are only of secondary importance and arise from time to time to meet the varying conditions of reasonable creatures. Those who require bodies are clothed with them, and contrariwise, when fallen souls have lifted themselves up to better things, their bodies are once more annihilated. They are thus ever vanishing and ever reappearing."[53]

I was not able to find anything directly from Origen that shows the church father believed in reincarnation, but I think it is at least possible that he did. The above quotation of Origen from Jerome reminds one of Paul, who said, "We would rather be away from the body and at home with the Lord" (2 Corinthians 5:8, ESV).

But that does not mean bodies are evil, as the Gnostics believed. Certainly, the physical body is prone to sin. "The spirit is willing, but the flesh is weak" (Matthew 26:41, NIV). But we look forward not to being unclothed, but being further clothed in our heavenly bodies.

> For in this tent we groan, longing to put on our heavenly dwelling, if indeed by putting it on we may not be found naked. For while we are still in this tent, we groan, being burdened—not that we would be unclothed, but that we would be further clothed. (2 Corinthians 5:2-4, ESV)

Origen did believe in the preexistence of souls, worlds before ours, and the unerring propagation of Divine Providence. It is to the latter where we may find a reason for Origen's fixation on the preexistence of souls. He did not want to implicate God in any way for the condition of man in this life and preferred to see it as a result of our past actions. Origen would not entertain any thought of an unjust God, creating bad vessels for no good reason.

> …the judgment of Divine Providence on each individual thing; and that, of those events which happen to men, none occur by accident or chance, but in accordance with a plan so carefully considered, and so stupendous, that it does not overlook even the number of the hairs of the heads, not merely of the saints, but perhaps of all human beings…[54] For the Creator makes vessels of honor and vessels of dishonor, not from the beginning according to His foreknowledge, since He does not condemn or justify beforehand according to it; but (He makes) those into vessels of honor who purged themselves, and those into vessels of dishonor who allowed themselves to remain unpurged: so that it results from older

causes (which operated) in the formation of the vessels unto honor and dishonor, that one was created for the former condition, and another for the latter…that a more ancient cause for Jacob being loved and for Esau being hated existed with respect to Jacob before his assumption of a body, and with regard to Esau before he was conceived in the womb of Rebecca…[55]

Origen talks about prior causes being to blame for the present condition. Here he clearly suggests the pre-existence of the spirit or soul. Whether or not he is saying the soul lived in a prior life is hard to prove from the text. He may simply mean the acts of the soul prior to incarnation. But I would say the preexistence of souls concept does follow easily to reincarnation. Still, I think the main thing here is Origen wants to be sure not to implicate the Almighty for our state of unrighteousness.

> …no shadow of injustice rests upon the divine government, than by holding that there were certain causes of prior existence, in consequence of which the souls, before their birth in the body, contracted a certain amount of guilt in their sensitive nature, or in their movements, on account of which they have been judged worthy by Divine Providence of being placed in this condition. For a soul is always in possession of free-will, as well when it is in the body as when it is without it; and freedom of will is always directed either to good or evil. Nor can any rational and sentient being, i.e., a mind or soul, exist without some movement either good or bad. And it is probable that these movements furnish grounds for merit even before they do anything in this world; so that on account of these merits or grounds they are, immediately on their birth, and even before it, so to speak, assorted by Divine Providence for the endurance either of good or evil.[56]

Note: all quotes from De Principiis above are taken from New Advent.org unless otherwise noted. The pages can be retrieved at http://www.newadvent.org/fathers/0412.htm.

Final Thoughts on Origen

The preexistence of souls, if true, makes Origen's arguments flawlessly logical. I agree our spirits do have free will in or out of the body, whether or not we preexist prior to incarnation. Our free agency in the spirit realm is consistent with the Scriptures. Jesus said in the spirit we are "like the angels in heaven" (Matthew 22:30, NIV). "For when they rise from the dead, they neither marry nor are given in marriage, but are like angels in heaven" (Mark 12:25, ESV). And the Scriptures reveal how some angels, created to serve God, chose not to keep their proper place.

"And the angels who did not stay within their own position of authority, but left their proper dwelling, he has kept in eternal chains under gloomy darkness until the judgment of the great day..." (Jude 1:6, ESV). While some angels abused their freedom, it is to God's glory that He allows His creatures our free agency. "You, my brothers and sisters, were called to be free" (Galatians 5:13, NIV).

God gives His imagers free will. We humans have free will on earth. His angels who are spirits have free will in heaven, and we, when we become like angels, must as well.

I realize belief in reincarnation is denounced by the church. Perhaps she has always condemned it. But even the ancient confessions of our church must be considered, with a respectful awareness of the weight they carry, but also with the understanding that they are still only the reasoned understandings of men. They are not Scripture. And even if the consensus-finding denied reincarnation, and that verdict is old, it does not make the conclusion true.

Life Review versus Final Judgment

Whether or not Origen did, I do believe in reincarnation, not in the sense that we return as cats or insects, but I think we occupy many physical lifetimes in the journey of our spirit. This is just a personal belief, but I do not think it contradicts the Bible as most Christians say. Let's take a look at the main Bible verse used to refute reincarnation.

> Just as people are destined to die once, and after that to face judgment, so Christ was sacrificed once to take away the sins of many; and he will appear a second time, not to bear sin, but to bring salvation to those who are waiting for him. (Hebrews 9:27-28, NIV)

Many Christians think the statement, "people are destined to die once" precludes the possibility of returning to earth in successive lifetimes. But that may not really be what the verse above is saying.

Of course, each individual physical body will face an ultimate and final death. And as the verse says, the spirit goes on "to face judgment."

But consider this: in almost all cases of NDE, the person reports undergoing a life review. In other words, they do face judgment of a kind. Following the NDE, the person gets to return to their body, with a unique insight and opportunity to make changes in that very life; but of course, in most cases of death, we do not make it back to that same life with our soul lessons learned because we simply die—I would argue, until the next lifetime, perhaps to continue learning.

The final judgment of the dead, though, will apparently not happen until the return of Christ, and the "Great White Throne Judgment" prophesied in Revelation 20 and also in Matthew 25. But as I mentioned earlier in Chapter 1, for the believer our misdeeds will be considered as forgiven sins—as Jesus will tell us, "Come, you who are blessed by my Father; take your inheritance, the kingdom prepared for you since the creation of the world" (Matthew 25:34, NIV). Indeed, "There is no judgment against anyone who believes in him" (John 3:18, NLT).

But who is to say how many incarnations a soul can occupy until then? I would say we even see a parallel to transmigration happening in our current lifetimes!

Many Faces, One Soul

Is it so strange to imagine the same spirit wearing different faces? Even in the same lifetime, we wear many faces. Consider a man's face at 10, then at 30, then at 50, then at 70 and so on—all very different faces, they almost look like different people—but still with a discernible similarity. I believe such to be the case with past lives.

There are many documented cases of people who have traced past-life memories to find evidence of the previous lifetime. Where pictures are found, the person from the past will often look eerily similar to the present individual.

Bloody Memories

Take, for example, the case of Confederate Brig. Gen. John Gordon and retired firefighter Jeff Keene. Mr. Keene came to believe he was the reincarnation of General Gordon after a flood of past-life memories surfaced at a chance visit to a place called the Sunken Road, an area of gigantic Antietam National Battlefield.[57]

The Battle of Antietam, which took place in 1862 near Sharpsburg, Maryland and Antietam Creek, was the site of the bloodiest battle in American history, with well over 22,000 casualties.[58]

I personally visited Antietam on Halloween 2018, and can attest to the enormity of scope and scale of the battlefield and the violent combat that spanned it. The fact that Keene would happen to tour the Sunken Road or "Bloody Lane" as it came to be known, amidst such an expansive area that encompasses some 3,000 acres, and experience strong, past-life memories, where he actually felt real emotions, like anger, is amazing, especially when you consider Keene previously had no interest in the Civil War or read any books about the subject.[59]

Upon researching the topic, Keene discovered the history of General Gordon who fell at the sunken road, an area of some of the fiercest fighting, where thousands of union and federal troops clashed for nearly four hours. It was said blood flowed like a river through the pass,

Born Again

hence the nickname "bloody lane." Gordon, then a colonel, valiantly led his men from the front despite being severely wounded.

Gordon was hit several times by enemy fire, including in the face, but survived drowning in his own blood as it drained out from a bullet-hole in his cap.[60]

Most astounding of all, the resemblance between Keene and Gordon is uncanny.

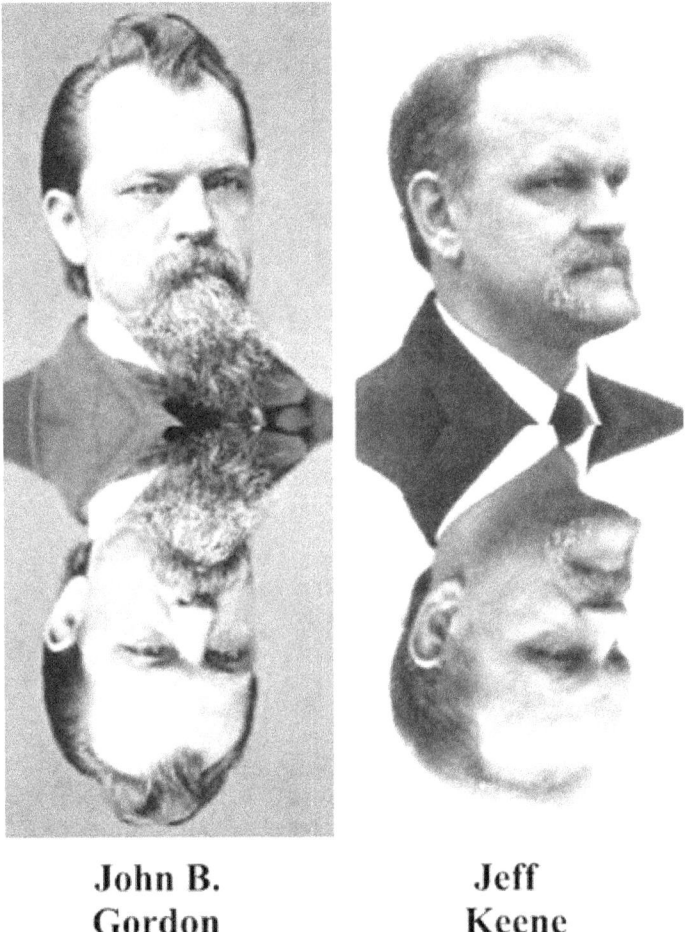

Figure 10.1: *Confederate Brig. Gen. John Gordon and Retired Firefighter Jeff Keene. Keene believes he is the reincarnation of the confederate general.*[61]

Figure 10.2: *The Sunken Road,* Antietam National Battlefield, October 31, 2018. This is the infamous "Bloody Lane" where Confederate Brig. Gen. John Gordon fell, but miraculously survived, during the Battle of Antietam, September 17, 1862. Photo taken by the author.

Figure 10.3: *The Sunken Road,* Antietam National Battlefield, October 31, 2018. Here I stand at the "Bloody Lane" just a few steps from where Brig. Gen. Gordon fell. Photo taken by the author.

Chapter 11

The Argument for Reincarnation

Jesus himself said we must be "born again" (John 3:7). Now, most Christians—myself included—take this statement, which literally means "born from above," to mean the spiritual re-birth needed to enter God's kingdom. But it is interesting to note the mysterious way Jesus explains this process—comparing the spirit's coming and going like the procession of the wind.

> "...Do not marvel that I said to you, 'You must be born again.' The wind blows where it wishes, and you hear its sound, but *you do not know where it comes from or where it goes* [emphasis added]. So it is with everyone who is born of the Spirit." (John 3:7-8, ESV)

This coming and going of the Spirit is "with everyone born of the Spirit." Consider Young's Literal Translation "that which hath been born of the Spirit is spirit" (John 3:6, YLT). So, if this coming and going is true of all spirits "born from above," it might imply pre-existence, as Origen believed, if not reincarnation.

If reincarnation is true, the period of time between incarnations seems to vary. Some report returning after many decades, others after only a few years or less—some even returning to the same family.

I believe this cycle of reincarnation is real, and will continue, until the Lord returns at the end of the age. "But of that day and hour no one knows," said Jesus, "not even the angels of heaven, but My Father only" (Matthew 24:36, NKJV).

At that that point in time, there will no longer be any need for reincarnation. We will inhabit a new earth, with glorified bodies (1 Corinthians 15:44).

The New Earth

This may sound like science fiction, but it is the ancient teaching of Scripture. "Then I saw "a new heaven and a new earth," for the first heaven and the first earth had passed away…" (Revelation 21:1, NIV). This is what Origen was talking about with his plurality of worlds (*De Principiis*, Book III, Chapter 5, Paragraph 3). And Origen noted the new heaven and new earth is something the Prophet Isaiah spoke about (see Isaiah 65:17-25).

Although scholars may argue over which passages in Revelation are to be taken literally versus figuratively, it seems clear to me the finality of this new earth is something quite different. "There will be no more night. They will not need the light of a lamp or the light of the sun, for the Lord God will give them light. And they will reign for ever and ever" (Revelation 22:5, NIV). "…the sound of weeping and of crying will be heard in it no more. Never again will there be in it an infant who lives but a few days, or an old man who does not live out his years; the one who dies at a hundred will be thought a mere child…" (Isaiah 65:19-20, NIV).

Some have interpreted the above to mean there will still be death in the new world, but Isaiah is using poetic language here; so, he is most likely emphasizing immortality with the idea that someone a hundred years old would be considered a mere child.

In a 2016 online article, titled "Reconciling Isaiah 65:20 with 'No more death,'" James Johnson advances the troublesome idea that some Old Testament Scriptures were eliminated or altered by Jewish leaders to quell the explosive growth of Christianity. He cites the church father Justin Martyr levying this accusation in *Dialog With Trypho* (LXXI-LXXIII) as proof.[62]

Our current NIV says, "The one who dies at a hundred will be thought a mere child." Johnson says Justin Martyr's Septuagint reads: "For the young man shall be an hundred years old." Johnson says the word "death" has moved from where it was in Justyn Martyr's Septuagint, and was previously associated with the sinner who we know will die: Justin Martyr: "but the sinner who dies an hundred years old, he shall be accursed."[63]

This idea of the Jewish religious leaders rejecting their own Scriptures, which spoke of Christ, was also hinted at by Tertullian, writing circa AD 198. While Tertullian allowed they may have rejected the Book of Enoch, believing that it could not have survived the Flood of Noah, he also implied it may have also been for reason of the Messianic verses in Enoch.

> [The Book of Enoch] may now seem to have been rejected for that (very) reason, just like all the other (portions) nearly which tell of Christ. Nor, of course, is this fact wonderful, that they did not receive some Scriptures which spake of Him whom even in person, speaking in their presence, they were not to receive. To these considerations is added the fact that Enoch possesses a testimony in the Apostle Jude. [Jude 14,15]. (Ante-Nicene Fathers Vol 4, On the Apparel of Women, Book I, Chapter III—Concerning the Genuineness of "The Prophecy Of Enoch."[64]

I did find there is a lost Scripture in the Book of Enoch that references the "Son of Man," one of the Lord's favorite references to himself. We see this in Scriptures such as Matthew 8:20, 9:6, 11:19, 16:13,

18:11, 20:28, 24:27, Mark 8:38, Luke 18:8, John 5:27, 6:53, 12:23, 13:31 and Acts 7:56.[65]

The passage in question comes in the Book of Enoch, The Parables, LXXI (Chapter 71), between verses 13 and 14. "[Lost passage wherein the Son of Man was described as accompanying the Head of Days, and Enoch asked one of the angels (as in XLVI.3) concerning the Son of Man as to who he was.]"

Then the book picks up again at verse 14:

> 14 And he (i.e. the angel) came to me and greeted me with His voice, and said unto me
> 'This is the Son of Man who is born unto righteousness,
> And righteousness abides over him,
> And the righteousness of the Head of Days forsakes him not.'
> 15 And he said unto me:
> 'He proclaims unto thee peace in the name
> of the world to come;
> For from hence has proceeded peace since the creation
> of the world,
> And so shall it be unto thee for ever and for ever and ever.'[66]

The verses above are clearly referring to Jesus Christ, Son of Man, Prince of Peace (Isaiah 9:6) since the creation of the world (John 1:1-4).

Could the missing passage have been dropped by scribes of the Hebrew faith, in an attempt to quell the growing Christian faith? Or perhaps the passage was just lost to time.

I find it hard to believe faithful leaders of the Jewish religion would alter or eliminate their own sacred Scriptures, but Isaiah is so full of Messianic prophesies it is sometimes called the "fifth Gospel." I am sure it must have been vexing for 1st and 2nd century adherents to the faith of Abraham to try and explain away Jesus of Nazareth as their Messiah, when He so clearly fulfilled all the requirements. There is simply no doubt then or now that Jesus was and is our Christ, the Messiah who was promised.

As to the proposed issue with Isaiah 65:20, it is also possible the word "death" simply moved by an accidental error in translation over time.

Either way, the Scriptures are clear: death will be wiped away in the world to come.

The Christian teachings espoused in Revelation appeared around AD 95. Revelation 21:4 says, "He will wipe away every tear from their eyes, and death shall be no more, neither shall there be mourning, nor crying, nor pain anymore, for the former things have passed away" (ESV).

The seeming contradiction in Isaiah must remain a mystery for now. Isaiah clearly taught there would be no death in the world to come. "He will swallow up death forever; and the Lord God will wipe away tears from all faces, and the reproach of his people he will take away from all the earth, for the Lord has spoken" (Isaiah 25:8, ESV). So, the Old Testament and New Testament do correlate.

If there really is a perpetual succession of worlds as Origen and many others believed, with a cycle of death and rebirth, and a similar cycle of death and rebirth progression of our own physical body incarnations, then it seems that all of it must come to an end at the Lord's return.

Got Questions Ministries explains the new earth like this:

> The heaven that believers will experience will be a new and perfect planet on which we will dwell. The new earth will be free from sin, evil, sickness, suffering, and death. It will likely be similar to our current earth, or perhaps even a re-creation of our current earth, but without the curse of sin.[67]

The Lord has tarried in His return now for nearly 2,000 years. Who is to say He will not delay thousands, even millions more years? Remember, "no one knows the day or hour" (Matthew 24:36, NLT). Of course we must also keep in mind that "with the Lord one day is as a thousand years, and a thousand years as one day" (2 Peter 3:8, ESV).

But consider this:

Well over 100 billion people have inhabited our planet since the beginning of time, according to an online Population Reference Bureau article titled "How Many People Have Ever Lived on Earth?" by Toshiko Kaneda and Carl Haub.[68]

Imagine all the believers from then until now, all those discarnate spirits, billions of them—just hanging out in paradise, the "old" heaven, and simply waiting for millennia upon millennia for what—millions, maybe even billions, more years? Of course, I am sure we have activities there, jobs even, in heaven. I do not believe the time is spent being idle, but still. Also, consider all those people tragically cut down early in life. Does it not make sense they would get another chance at life? Just imagine all the lessons and growth our souls would experience with each successive lifetime!

Yes, you may say. That all sounds well and good. A nice thought. But what does the Bible have to say about it?

Reincarnation in Scripture

A thoughtful look at Scripture reveals the Apostles themselves may have even believed in reincarnation. There are several verses that I feel corroborate this argument.

> When Jesus came to the region of Caesarea Philippi, he asked his disciples, "Who do people say the Son of Man is?" They replied, "Some say John the Baptist; others say Elijah; and still others, Jeremiah or one of the prophets." (Matthew 16:13-14, NIV)

Note the casual manner in which the disciples discuss the possibility Jesus was the rebirthed return of an earlier prophet. Is that not reincarnation? It seems many people thought Jesus *was* the reincarnation of the Prophet Elijah. Jesus clarified that he was not Elijah returned; however, He went on to say Elijah *had* returned in the person of John the Baptist!

> From the days of John the Baptist until now the kingdom of heaven suffers violence, and violent men take it by force. For all the prophets and the Law prophesied until John. And if you are willing to accept *it*, <u>John himself is Elijah</u> [emphasis added] who was to come. He who has ears to hear, let him hear. (Matthew 11:12-15, NASB)

Notice how Jesus said, "if you are willing to accept it." To this day people are still unwilling to accept it. Whether or not they understood it at the time, John's arrival on the scene was a fulfilment of prophesies from the Book of Malachi.

"Behold, I will send you Elijah the prophet before the great and awesome day of the LORD comes. And he will turn the hearts of fathers to their children and the hearts of children to their fathers" (Malachi 4:5-6, ESV).

> Then an angel of the Lord appeared to him, standing at the right side of the altar of incense. When Zechariah saw him, he was startled and was gripped with fear. But the angel said to him: "Do not be afraid, Zechariah; your prayer has been heard. Your wife Elizabeth will bear you a son, and you are to call him John. He will be a joy and delight to you, and many will rejoice because of his birth, for he will be great in the sight of the Lord. He is never to take wine or other fermented drink, and he will be filled with the Holy Spirit even before he is born. He will bring back many of the people of Israel to the Lord their God. And he will go on before the Lord, <u>in the spirit and power of Elijah</u>, [emphasis added] to turn the hearts of the parents to their children and the disobedient to the wisdom of the righteous—to make ready a people prepared for the Lord." (Luke 1:11-17, NIV)

We must be willing to consider there may be truths in Scripture that go beyond or against popular interpretation, even long-held beliefs. Hear, again, the words of Jesus:

> But I tell you, Elijah has already come, and they did not recognize him, but have done to him everything they wished. In the same way the Son of Man is going to suffer at their hands." Then the disciples understood that he was talking to them about John the Baptist. (Matthew 17:12-13, NIV)

Jesus said, "John himself is Elijah," not John is like Elijah. He said, "Elijah has already come," not one like Elijah has already come. This seems to imply more than just John coming in the spirit and power of Elijah, but John coming as Elijah returned. "John himself is Elijah who was to come" (Matthew 11:14, NASB). The New King James Version translation says "he is Elijah" and the American Standard Version says, "this is Elijah." John was Elijah returned!

The prophesy of Elijah returning was very important to 1st century believers, as it should be to all Christians. For Jesus to be the Christ, Elijah had to return first and set the stage for our Messiah.

> "I will send my messenger, who will prepare the way before me. Then suddenly the Lord you are seeking will come to his temple; the messenger of the covenant, whom you desire, will come," says the LORD Almighty. (Malachi 3:1, NIV)

> And they asked him, "Why do the teachers of the law say that Elijah must come first?" Jesus replied, "To be sure, Elijah does come first, and restores all things. Why then is it written that the Son of Man must suffer much and be rejected? But I tell you, Elijah has come, and they have done to him everything they wished, just as it is written about him." (Mark 9:11-13, NIV)

> "See, I will send the prophet Elijah to you before that great and dreadful day of the LORD comes. He will turn the hearts of the parents to their children, and the hearts of the chil-

dren to their parents; or else I will come and strike the land with total destruction." (Malachi 4:5-6, NIV)

And the land *was* smote with total destruction, as the Romans sacked Jerusalem in AD 70, and destroyed the second temple, a destruction that remains in perpetuity to this day. The city suffered unimaginable horrors in which over one million people, mostly Jews, perished. This according to the account of the historian Josephus.[69]

Destruction of Jerusalem

Titus Flavius Josephus, who had been acting as a mediator for the Romans prior to the siege, describes in explicit detail the events leading up to, during, and the harrowing aftermath. In his account, *The Judean War*, Josephus said, "the multitude of carcasses that lay in heaps one upon another was a horrible sight, and produced a pestilential stench."[70]

> Now as soon as the army had no more people to slay or to plunder, because there remained none to be the objects of their fury (for they would not have spared any, had there remained any other work to be done), [Titus] Caesar gave orders that they should now demolish the entire city and Temple, but should leave as many of the towers standing as they were of the greatest eminence; that is, Phasaelus, and Hippicus, and Mariamne; and so much of the wall enclosed the city on the west side. This wall was spared, in order to afford a camp for such as were to lie in garrison [in the Upper City], as were the towers [the three forts] also spared, in order to demonstrate to posterity what kind of city it was, and how well fortified, which the Roman valor had subdued; but for all the rest of the wall [surrounding Jerusalem], it was so thoroughly laid even with the ground by those that dug it up to the foundation, that there was left nothing to make those that came thither believe it [Jerusalem] had ever

been inhabited. This was the end which Jerusalem came to by the madness of those that were for innovations; a city otherwise of great magnificence, and of mighty fame among all mankind.[71]

The words of Josephus give great insight into why Jerusalem today remains a desert remnant of the fertile city she once was.

And truly, the very view itself was a melancholy thing; for those places which were adorned with trees and pleasant gardens, were now become desolate country every way, and its trees were all cut down. Nor could any foreigner that had formerly seen Judaea and the most beautiful suburbs of the city, and now saw it as a desert, but lament and mourn sadly at so great a change. For the war had laid all signs of beauty quite waste. Nor had anyone who had known the place before, had come on a sudden to it now, would he have known it again.[72]

Of course, all of that terrible destruction was prophesied by Jesus, who, referring to the temple buildings, said, "there will not be left here one stone upon another that will not be thrown down" (Matthew 24:2, ESV) and "let those who are in Judea flee to the mountains" (24:16). "And alas for women who are pregnant and for those who are nursing infants in those days!" (24:19).

Figure 11.1: *Stones from the Western Wall of the Temple Mount (Jerusalem, Israel) thrown onto the street by Roman soldiers.* Photo taken by geologist Mark A. Wilson, May 27, 2009 (public domain). Here we see excavated stones from the Western Wall of the Temple Mount, knocked onto the street below by Roman battering rams in AD 70. This 1st century street is located at the base of the Temple Mount where the western and southern walls meet.[73]

Reincarnation is Compelling

From a philosophical standpoint, reincarnation is a compelling concept. Our human lives are far too short to learn and experience everything we need to grow and become all God wants us to be. But also think about all the people who have died as children, or babies, or even those unborn from the womb. Do you really think that is the extent of their mortal lives, that God does not give them another chance at life on this earth?

Now, I know Christians have obvious questions about this, like which of their bodies then will be renewed in the resurrection? But that is not thinking deeply enough. Paul already answered that question in 1 Corinthians 15:

> But someone will ask, "How are the dead raised? With what kind of body will they come?" How foolish! ...it is sown a natural body, it is raised a spiritual body. If there is a natural body, there is also a spiritual body... I declare to you, brothers and sisters, that flesh and blood cannot inherit the kingdom of God, nor does the perishable inherit the imperishable... For the perishable must clothe itself with the imperishable, and the mortal with immortality. (1 Corinthians 15:35-36, 44, 50, 53, NIV)

The resurrection body will be something new. It will be different. It will be everything you have ever been and nothing you were before. Just like a seed that falls into the ground, splits apart, casting its casing away—we will arise as something new and glorious, but still connected to what we were before. That is what the resurrection body will be like.

"When you sow, you do not plant the body that will be, but just a seed, perhaps of wheat or of something else. But God gives it a body as he has determined" (1 Corinthians 15:37-38, NIV). Could this mean the spirit is clothed with the new body at death? That could very well have been what was meant by the aforementioned Calvary Chapel movement founder, the late Pastor Chuck Smith, who thought believers received the resurrection body after death.

If true, that does not preclude the resurrection body being both physical and spiritual, as we saw Jesus' was (Luke 24:30-31, 36-37, 39, 41-43, John 20:26-27, 21:9-13, Acts 1:9-11). It also does not necessarily contradict our being raised on "the last day" (John 6:40, 44) as

God "inhabits eternity" (Isaiah 57:15, ESV). The spirit world exists outside of our space-time continuum (2 Peter 3:8, ESV). Remember, the dead in Christ rise first, and Jesus will bring them with Him when He returns (1 Thessalonians 4:14-17).

And none of this precludes the possibility of reincarnation, in my opinion. Still unconvinced? Let's take a look at some of the evidences of reincarnation.

Past-Life Memories

There are many striking, albeit anecdotal, evidences of reincarnation. Let's delve more into one of the most convincing—the many cases of past-life memories. I already covered the amazing story of Jeff Keene. His case is one of many. Evidence of belief in past-life memories goes back at least as far as the 2nd century BC., with an uptick in claims, along with past-life regression becoming mainstream, finding clinical uses in psychology and psychiatry since the 1950s.[74] Now, it seems, more and more stories of past-life memories are coming to the surface, especially among children.

A 2014 *Psychology Today* article by Michael Jawer titled, "Children Who Seemingly Remember Past Lives" reports, "…young children around the world spontaneously volunteered—in great detail—recollections that seemed to be about someone else's life. Much of the time, the person being spoken of had died violently or unnaturally…"[75] Jawer does not offer any plausible explanation for the phenomena and notes that in many cases the families are devout Christians for whom the concept of reincarnation is foreign.

"Between them, Stevenson and Tucker have compiled more than 2,500 cases… In many of these cases, the person being spoken of could be identified through the specificity of information volunteered…"[76]

Following is one such story, in print for the first time here.

I Carried You

In one of the many interviews I conducted for this book, l learned about Maria Hernandez, who was a typical grandmother living in

Atotonilco, a charming town in the state of Jalisco, central-western Mexico. The area is rugged and rural, steeped in ancient traditions blending Medieval Catholicism along with lingering native mysticism. The strange workings of the supernatural and paranormal are not unknown, but still surprising at times. Such was the case with Maria's granddaughter Paulina. The events I am about to describe took place around 1968.

Paulina was about four years old when she started asking her grandma, "Do you remember when I used to carry you?"

Her relatives would laugh this off, saying "No, *maha*, you are little. We used to carry *you*." But the little girl persisted, so serious—and every time she saw her Grandma Hernandez she would say, "I used to carry you." Amusement turned to annoyance, as the girl's insistence was bordering on disrespect to her elder.

One day Grandma said firmly, "No, you are little. I carried you."

Paulina, just as firmly, shot back, "No! I used to carry you when we lived in Zacualtipan."

Annoyance turned to shock. Grandma Hernandez grew up in Zacualtipan. Little Paulina had never been to or even heard of Zacualtipan, and Maria Hernandez had not been there since she was a child some 60 years earlier. How could Paulina know?

More and more such cases are being revealed in which people demonstrate accurate memories of lifetimes past—lives of real people of whom the experiencers had no prior knowledge. Often times the phenomenon appears in early childhood, but is typically forgotten by adulthood. Paulina, now in her mid-50s, no longer remembers saying "I carried you," but her Grandma would never forget it.

There are many other examples such as this. One of the most remarkable cases is the story of James Leininger.

Soul Survivor

James was born in 1998 to Bruce and Andrea Leininger, a conservative Christian couple who did not believe in reincarnation. Their belief system was about to change. Right around two years after the boy was born, James started having frightening nightmares. The incredible experiences of this family are documented in the couple's 2009 biographical account, *Soul Survivor: The Reincarnation of a World War II Fighter Pilot.*

Over time, the parents of James Leininger became convinced, against all their Christian beliefs, that their son was the reincarnation of World War II fighter pilot James Huston, who was shot down and killed in 1945 in the Pacific Theatre.

About two months into the nightmares, they overheard their boy in diapers screaming chillingly in his sleep, "Airplane crash! Plane on fire! Little man can't get out!" The boy was kicking and clawing at the covers as if trying to escape something.[77]

The toddler had an unusual interest in World War II items and displayed an uncanny knowledge about them. The parents reported a particular instance where Andrea gave her son a model airplane. She pointed out to the boy, who had barely learned how to form complete phrases, that there was a bomb on the bottom of the plane.

"That's not a bomb, Mommy," the boy replied. "That's a dwop tank."

How would a two year old still in diapers know what a drop tank was? Most adults would not know. This began an amazing journey for the Leininger family, who followed the trail of their son's past-life memories all the way to the family of James Huston, as well as the squadron and veterans he served with. Reportedly, James even recognized the men he once served with when he met the living veterans—the boy knew them by name!

As remarkable as the Leininger case is, it is still just one of many. A lot of children report past-life memories. Carol Bowman, in her foreword to the book, reports:

> Some children begin to speak of these memories as soon as they can talk—some still in diapers! They surprise their parents with comments such as 'When I was big before,' or 'When I died before.' Or they exhibit unusual behaviors: phobias, nightmares, unlearned talents and perplexing

abilities, or uncanny insight into adult affairs they couldn't possibly know about in their only two or three years of life.[78]

A final thought on reincarnation. Proponents say at some point the cycle of rebirth will end. The Scriptures may actually allude to this, seemingly implying the spirit goes out and returns and goes out again. But at some point, the spirit will rest. "He who overcomes, I will make him a pillar in the temple of My God, and he shall go out no more" (Revelation 3:12).

Figure 11.2: *The Last Judgment* by Michelangelo, located at the Sistine Chapel, Vatican City (public domain). The fresco was completed between 1536 and 1541 and covers the entire altar wall.[79]

They were startled and frightened, thinking they saw a ghost.
He said to them, "Why are you troubled, and why do doubts rise in your minds?
Look at my hands and my feet. It is I myself! Touch me and see; a ghost does not have flesh and bones, as you see I have."
Luke 24:37-39
Holy Bible, New International Version (NIV)

Chapter 12

Ghosts

Trick or Treat

I must have been no more than three years old when I watched as Mom came into my room carrying my first Halloween costume. It is one of my earliest memories. I was about to embark on my inaugural trick or treat outing; and it was already dark outside. My room was dimly lit, illuminated by a single nightlight casting shadows on the wall. Mom no doubt had put me down for a nap so I would have enough energy for the evening festivities—but I was wide-awake now.

I remember clearly standing in my crib, beaming at Mom as she held out the Romper Room costume box, a treasure to be cherished.

"Look, Richie!" she said, presenting the box, perhaps even more excited than I was. I can still remember the crackling sound that see-through cellophane made as Mom opened the prize. I also remember when we picked it out at Kmart some days earlier.

Back then, practically all Halloween costumes came in these glorious, colorful boxes, with the transparent cellophane window. They each contained a folded, mylar smock, hidden beneath a plastic mask.

I can still smell the stiff but bendable, smooth plastic and feel the prickly elastic band stretching around my head as Mom helped me don the mask. Within a few moments, I could feel the sweat condensing under the nose and mouth area.

"Rich, you're gonna be a ghost," Mom purred. "But he's Casper, the *friendly* ghost."

Mom freed me from the smothering plastic. Cool air met the sweat on my face.

"Now you know, Rich, there's no such thing as ghosts…"

"Yes, Momma."

(Mom actually believed in ghosts, but I am sure she did not want to scare me.)

Soon we would be off on that first Halloween excursion, haunting the streets of Greensboro.

I know many Christians find Halloween problematic, and I can understand why. But, for me, I always found it to be harmless fun.

To a child, dressing up as our favorite cartoon character or superhero was so exciting. And walking from house to house, over-filling our bags with snack-size candy bars and other goodies, then coming home to sort out and eat our spoils while watching scary movies and reading comic books—what's not to love about that?

Six years later, on Halloween night, I would have another "ghost" experience—a haunting of a new and altogether different kind.

The Prettiest Ghost

On October 31, 1978, age nine, I went on a hayride with some other kids my age. It was my first time on a hayride. The sweet smell of hay enveloping us met the cool night air, which was filled with hints of pine needles and fallen leaves crunching under our wheels, while the bitter scent of wood burning in stove-heaters drifted by, from homesteads far off in the distance.

We were driven not by horses, but by a powerful Ford truck, piloted by a friendly neighbor whose daughter had caught my make-up-covered eyes.

We made our way around that night, collecting candy from the old farmhouses and mini-mansions in rural Summerfield, North Carolina. But a new awareness had captured my attention far more than the want of treats.

I remember it was very dark outside that night. With a new moon waxing, out there in the country landscape, you could see every star in the sky. It was the perfect setting for a budding, adolescent romance.

I was clothed as a hobo/scarecrow and soon got myself snuggled up to this adorable little blonde girl dressed up as a ghost. This was as close as it gets to love at first sight for nine year olds. She was sweet and sassy and cute. I remember telling her she was the "prettiest little ghost I ever saw." To this day, I think she probably was.

"There's no such thing as ghosts," she shyly replied, but beamed at the compliment nonetheless. And then she held my hand. What a wonderful Halloween night!

I would eventually leave the hay fields of country living with my dad and stepmom to move back in with my mom and stepdad. They preferred the inner city of urban Greensboro, North Carolina. There, it was motel living, driving around downtown, and by 1981, we were watching the delightful Jamie Lee Curtis run screaming away from Michael Myers in *Halloween II* on a newly expanded 24-hour cable network called HBO.

After living a few years with Mom and Stepdad in the city, I was back in Summerfield again for country living. But by the first day of 10th grade history class, nearly six years had passed since that moonless hayride so long ago.

I walked into class that day and to my surprise *there she was*, sitting at the back of the room. She was all grown up now, blossomed and even more beautiful than I remembered—but, I instantly recognized my pretty little ghost from Halloween past—and she immediately remembered me! As we were the first into class that day, we had a few moments to catch up.

She recounted her memory of that night, and it was as vivid and meaningful to her as my recollection was to me. I wish I could say we reignited the flame of our star-crossed romance—but alas, this young woman had already met and was dating the high-school sweetheart she would end up marrying. She did tell me though that the hayride rendezvous made me her first boyfriend.

Other than the butterflies I felt in my stomach that 4th grade night as I left the hayride, I remember clearly the feel of that heavy treat bag on my shoulder, all weighed down with candy. I dumped it out on my bedroom floor in our mobile home and tuned in to watch a re-broadcast of the *Fat Albert Halloween Special* from the year before, on my little 13-inch black and white TV.

Many kids remember the Charlie Brown *Great Pumpkin* special from 1966, a classic no doubt—but, for me, the one that really sticks out in my mind for some reason is that Fat Albert cartoon from 1977. Ah, nostalgia! And remember what they used to say on those old cartoons? "There's no such thing as ghosts."

Well, that may help little kids sleep better at night—but is it really true?

According to a 2013 Harris Poll, 42% of Americans believe in ghosts.[80]

A careful look at the Scriptures reveals the Bible also supports a belief in ghosts, and perhaps even the existence of ghosts, implicitly at least.

Ghosts in the Bible

When Jesus met the Apostles after His resurrection, they thought He was a spirit or ghost. He demonstrated His resurrection body was physical. Yet, it must have somehow also been spiritual, as He appears in the midst of them when they were behind closed doors (John 20:19).

But the physicality of His nature is without question, as He also invites them to touch His body and He even eats food with them.

> As they were talking about these things, Jesus himself stood among them, and said to them, "Peace to you!" But they were startled and frightened and thought they saw a spirit. And he said to them, "Why are you troubled, and why do doubts arise in your hearts? See my hands and my feet, that it is I myself. Touch me, and see. For a spirit does not have flesh and bones as you see that I have." And when he had said this, he showed them his hands and his feet. And while they still disbelieved for joy and were marveling, he said to them, "Have you anything here to eat?" They gave him a piece of broiled fish, and he took it and ate before them. (Luke 24:36-43, ESV)

Some would argue in the account above it is not implicit that He *miraculously* appeared, walking through walls or locked doors. Perhaps the disciples simply let Him in. But the Scriptures make a point to keep emphasizing how the doors were locked, and yet He appeared.

> Eight days later, his disciples were inside again, and Thomas was with them. Although the doors were locked, Jesus came and stood among them and said, "Peace be with you." Then he said to Thomas, "Put your finger here, and see my hands; and put out your hand, and place it in my side. Do not disbelieve, but believe." Thomas answered him, "My Lord and my God!" (John 20:26-28, ESV)

The resurrected body is a mystery indeed. It is obviously something altogether different than a discarnate human spirit, as the risen Christ had both "flesh and bones" (although some hold the position the Apostles shared an entirely spiritual experience, something like a waking dream; to me that explanation stretches belief, especially as one considers the number of witnesses who saw the risen Lord).

In his first epistle to the Corinthians, Paul confirms that well over 500 people saw the Christ, post resurrection, and most of those witnesses were still alive at the time his letter was written! (1 Corinthians 15:6).

But back to my original assertion—that the Bible supports not only a belief in ghosts, but perhaps the existence of them as well.

In further examination of the Lord's appearance to the disciples, this time in Luke's gospel, Jesus seems to affirm the existence of ghosts by simple reverse logic.

> Jesus himself was suddenly standing there among them. "Peace be with you," he said. But the whole group was startled and frightened, thinking they were seeing a ghost!
>
> "Why are you frightened?" he asked. "Why are your hearts filled with doubt? Look at my hands. Look at my feet. You can see that it's really me. Touch me and make sure that I am not a ghost, because ghosts don't have bodies, as you see that I do." As he spoke, he showed them his hands and his feet. (Luke 24:36-43, NLT)

Many translations render the Greek word *pneuma* as "spirit" rather than "ghost." Strong's says the transliteration *pneuma*, means air, wind, breath, spirit. Although the word literally means air/wind or breath, by analogy and in a religious context, *pneuma* means spirit or soul.[81]

Perhaps the word *spirit* sounds less archaic or sensational than ghost; but either way, we are talking about a discarnate presence, an apparition. A ghost.

The disciples were afraid Jesus was a ghost. The Lord reassured them He was not a ghost, by arguing "ghosts don't have bodies, as you see that I do." He could have corrected their belief in ghosts with the classic, 'there's no such thing as ghosts,' or some variation, but He did not. The Lord's statement, "ghosts don't have bodies," suggests there *are* such things as ghosts.

There is no doubt the Scriptures support the existence of discarnate human spirits (Ecclesiastes 12:7). I would also argue the story above from Luke implies it is not outside the realm of possibility to actually see a discarnate spirit. When you add to this the anecdotal evidence, the simple fact that humans have reported seeing phantoms since antiquity, the argument approaches sublimity. By the way, this was not the first time His followers mistook Jesus for a ghost.

> Immediately He made the disciples get into the boat and go ahead of Him to the other side, while He sent the crowds away. After He had sent the crowds away, He went up on the mountain by Himself to pray; and when it was evening, He was there alone. But the boat was already a long distance from the land, battered by the waves; for the wind was contrary. And in the fourth watch of the night He came to them, walking on the sea. When the disciples saw Him walking on the sea, they were terrified, and said, "It is a ghost!" And they cried out in fear. But immediately Jesus spoke to them, saying, "Take courage, it is I; do not be afraid." (Matthew 14:22-27, NASB)

The Paranormal Christian

Figure 12.1: *Jesus Walks on Water* by Ivan Aivazovsky, 1888. Oil on canvas (public domain). This beautiful painting is housed in an undisclosed private collection.[82]

History, Belief, and Skepticism about Ghosts

Although the overall consensus of science may be that ghosts do not exist, a belief in ghosts is widespread across nearly every people, culture, and time. But even while recognizing the strong anecdotal and even biblical basis for a belief in ghosts, I point out that one must first rule out all natural explanations for ghostly encounters. Indeed, nearly any suspected ghost experience can be explained away, as skeptics are keen to point out. Cold spots, creaking sounds, and strange noises can be found in almost any home, especially old ones. Add in some imagination and confirmation bias, and viola—you've got a haunted house.[83]

Also, when it comes to the sensed presence phenomena, researchers say monotony, darkness, cold, hunger, fatigue, fear, sleep deprivation, and even carbon monoxide poisoning, can lead to the feeling that someone is watching you.[84]

Still, we proceed with the open-minded but cautious understanding that, natural causes aside, the weight of witness testimony over time implies that there must be something to all this ghost business. So, moving forward, and assuming that natural causes are eliminated, now what do you have?

The English word "ghost" has Germanic, proto-European and Old Norse influences denoting fury or rage as in an angry ghost.[85] Not all ghosts are discarnate human spirits. A ghost could also represent an angelic or demonic manifestation or perhaps even a dead animal. But for the purposes of our discussion, when I refer to ghosts as spirit manifestations, I am talking about discarnate human spirits, unless otherwise noted.

Human souls persisting to haunt the physical earth plane would tend to be an unnatural state, and commonly lead to unpleasant or negative effects. Such a ghost that would remain earthbound to seek out physical gratification through the living, certainly those who would torment or even try to possess people, would be demonic in nature. Most Christians would say such beings are simply demons, but many believe discarnate human spirits can act out in this way.[86]

On the other hand, as I have said before, I do believe God allows some measure of grace for our departed loved ones to temporarily and/or occasionally visit us. This is far too commonly experienced and reported to rule it out.[87] And while this too can be unsettling, more often than not, it has a comforting effect on the person to know their departed loved one is alive and well on the other side.[88]

Human spirits normally progress to the afterlife following death as "the dust returns to the ground it came from, and the spirit returns to God who gave it" (Ecclesiastes 12:7, NIV). Some disagree with that viewpoint and hold that spirit in the above context simply means breath, citing the creation account in Genesis where "the Lord God formed a man from the dust of the ground and breathed into his nostrils the breath of life, and the man became a living being" (Genesis 2:7, NIV). Such proponents say we sleep in the grave until the Lord's return; however, my experience and research, literature on the topic, anecdotal evidence, as well as the viewpoint of orthodox Christianity and the Bible, all point to a conscious spirit continuing on after death.

Dr. A. L. Barry, former president of the Lutheran Church, Missouri Synod, in his 1998 pamphlet from the *What About* series titled "What About Death and Dying," said the following: "At the moment of death, our souls, and the souls of all those who die in faith, immediately are in the presence of Christ, and will enjoy His presence, peace and joy until the great day of the resurrection of all flesh."[89] Likewise, Jesus told the story of a poor man named Lazarus, who when he died, was carried by angels to Abraham's bosom (Luke 16:22).

But who can say for sure we are *immediately* in God's presence following death? Can theologians prove that through the biblical account alone? I say not. "Can two walk together, except they be agreed?" (Amos 3:3, KJV).

Humans have free will (Genesis 2:16, Joshua 24:15, John 7:17, etc.), but God has a best plan for our lives that we cooperate with by making the right choices, as "a man's heart plans his way, but the Lord directs his steps" (Proverbs 16:9). As in life, so in death. God never imposes on our free will in life; so I am of the belief we maintain our free will after death. Some spirits, apparently, choose to stay here, at least temporarily. Most, it seems, hang around long enough to at least say goodbye, and occasionally return to say hello.

People choose to go to hell, which is separation from God, and choose to stay in hell by choosing to reject God. "These will pay the penalty of eternal ruin, separated from the presence of the Lord and from the glory of his power" (2 Thessalonians 1:9, NABRE).

The rest of us who do not reject our free gift of salvation go to paradise and dwell with our Lord.

Reconciling reincarnation, if it is true, is then quite easy to do. For if the Lord really does allow it, then at our choosing and His agreement, we return again at a later date to this earthly plane and so on, until the Lord returns and the cycle of death and rebirth is broken.

So, what of the dead who tarry too long, afraid to cross over?

In my Angel Therapy Practitioner training (see Book I), Doreen Virtue taught that spirits may get stuck in the earth plane and end up cut off from God. Being in such a state where they are not in contact with God's Spirit would lead them to eventually become wild and irrational, perhaps explaining the behavior of poltergeists or angry ghosts.

While the theories and explanations about ghosts and what they are may vary, I can tell you this: ghosts *are* real.

I have seen them.

Nature of Ghosts

Ghosts are widely reported to appear in many forms. They may be visible or invisible, emit odors, move objects, and make sounds. They may appear formless, as in a mist, or emerge as floating orbs, cold spots, or manifest in the likeness of the departed. And, according to modern paranormal understanding, ghostly manifestations may be cognizant spirits or energy signatures.[90]

A place thought of as haunted is believed to be inhabited by disembodied spirits, usually thought of as the deceased, such as former residents or those otherwise connected to the property. Hauntings are often attributed to locations of violence, such as murder, accidental death, or suicide. But not all hauntings are at a place of violence. They may simply be a locale where the person's memories and energies are strong.[91]

Ghosts often appear as conscious spirits, deliberately roaming the earth plane. But the energy signature manifestations seem to be more of a reflection, almost like a video playing in a loop. In the case of those ghostly apparitions, perhaps something of a highly charged emotional impact happened to the person at that locale, or perhaps they simply feel connected to the place—it was a beloved home, or maybe a relative lives there now. If they were a heavy drinker, maybe they still choose to frequent their favorite haunt. Or maybe the site could be some kind of a portal, energetic gateway, or other mysterious void. Again, as Christians rightly point out, ghostly phenomena may also be attributed to demonic or even angelic activity; but I believe in many, if not most, cases we are encountering the activity of departed human spirits.

I consider seeing a ghost to be something like the spiritual equivalent of spotting a meteor or "shooting star." Such sightings are rare, seemingly mystical, yet altogether natural. A person could go their whole life without seeing one; but perhaps being observant or even expectant of them, they are more likely to appear. People seem to be more prone to seeing ghosts when they are just falling asleep or waking up, and spirits have been reported to appear in dreams—for probably as long as people have had dreams.

In my case, the times I have seen ghosts it has been when I was *not* expecting to. And after seeing a ghost for the first time, perhaps one is more likely to see them again.

Ghosts may interact with you and the surrounding environment, or they may play like a movie clip on repeat. They may see you and react to what you say or do, or they may go about their movements seemingly oblivious to our world.

Reflections in Time

There is a fascinating theory that in some cases the apparitions may actually be us! That is to say, the ghosts we see may simply be our fellow humans simultaneously living alongside us but at a different point in time—meaning some type of portal is opening in time and space and allowing us to see them—and/or likewise, them to see us. So, maybe the Civil War soldier is simply going about his daily chores at that moment in time, when/where the fabric of time is peeled back, and suddenly we see a ghost, that soldier, but to him, we are the ghosts! A mind-blowing concept, no doubt. But is it so hard to believe? Time is really just an illusion. The Spirit from which we come, that which created the reality of the natural world must exist outside of it, therefore outside of time and space.

This is why the Scripture says, "do not forget this one thing, dear friends: With the Lord a day is like a thousand years, and a thousand years are like a day" (2 Peter 3:8, NIV).

In 2014, scientists from the University of Queensland in Australia showed mathematically that light particles could be sent back in time, demonstrating the resultant causal loops in space-time. Although nothing was actually sent back, the experiment proved a single photon could pass through a wormhole, creating a reaction in its older-self in the present. These results were published by *Nature Communications* in an article titled "Experimental simulation of closed time-like curves."[92]

The Bible teaches that Jesus is the Alpha and the Omega, the beginning and the end (Revelation 22:13). Time exists in a linear fashion to us in this material earth plane during our physical lives. But God, the creator of time, *must* exist outside of time. Therefore, all of time is happening concurrently, from God's viewpoint.

That is the perspective of God's realm, the spiritual world.

Figure 12.2: *Witch of Endor* by Nikolai Ge, 1857 (public domain). This mysterious painting depicts King Saul encountering the ghost of the prophet Samuel as recorded in 1 Samuel 28.[93]

Chapter 13

Strange Encounters

Ghosts or Daemons?

It is important to remember that ghost phenomena may represent other entities, not just discarnate human spirits. Inhuman spirits can run the gamut from angels to demons to who knows what? But ghostly apparitions generally seem to be less severe than demonic manifestations—so, I defer to the common understanding that ghosts are typically human spirits.

Still, human or not, some ghosts are more malevolent in their demeanor than others; and what appears to be a ghost might actually be a demon—but I do not hold, as do some Christians, that every ghostly encounter is demonic.

And when I say demon, I am referring to the classical Christian interpretation, of a fallen angel. However, as we discussed in Chapter 2 of Book I, the English word for demon comes from the Greek word daimon (daemon in Latin). To the Greeks, a daimon was a guiding spirit, not necessarily evil—a lesser deity, for sure—but not strictly a fallen angel, as Christian tradition holds.[94]

Plato's muse was a daimon, and the ancients believed a human spirit could be a daimon.[95] In the view of the Greeks, a daimon was something like a guardian angel. In his *Apology of Socrates*, Plato documents the defense of his friend and teacher, Socrates, tried in 399 BC for corrupting the youth and believing in the wrong daimons. Socrates claimed to have a daimon, or "divine something," that frequently warned him—in the form of a "voice"—against mistakes.[96]

We get the word demon from daemon and daemon from daimon, which simply means spirit. We get clues on the nature of a spirit by the context of its communication. If the voice is angry, overly critical, discouraging, it would not be from God.

Readers of *The Paranormal Christian: Book I* will recall my explanation of The Voice, as a form of communication from the divine. It can be the voice of God, a kind spirit, or guardian angel. Likewise, a negative spirit can speak to us too, requiring discernment on our part (1 John 4:1). So this understanding of spirits defies rigid interpretations and explanations and requires nuance. And when it comes to ghosts, they do not easily fit a simple good/bad construct.

What then are these ghosts? Angels? Guides? Departed loved ones? Actual Demons? Aliens…? Some people think cryptids like Bigfoot and Mothman are spiritual beings. Perhaps things of the unseen universe are not always a black-and-white, either-or, matter. Again, I tend to think ghosts are typically discarnate human spirits, but the bottom line is, we really don't know who these or any spirits really are, whether ghosts or angels or fallen angels or demons or human spirits, pre-Adamic spirits, or deceased Nephilim. Honestly, we really don't know—and anyone from the New Age mystic to the protestant evangelist, is presumptuous to say anything to the contrary.

What we can do is test the spirits as John advised, to see if they are from God (1 John 4:1-3) and pray for the gift of discernment of spirits as Paul described (1 Corinthians 12:3-4, 7-11) or seek advice from those in the church who do have that gift. And of course, we have our good old common sense to know the spirits by their fruits. If they are saying negative things, or influencing us to do bad things, or in any other way are speaking in contrast to the Scriptures or the faith, then we know they are not from God (1 John 4:1-3, 1; Corinthians 12:3-4). Other than that, those of us here in the physical realm are left to speculate.

Ghostly visitations have been, and continue to be, observed by people all around the world. Following are some real-life examples from myself along with others who have experienced strange encounters.

Phantom at Big Lake

Big Lake, Minnesota is a small, rural town about 41 miles northwest of Minneapolis. I was there visiting with family during the summer of 2005, when I saw a strange apparition one evening. It was close to midnight under a full moon. Everyone was already in bed, and I had gone outside for a cigar before turning in myself.

I could hear crickets chirping nearby and echoing across the distant fields into the woods. I was standing beside an old, ash-colored shed, looking across a timeworn, wooden fence, which bordered a deserted meadow. The bright moonlight overhead was casting dark shadows on the ground.

As I stood there enjoying my cigar, a mysterious orb came into view. It was globular with shimmering colors, and wobbled in motion as it floated by. I followed its movement and watched as the specter disappeared into the shed I was standing by.

Curious, I placed my ear to the shack, right at the spot where the orb had entered.

At the same instant I registered the rough, wood surface against my cheek, I heard a woman sobbing. Startled, I jumped back. My heart was pounding.

"Oh Lord, in Jesus' name," I cried. "Please free this suffering spirit and bring it home, or if this be a deceiving spirit, I pray it also be removed from this place. In Jesus' name, amen."

I slowly returned my ear to the side of the shed. To my relief, the sobbing was gone.

And I saw the orb no more.

The Presence

In 2016, my niece, Kimberly Garcia, complained of a presence in her room. At the time, she lived with her family, a devout, Christian household in beautiful Corona, California.

Her dad Louis reminded Kim that the Blood of Christ covers her. But still the presence would not go away. I advised Kimberly to place blessed objects around her room and pray. I also counseled her to sever ties with any unwholesome friends or behaviors that may be negatively affecting her life.

Over time, as Kimberly grew closer to God and distanced herself from bad friends and behavior (also the family moved from Corona to Trabuco Canyon), the presence went away.

Feeling that a room is haunted is not an uncommon experience. In some houses there are certain rooms one is afraid to enter. You get a cold feeling—chills go up and down the spine.

Children's rooms are no sanctum from hauntings. Youngsters become frightened something is under the bed, or hiding in the closet. It can be unsettling for both kids and parents—the feeling you are being watched.

Ghost in the Closet

Shannon Healey is a typical, young Southern California woman: big smile, slight valley-girl accent, and careful attention to detail as she clips your hair. She is co-owner of The Ave, a hip barbershop for men and women on Avenue L in Redondo Beach. It is the kind of place you can play foosball or sip an icy-cold Pacifico beer while you wait to get a trim or a shave.

Shannon is caring and down to earth, quick-witted and warm; pragmatic enough to easily juggle the dual roles of stylist and business owner, but girly enough to admit her frustration at having her credit card spending-limit flagged when she is trying to buy make-up. Shannon is also a young mom.

In 2016, the same year Kim was dealing with her ghostly presence, Shannon was home, happily doting on her three-year-old son Julian and 10-year-old stepson Rob. She was not so enthusiastic about the ghost in the closet in Julian's room.

"I get creeped out every time I pass that closet," she said.

Shannon never shared that feeling with anyone until her stepson Rob asked her about "the man in the closet."

"I see it," said Rob. "I see him standing there."

Shannon thinks it could actually be her dad, who died when she was only 16. "I've seen my dad in my dreams."

Shannon's father died serving the country in the military, so he never lived to see his little girl grow up into the woman she is today—a successful business owner with a beautiful, young and growing family. Shannon had just added an adorable baby girl named Scarlett Rose to her brood in January 2018. I would not be surprised if it really was her dad, just stopping by to visit the family he never got to meet. Perhaps Grandpa is just there to watch over the little ones.

Children and Spirits

There is something about little children and spirits. Whether it is a departed loved one, or guardian angel watching over a child, a curious ghost, or (hopefully not) even a negative entity, young children seem to be of special interest to spirit beings.

Also, kids (and animals) are apparently more receptive to seeing ghosts. Children, especially young infants and toddlers, are closer to the other side than they are to this world. They have not had years of distractions, concerns, and parents saying, "There are no such things as ghosts," to shut down their innate spiritual senses. Scores of families report their young ones describing "imaginary friends." I would suggest these encounters may not be imaginary at all.

I See God

My daughter Miranda stunned us one afternoon many years ago, as we were driving around in the Riverdale area of Ogden, Utah. She was only four or five years old and sitting in the back seat of our blue, Ford Taurus station wagon, looking out the window and riding along. Then, out of nowhere, Miranda says, "I see God."

"What?!" I thought. Both her mother and I looked at each other, an amazed smile, rising on our faces.

"What did He look like honey?" I asked. But my baby girl just started mumbling about something else—she was already moving on. I tried again to backtrack and ask her more about what she saw, but she would not be bothered much about it and just returned to normal things little children in the back seat say and do.

Peek-a-Boo, I See YOU!

Samantha Domenick was a young, single mom, who worked at Peak Orthopedic Physical Therapy, in Redondo Beach, California, when I interviewed her there in 2017. She is a quiet and reserved, dark-haired beauty, with powerful, muscular legs and stern demeanor if you try to skip the dreaded cable side-steps in your knee-rehabilitation routine.

Sam was pursuing advanced education in PT studies, and dreamt of one day being an officer in the Navy Reserve (once she pulled her credit score up). Finances notwithstanding, there are many other challenges for a single parent. Although paranormal activities are not usually at the top of the list, such concerns quickly rise to the forefront when something strange happens.

Sam had just moved into a new apartment in April 2017 with her 20-month-old daughter Mia. Mia had a toy in her room that began to weird her mother out. The toy is called the V-Tech Sit-to-Stand Learning Walker, an interactive play device designed to encourage a baby to develop, stand, and walk.

Sam started feeling a strange sensation when she came into Mia's room to put her daughter to bed.

"Peek-a-Boo, I see you!" The toy squawked.

A chill ran down Samantha's spine. This toy is only supposed to speak when someone presses the appropriate button. But Sam is a tough girl. So she just shook it off and tucked her child into bed.

Later that night, as Sam passed the room, the light suddenly turned on.

The toy squealed, "Peek-a-Boo, I see you!"

Now Sam was breathing heavy. She picked up the toy to remove it from her daughter's bedroom. "Peak-a-Boo, I see you," it said again.

"Oh, be quiet," Sam chided as she hid the object away.

For the next several days, the light in Mia's room would suddenly turn on in the middle of the night.

After sharing this story with several people, Sam told me the frequency of the light in Mia's bedroom turning on unexpectedly has decreased. But as of November 2017, it was still happening. Sam told me she would be giving that toy away.

There is an interesting thread on Reddit where parents discuss toys like the Sit-to-Stand Learning Walker creeping them out.[97] Based on that discussion, there seems to be a higher frequency of "haunted" toys among those which were obtained second-hand.

You can imagine my surprise when Janet came home one night in March 2021 with a Sit-to-Stand Walker for our grandson Ever. I did not make the connection until I was fumbling around with the detachable panel and heard, "Peek-a-Boo, I see you." It was a little startling, but we just laughed it off. So far, so good. Janet bought the toy new and it has not gone off unexpectedly. Janet's co-worker tells a different story about a child and a phone.

Stories from Janet

Picture, Picture

There is a lady named Veronica who works with my wife Janet at the Sigma Alimentos—Bar-S Foods, Los Angeles distribution center—in Vernon, California. Veronica's cousin, Camila, has a school-age daughter named Luna, who makes the family worried. Veronica has been encouraging Camila to get her daughter baptized, but the cousin refuses. Instead, she spends her time involved in occult practices like palm-reading.

In February 2018, Camila got a great scare. While she was working in the kitchen, her six-year-old daughter Luna was busy posing, speaking to the camera on the smartphone.

"Picture, picture!" she said. The little girl continued to stand there posing, as if she was expecting the phone to capture her image.

From the kitchen, her mom began hearing a little boy's voice on the other end of the phone also saying, "Picture, picture."

"Who the heck is she [her daughter] talking to?" Camila wondered. She continued to hear the boy's voice on the phone as Luna continued posing, saying "Picture, picture." Then the mother picked up the phone and a growling, demonic voice roared, "PICTURE-PICTURE!" *but there was no one on the phone.*

Scared, Camila immediately called her cousin Veronica, who immediately called her coworker, Janet. I was standing right there when Janet got the call. My wife was speaking in the rapid Spanish that I have learned means something concerning is going on. Knowing we are a devout, Christian family, Veronica requested our intercessory prayers for Camila and Luna.

The Black Witch Moth

Ascalapha odorata, more commonly known as the "Black Witch Moth" is a large, dark, bat-like moth known in the folklore of Mexico, Latin America, and the Caribbean as a harbinger of death.[98] Many people, including Christians, view such stories as superstition, bordering on the occult. As a Paranormal Christian, I view these signs as a gift from God. It is not that we go searching for signs—the signs come and find us.

Tia Merced

When my wife Janet was a little girl growing up in Mexico City, she had a beloved auntie named Merced, who was stricken with tuberculosis. Tia Merced, her dad's sister, ran a store where Janet would come in the afternoons to reach her skinny arms up onto the counter to receive goodies from her aunt. Little 10-year-old Janet waited with anticipation as her auntie would emerge from the back room, always bringing extra treats and candies for little Janet.

Merced was a pretty woman, slim and elegant. She must have caught the eye of many a young man in her youth. But Janet could see pain in her old auntie's face now, as she forced a smile for the little one. Janet's brow squinted into a concerned furrow.

Merced was trying to hold in her suffering, shuffling slowly on a foot that had turned under, and slowly raising her bony but still beautifully long, feminine fingers, to reach out and touch her niece's waiting hands.

Janet's dad, Merced's brother, was a tailor who ran a clothing factory that he owned. The factory was also the same building in which the family lived. The year was 1984.

One day back then, a black witch moth suddenly appeared in the factory bathroom. The creature was huge. Some thought it was a bat at first. This appearance created quite a stir among the workers and the children who all came around to take a look.

"Don't touch it!" warned Janet's mom. "It will go out when it is ready. It is here to tell us that someone is dead or will die very soon."

This ominous warning sent chills down Janet's spine.

Three days later, Tia Merced passed away.

Janet had a dream around that time, where Merced appeared to her. As in life, her auntie reached her bony fingers toward the child, but Janet was afraid to touch them.

"She wants to take you with her," Janet's mom told her. Janet never forgot the experience with Tia Merced.

Primo Beto

Years later, the family moved from the city to the rural area of Hidalgo, to the tiny village of Atotonilco, where her dad set up a modest clothing shop next to their house.

The home complex has a small courtyard outdoors with an outside bathroom. A few steps away is the bedroom Janet occupied as a teenager. One night, the children were all marveling at the astonishing appearance of a black witch moth in the bathroom. Janet ran to take a look.

This one was smaller than the moth who came for Merced. It was pretty, Janet thought, very dark, but she could make out circles on the wings that almost looked like eyes.

Janet's younger brothers were getting agitated by the creature, itching to remove it.

"Don't touch it!" Janet's mother warned. "It will leave."

But this time, her mom made no mention of the meaning of the omen. She nodded slightly toward her daughter, then turned and left.

Janet, now 14, thought to herself, "Someone is going to die."

Later that night, Janet awoke to screams in the house.

Her cousin Beto had just passed away.

Photographic Evidence

Ghost at Brookstown Inn

Consider the following photo taken by my good friend from high school, artist and photographer, Scott Blaylock. Scott is a level-minded conservative not taken to flights of fancy; but he has experienced the reality of ghosts, first-hand. Although we grew up together in rural Summerfield, North Carolina, Scott currently lives on the Atlantic coastline in historic Georgetown County, which he says is "the most haunted county in South Carolina." But Scott's ghost experiences go way back before he moved there.

In the 1990s, Scott worked for a firm that took up residence in the old Brookstown Inn, Winston Salem, North Carolina. Built in 1837, this impressive red-brick structure and former cotton mill sits near historic Old Salem.

Scott's company had rented out the third floor, where employees often reported noises and strange disturbances. Scott worked in photography there and decided to do a long-exposure photo of a deserted archway, as the late afternoon sun cast a striking ray of light from an upper window onto the exposed brick walls.

Unbeknownst to Scott, the image of a man's face appeared on the film—his floating head peering right into the camera, with an arm casually leaning on the archway. The amazing thing is Scott had no idea the specter was there, until his wife Cami noticed it on the negative years later. So, Scott had the photo developed.

Figure 13.1: *Ghost image at Brookstown Inn,* circa 1990. Photograph taken by Scott Blaylock. Used by permission of Mr. Blaylock.

Ghost Face

Another time, Scott visited a nearby cemetery, which was supposedly haunted by a woman in a red dress. Scott set up his camera and pointed it at the gravestone of the woman people claimed were haunting the site.

An interesting image appeared on the marker. It is not the form of a woman, though—more of a ghastly face, something you might see on a Halloween card.

Figure 13.2: *Photo of an apparition in front of a gravestone,* taken by Scott Blaylock. Used by permission of Mr. Blaylock.

Chapter 14

Other Hauntings

Pacific Crest Cemetery

I lived in Redondo Beach, California across from El Nido Park for many years. After a wave of paranormal activity began in my home, my friend Joe Juarez reminded me of the nearby Pacific Crest Cemetery just a few steps away. Although I had never heard about any stories of hauntings there, in a 2017 article on George Cate, founder of Pacific Crest, the *Daily Breeze* reported the site as the probable location of an ancient, Indian burial ground.

And Pacific Crest may well have been the origin of the most incredible, and frightening, series of ghostly phenomena I have ever observed.

But first, let's take a look at a couple of other strange hauntings. One, is a visitation I personally encountered.

I will share with you the mystery of this unseen watcher.

The Birdman

Whether he is an angelic guardian and friend, or malevolent immortal, I do not know—but, in either case, the Birdman is real. I am sure this entity, or family of beings, is related to the hawkman spirit I saw during that reading at Angel Camp, reported in Chapter 25 of *The Paranormal Christian: Book I.* To my surprise, a birdman would appear to me not long after that.

Birdmen show up in early folklore and religions around the world, from such places as ancient Egypt, Greece, Mesopotamia, India, Germany, China, Japan, Russia, Easter Island, and even in Norse mythology.[99] Depictions of winged beings are widely seen throughout practically all cultures since antiquity.

Other Hauntings

Figure 14.1a: *Ritual Water Jar Depicting Deities and Allegorical Figures.* Origin: Greek, made in Taras, about 330 BC. This ornate piece is currently on display at the Getty Villa in Pacific Palisades, California. Photo taken by the author on July 22, 2021.

Figure 14.1b: *Ritual Water Jar Depicting Deities and Allegorical Figures*. This is a close-up image of Astrape (Lightening). Depictions of winged beings have appeared in cultures and religions around the world since antiquity. Origin: Greek, made in Taras, about 330 BC, currently on display at the Getty Villa in Pacific Palisades, California. Photo taken by the author on July 22, 2021.

The Birdman figures prominently in the ancient Mississippian culture of North America, whose descendants include Native American tribes like the Cherokee, Seminole, Creek, and Choctaw. Interestingly, the native peoples seemed to view birdmen in much the same way Christianity sees angels—as winged messengers from God. Author and historian Linda Alchin, of the Native Indian site Warpaths2peacepipes.com, explains:

The link between the Upperworld (heaven) and the earth was the sky and the bird man was able to move between the two realms as messengers to the gods. The bird man was portrayed in the guise of an eagle, hawk or falcon.[100]

Birdmen are ubiquitous in ancient beliefs and customs; and represent watchers, guides, and even gods. Some have connected the Birdmen to the Watchers, from the non-canonical Book of Enoch as well as the biblical Book of Daniel—where the term is referenced in Daniel 4:13, 17 and 23. For example, "I saw in the visions of my head as I lay in bed, and behold, a watcher, a holy one, came down from heaven" (Daniel 4:13, ESV).

If birdmen and watchers are one in the same, that would mean they are angels from God. Remember, in Ezekiel's vision, he mentions seeing angels having four faces, including the face of a bird (eagle).

> Their faces looked like this: Each of the four had the face of a human being, and on the right side each had the face of a lion, and on the left the face of an ox; each also had the face of an eagle. Such were their faces. They each had two wings spreading out upward, each wing touching that of the creature on either side; and each had two other wings covering its body. (Ezekiel 1:10-11, NIV)

But watchers could also apply to the sons of God—fallen angels—alluded to in Genesis 6 and directly attributed in the Book of Enoch.[101]

So, a birdman is a spiritual being, an angel, one which may be good or wicked.

Of course, I never knew any of that until I personally saw the Birdman for myself, the first of many times, starting in 2003. Later, I began researching the topic to try and understand what it was I was seeing. Strangely, the first visitation occurred following a grueling session of physical therapy for my left knee.

I lay back on the table at Redondo Orthopedic (now Peak) Physical Therapy, in Redondo Beach, California. Dr. Steve Tysee and his assistant wrapped a cold, ice-pack around my knee. It burns with icy frost as knee pain is quickly replaced by a deep freeze. Below that, pulsing electric jolts from the TENS-unit, probed, tickled, and massaged the knee. The pain ebbs away.

As I lay there staring at the buzzing fluorescent lights in the ceiling, the adrenaline dump from exercise drains away. With the chatter of PTs and patients fading into the distance, I almost fall asleep.

I have found the time between waking consciousness and sleep is one in which people are particularly prone to seeing into the spiritual dimension. It is a mid-point where the veil of the natural world is lifted prior to the sleep-state taking over. Once asleep, you are definitely open to communication from the other side. Let's look at Job chapter 33, verses 14-18 again.

> Indeed God speaks once,
> Or twice, *yet* no one notices it.
> In a dream, a vision of the night,
> When sound sleep falls on people,
> While they slumber in their beds,
> Then He opens the ears of people,
> And seals their instruction.
> - Job 33:14-18, NASB and NASB 1995

Notice the above cites not one but two of the ways God speaks to us—one, through dreams (verse 15), and two, through our ears (verse 16). There are many more examples in the Bible where people have received messages in their dreams (Genesis 20:3, 40:8, 41:12, 25, 42:9; Numbers 12:6; Daniel 7:1-3; Joel 2:28; Matthew 1:20, 2:13, 19, etc.).

Like Nebuchadnezzar in Daniel 4:13, I caught the vision, "as I lay in bed."

Just as I was about to doze off, I was startled awake. In that mid-twilight state, I saw him standing right over me—the Birdman!

My Birdman

My Birdman had the body of a man and the presence of a warrior. His face was clearly that of a bird, almost cartoon-like—an eagle or a hawk. The beak was smiling at me. The eerie thing is, this spirit-being was literally beak-to-nose with me!

Startled, I gasped awake to full-consciousness.

"You ok?" The therapist smiled.

"Yes," I replied. "Just fell asleep for a moment."

Steve chuckled. I could talk to him about anything—but not this. I did not want my friend to think I had gone crazy. Steve smirked, but turned away and attended to other patients.

I saw the Birdman that day and again several other times as I was falling asleep. As before, my birdman was staring down, beak to nose, strangely smiling at me.

I was frustrated at first, trying to find a representation in the literature for what I saw. This was long before the *Birdman* (2014) movie starring Michael Keaton, which populates any internet search on the topic these days.

I found many accounts of Birdmen, but none really matched the one I saw, until one day when I took a closer look at the Japanese Tengu. Tengu are birdmen appearing in Shinto and Buddhist religions as guardian spirits of war and mischief. An online article by Mark Schumacher titled "Tengu: The Slayer of Vanity," defines the Tengu as the patron of martial arts.[102] Schumacher says Tengu oppose the haughty and vainglorious, punishing those who willfully misuse knowledge and authority. In the past, he says they were known to punish vain and arrogant samurai, and they dislike anyone who corrupts the Dharma (Buddhist Law).

This was fascinating to me. I have had a life-long interest in martial arts and samurai culture. I even have a framed *Kill Bill* (2003) movie poster and replica samurai swords hanging on my walls at home. Could I have possibly attracted a Tengu spirit through my preoccupation with kung fu movies and karate classes?

To my amazement, I found an image of Japanese Tengu samurai armor, with a "face" that looks almost *exactly* like the Birdman who visited me! The Tengu *tōsei gusoku* armor, Kiyotoshi, Munekiyo, Ryūsuiken, from the Late Edo period of Japan, 1854, was part of an exhibition by the Los Angeles County Museum of Art in 2014-2015, on loan from The Ann & Gabriel Barbier-Mueller Museum collection in Dallas.

Figure 14.1: *Tengu Tōsei Gusoku Armor,* Kiyotoshi, Munekiyo. Ryūsuiken, Japan. Late Edo period, 1854. The Ann & Gabriel Barbier-Mueller Museum, Dallas. Photograph by Brad Flowers.[103]

It was validating to see an actual physical representation of something that had appeared in my mind's eye many times, yet altogether unnerving to see the same, cartoon-like face, captured almost identically in such an ancient relic.

In the end, I think Birdmen are really are angelic beings, either good or bad. It has been a long while since I have had a visitation from the Birdman. Whether mine was there in the role of guardian spirit or mischievous wraith sent to vex me, I do not know.

What I do know is it was always very unsettling to see the Birdman staring down at me, even though he *was* smiling.

Look at the smiling face on the Tengu *tōsei gusoku* armor and decide for yourself. Does the Birdman look like a friend or a foe?

Now onto another strange being many have reported encounters with.

Bigfoot and Other Critters

Bigfoot or Sasquatch stories have appeared in American folklore by settlers and the native peoples of North America for nearly 200 years. They originate primarily from the Pacific Northwest, but also appear in accounts from the Great Lakes region all the way down to the Southeast.[104] In Himalayan folklore they are known as the Yeti.

But who or what are these creatures? If the theory that alien visitations represent some kind of demonic manifestation holds true, could the same be said for Bigfoot and other cryptids?

Some researchers believe Bigfoot is a hominid offshoot from our own family tree, or even a prehistoric "Wildman" akin to our cousin, Neanderthal. Geoffrey H. Bourne and Maury Cohen say Bigfoot could be a remnant population of Gigantopithecus.[105]

But how likely is it that such a species could continue to remain hidden in the modern world? In fairness, scientists discover new forms of animal life all the time—and Bigfoot, Sasquatch, and Yeti encounters normally occur in vast, wilderness areas with hundreds of square miles of untamed forests or mountain ranges, such as the Pacific Northwest, Canada, and the Himalayas.

Still, it stretches the imagination to think a great ape or sapiens cousin could evade us—unless the being really is paranormal. Ancient Buddhist traditions in Tibet say Yeti guard the gates to Shamballa, which is an obvious religious, spiritual connection. Why would an ape-man guard Shamballa? But a spiritual creature would imply a different story altogether.

Bigfoot creatures slipping in and out of open portals or etheric gateways could explain how they never get caught. Several accounts say that is what is happening at Skinwalker Ranch (Sherman Ranch) near Ballard, Utah. Of course, Bigfoot's not even being real would be another possible, if less stimulating, explanation. But that is not the case, according to my friend and former mentor, who says Bigfoot is very real.

The Inscrutable Richard Meyer

I met Richard Meyer when I got out of the Air Force in the late 1990s and began working for a commercial TV production company in Salt Lake City called Arrow America Video.

Richard, the producer who hired me, had a full complement of film production cameras and grip equipment, which he had inherited from his dad, a documentary filmmaker.

When Richard was a young man, he learned the craft of film production from his father. In like manner, Richard, by then in his late 40s, passed on the precious filmmaking knowledge to me and my counterpart in the production department, Mr. Brian Paul. We were both in our 20s at the time.

During slow afternoons, Richard would show Brian and me how to load the film magazines that mounted on his wonderful Arriflex BL camera. It was tricky, as you had to load the 400-foot rolls of motion picture film blindly, the heavy magazine and your arms buried deeply in the black, changing bag, so sunlight would not expose the negative.

It was during one such afternoon in our cramped, production office reception area, that Richard relayed the story of a documentary film he apprenticed on with his dad. We took turns practicing loading the film as Richard spoke. He sat opposite us in the computer desk chair, while Brian and I sat on the tan leather couch where we pitched clients on our production services.

All around the room were totems of Richard's career: an antique Hollywood clapboard, still chalked with an old production title and scene number, a dusty 1940s Mole Richardson studio light, and a large bookshelf, filled from top to bottom with volumes on the art and craft of filmmaking, classics such as John Alton's *Painting with Light*. I used to check out and read those books, one-by-one, and Richard would sign them out to me like a bearded librarian.

As Richard purposefully loaded the 400-foot roll of unexposed celluloid into the magazine, golden light from the late afternoon sun beamed through the blinds in the production office, threatening to creep into the black bag and lighting up Richard's scruffy red beard.

He smiled up at Brian and me, his blue eyes reflecting the sun, and told us the story.

Richard claimed he worked with his father on the 1976 Ivan Marx documentary *The Legend of Bigfoot*. He said they trekked around places like California and Oregon gathering lots of footage. Richard said they were well into the production with several interviews and location shots in the can when the production came to an abrupt halt.

"They asked us to stop filming," Richard said.

"They? They who?" I asked, frustratedly fumbling with the film magazine in the bag.

"The government," Richard replied, stoic.

"Who in the government?" I asked.

"I don't know," but they must have been credible because we stopped filming and never resumed production.

Richard claims Marx had enough film with all the nature shots they had already taken to finish the film, but they were not allowed to continue and missed out on getting real proof for the documentary.

"What?" I said, in awe.

"Apparently, we were onto something."

By now, Brian seemed bored with the story. I must admit, it all sounded like so much bunk, but I was hooked. There were so many specific details—and something so matter-of-fact, yet nonchalant, about the way Richard told the story—I couldn't help but believe it.

"So, Bigfoot is real?" I asked.

"Oh yeah," Richard smiled. "He's real."

"Well, what is 'he'?" I asked.

"He's a critter," Richard replied.

Brian chuckled and stood up, still smiling as he made his way back to his video editing room.

"So, he's not some kind of a…person."

"Nah," Richard rasped. "Bigfoot's a critter."

I have no idea if Richard and his dad really worked on that film or not, but the doc is made up mostly of wildlife and nature footage, so I suppose it is possible they participated as uncredited crew, trudging along, grabbing pick-up B-roll shots for the film—that kind of thing is not unheard of, especially on a guerilla (pardon the pun) indie film like that. I will say this: I personally saw outdoor footage that Richard shot for our productions while we were working together at Arrow using his old ARRI BL, and it is the most beautiful, outdoor footage I have ever seen anyone capture.

And as to the alleged call from the government. The FBI did have some involvement in Bigfoot investigations back then, at least a little. In 2019, the agency released 22 pages of documents from analysis they conducted in 1976 on a hair and skin sample they were given by researcher Peter Byrne, at the time, the director of the Bigfoot Information Center and Exhibition in The Dalles, Oregon.[106]

Located on the shores of the Columbia River near the Deschutes River, The Dalles is the eastern gateway to the Columbia Gorge National Scenic Area, at the end of the Oregon Trail. It was once a major Native American trading center. A frontier land, it's where Lewis and Clark once encamped, and the fur trade was active. The Dalles is the kind of place one could imagine encountering a Bigfoot on a scenic hike through remote trails.[107]

But in the case of the hair sample provided by Byrne, the FBI thoroughly tested it and concluded the hair was of "deer family origin."[108]

Some people, like Richard Meyer, say Bigfoot is a beast. Some say the creature is a hominid relative to the human race and other great apes. Others say the infamous cryptid is nothing more than a myth. Still others believe Bigfoot, and various such beings, are creatures of another dimension who access Earth through mysterious energetic gateways, or portals (this is also a theory growing in popularity for alien ETs as well).

Cryptid sightings are often said to be accompanied by a foul odor, something like sulfur. This would lend weight to the portal theory.

Could these beings be the denizens of a hellish underworld? While hard to believe, it is very intriguing and provoking to imagine the possibility that strange creatures such as cryptids and other beings could come to us from other dimensions.

Our folklore is filled with such tales.

Haunted Military Bases and Homes

Warren Air Force Base

Military bases often carry tales of hauntings and sightings in certain areas and buildings. In my travels to F.E. Warren, near Cheyenne, Wyoming, I encountered many airmen who swear the base is haunted. Warren is the oldest continuously active military installation in the Air Force.[109] The missile base, once an army installation, dates back to the building of the transcontinental railroad, when the U.S. government set plans to build a military base in the area to protect Union Pacific workers toiling away in the untamed frontier.

Ghosts at Mather

Rod Jones was an enlisted Airman stationed at Mather Air Force Base in the 1980s. "That place is haunted," said Jones. The former Strategic Air Command and training base had a long history dating back to World War I. The facility was located 12 miles east of Sacramento, on the south side of U.S. Route 50 in Sacramento County, California.[110] Mather, which closed in 1993, was built on ancient Indian burial grounds, according to Jones and others. Here's one such account, where a military family say they saw ghosts and other apparitions, and had electronic equipment and water faucets turn on all by themselves. The man who reported it, then a teenager, said one time he watched the dial on his radio turn all by itself and change channels! He also mentioned the connection to Native American burial grounds.

> We lived in the old base housing…the history of the land goes back thousands of years to the Native Americans and Pre-Archaic Period (10,000-8,500 BC). It was rumored and later confirmed that the base housing was built on Native American burial grounds.[111]

Here's a Mather story from another military member:

> I was stationed at Mather…We would often go to work and come home to find that all of the lights were on in the apartment…Then we started coming home to find things from the bathroom sitting on the kitchen counter—usually my deodorant or my wife's hair brush…Then we started seeing things in the bathroom mirror…you would see the reflection of someone walking behind you through the hallway into the bedroom.[112]

There are many stories about hauntings at Mather:

> When I was at Mather…I once felt a spirit walking behind me, I heard a spirit's voice call my name. My mother…once saw a man in white, and the ghostly entity walked away. When my mother went to investigate, there was nothing there.[113]

My friend Rod Jones also had a scare. He was having dinner at his best friend's house, when his buddy's daughter started pointing toward strange apparitions she saw in the living room. The girl saw an old woman standing over her friend and an old man sitting on her dad's chest. The dad was napping at the time.

"What did you do?" I asked.

"I got the hell out of there," Jones asserted.

Rod is now exploring a film project on the subject of 'creepers.'

"Creepers are spirits who follow you into your garage when you open it," says Jones.

Strange, the very night before he told me this, I was having a cigar in my garage. This is an unusual act for me, as I normally smoke outside, not wanting to fumigate my garage with strong cigar odors; but on that uncommonly cold Southern California night in November 2017, I retreated into the garage for shelter.

The whole time I was smoking, side door open to allow the acrid smoke to waft out into the chilly night air, I could not shake the feeling someone was watching me. So real was this sensation, I kept turning my head behind me, staring into the darkness, half-expecting to find eyes staring back at me. I ended up shining a light all around both cars to make sure no burglar had snuck inside.

Although there was no physical presence in the garage with me, I could not dismiss the feeling I was being watched. And it was quite bizarre to have Rod bring up the concept of garage 'creepers' to me the very next day. Unfortunately, this experience would not be the last time a force of spiritual oppression would manifest in the garage.

The Garage Door Incident

Tuesday, March 27, 2018 – I came home late from work. When I pulled into my garage, the garage door opener flew out of my hand and slid under the seat. I heard it hit inside the car alongside the left somewhere and ricochet around; but I could not locate it. I reached all around and under the seat but just could not find it. Even after parking the car, I still could not locate that pesky remote.

The strange way the garage door opener flew out of my hand made me suspect I was under a spiritual attack—that, along with the fact there were many people at work currently unhappy over recent management decisions. And as a management official, I sometimes became a target for their ire. There was ill will afoot, and they may have unwittingly (or wittingly, even) launched their demons at me.

Could that explain the "creeper" in my garage? Is that what I had sensed a few months earlier? Either way, I felt like a spiritual cause was at work, but was my garage truly haunted?

Unable to find the remote, I surrendered the situation to God and prayed He would allow me to find it. And I also prayed for protection against the unwelcome presence that seemed to be at work. After praying, I looked again and found the remote right away.

The next night was an uncommon Wednesday night choir rehearsal at church. Normally, the worship team practices songs on Thursday, but this was our special choir rehearsal for the upcoming Easter services. On my way to choir practice, my wife called and said she was not able to close the garage door. She had tried her remote several times, but the door would simply not close. She was concerned about leaving the car and other items exposed, such as the garage sale goodies her brother had stored in there.

Immediately, I got the sense this occurrence was connected to the spiritual attack I experienced with the garage door opener the night before.

I told my wife to relax and give it a break. Go inside the house and pray about it, and I would pray about it too. So, I joined the choir inside church and began praying silently for deliverance from this oppression.

After our prayers, my wife returned to the garage, and the door closed on the first try!

Chapter 15

The Ghostly Adventures of Uncle Ron and Friends

I am not the first sensitive in my family. My mother had the gift, as does my Uncle Ron. Ronald Lewis, my dad's baby-brother, is an easy-going man in his late 60s. Ron is quick to share a laugh, or the tuna-mac-and-cheese casserole he whipped up, doused with tabasco, of course, along with his famous ginger ale, sweet-Carolina-Muscadine wine concoction—not to mention a ghost story or two.

"First of all, Richard," says Ron, "there is nothing wrong with you. I have been seeing these things my whole life."

Uncle Ron said when he first started seeing ghosts he thought he was going crazy. But then he figured out it was all just normal.

"And it don't make you evil," he adds. Ron, who proudly declares he has read through the whole Bible, says Jesus was all about love; and believes Christians should not pass premature judgment on things they do not understand. Uncle Ron, a Vietnam veteran, has even seen a formation of UFOs. "Yes, I witnessed a formation of craft. I was called in [to] work [at] 3:00 a.m. one morning, winter time, maybe six in the group. They were there, then they weren't."[114]

Ron clicked the sound down on the TV to share a couple of spooky stories.

Haunted Crib

When Cousin Ron was a boy, they called him little Ron, or Ron-Ron, so as not to confuse him with Uncle Ron or "Big" Ron. When little Ron was a baby, he lived with his mom, my Aunt Beverly, on Barclay Street in Greensboro. The family was poor, so it is no wonder they accepted an old, hand-me-down crib for the child. One night, while baby Ronnie was sleeping, Uncle Ron noticed a "fog" hanging over the crib; so he moved closer to investigate.

"Hey, Bev, come here."

"What is it?" Aunt Bee replied.

"Do you see that?" He pointed to the mist.

"Yes, I see it," said Beverly.

Ron reached his hands into the crib where little Ron stirred.

"The air in the crib was at least 10-degrees cooler than that in the room," said Ron.

He immediately pulled my little cousin up out of there, carried the crib outside and dismantled it.

Later, Uncle Ron and Aunt Beverly learned a little baby had died in that old crib.

Sister-in-Ghoul

Another time, Ron was mowing his grass when he felt something… behind him.

"That's real," says Ron. "When you feel something behind you—it's there."

Then he caught a hint of his sister-in-law's perfume. What a lovely fragrance. Only she had committed suicide years earlier.

Another time, as he walked past her old car that the family kept parked in the yard, he saw her through the window, sitting inside at the driver's seat, smiling at him.

"It was plain as day," Ron says.

Departed Loved Ones

To corroborate Uncle Ron's story, I have seen the spirits of family members myself, and I've noticed they will smile at you. They smile—but in my experience it is often a frozen smile where their lips do not move. These beings rarely speak. If they do speak, it is telepathic, and they use few words.

"Because they're spirits," says my Aunt Catherine "Cathy," my mom's baby-sister—and she is right. Cathy looks serious for a moment, while staring over her lunch at me, country-style steak, sweet tea, and chocolate pie. I am eating my usual chicken-pan-pie. The venue is K&W Cafeteria at the Friendly Center on Northline Avenue, in Greensboro, 2017. We have been going here since I was a little kid; and I always pay K&W a visit anytime I am back home.

How odd to see the passage of time in my Aunt's visage, now looking back at me with her big smile. She reminds me more of Grandma Clara these days. It seems like just yesterday Cathy was racing me and Cousin Brian around in her yellow 1978 Camaro, and sunbathing in the side yard at Grandma's house on East Market Street, a young woman. Now, here we are—an entire lifetime lived, but the past seems more like the momentary reflection of an evening dream.

By 2018, we were favoring the Burlington K&W location. Its glorious chicken-pan-pie as fresh as possible, with buttery-flaky dough crust and creamy sauce, identical to the experience from my childhood. Only now Mom is long gone and not here to share in our Scots-Irish-English pedestrian feast. But Mom is alive in our conversation and memories of her.

So, why don't the spirits talk with their mouths? The answer is simple: Our vocalized communication involves a complex union of breath, mouth, teeth, lounge, throat, diaphragm—disembodied spirits have no need to mouth words. My experience has been that you will see their form appear like a reflection, their face frozen in a smile, like a still photo, while you only hear their voice. It is like receiving a radio transmission while watching a flat, black-and-white projection of a still image.

That is not to say ghosts do not make facial expressions. Those of you who read Book I will recall the spirits who sneered down at me during Angel Camp, as well as my departed mother who lovingly blew me a kiss. Still, in all those encounters, they never spoke mechanically the way we do in this earthly body.

Aunt Cathy has seen spirits too. Shortly after my Grandpa George Spence, her father, died, Grandpa appeared to Cat at the foot of her bed.

The same thing happened to my Cousin Tracy Fulk, also from Mom's side of the family. When her Grandpa passed, he appeared at the foot of her bed. Her mom, my Aunt Brenda, experienced his presence too.

"Dad showed up to me when I was sick," says Brenda.

The venue now is Tex and Shirley's in High Point, where we mop up our breakfast eggs and swap stories.

"I did not see him, but I felt the bed go down on one side like he was sitting down."

That feeling of the bed going down on one side as if someone's weight just sat on it is commonly reported. I have experienced it personally, along with scores of others.

"Then he put his hand on my head," says Aunt Brenda. "Like he was checkin' my temperature."

Cousin Tracy, a retired Greensboro police detective, has taken her gumshoe skills to the next level. She actually goes out on ghost-hunting excursions.

"We recorded a little boy's voice at one place," Tracy said.

"An EVP [electronic voice phenomena]?" I asked.

"Yep," she replied. "It was pretty cool."

It happened at a building that had been an insane asylum. Before that, it was a home for orphaned boys.

"We found out a boy had been murdered in that room," Tracy said.

Cousin Tracy even took her entire police squad out to graveyards with her ghost-hunting kit. Her boyfriend at the time, Phil, went along too.

I used to stay with Phil and Tracy when I would visit North Carolina. They were the ones who picked me up at the hospital after my mom passed. And even though Phil does not believe in ghosts, he did have an experience out there in the graveyard one night. But it was not a departed human.

"Where did that cat go?" Phil asked.

"What cat?" Tracy replied.

"The one that just rubbed up against my leg," said Phil.

But there was no cat around.

Uncle Chubby and the Night Lady

In another case with my Uncle Ron, he was hanging out with a lady friend, standing around in the yard outside her house. Off in the distance, he saw a man standing there with a hat that said 'taxi driver' on it, staring at him. The lady did not see it.

"You have any relation to you who was a taxi driver?" Ron asked the woman.

"Oh yeah, my Uncle Chubby," she replied. "But he passed away."

Another time, Ron was hanging out with some friends around an abandoned building. Guilford County is littered with these old structures, many of them from the turn of the century. Ron felt something strange about an old tree standing nearby.

Ron pulled a branch toward his nose and sniffed the acorns hanging on the tree.

"You smell that?" Ron asked, turning to his friend. The friend must have thought it was weird, but he took a whiff too.

"Smells like liquor," the friend replied.

"That's what I thought," Ron said.

Just then, Ron saw a beautiful young woman, standing in front of the building. Although his friend did not see the ghost, they found out about a 'lady of the night' who used to work there during the prohibition era. The woman served liquor to people from within that very building.

"What did she look like?" I asked. Ron's eyes furrowed for a moment.

Uncle Ron is a widow now, his large home an empty nest—it's expansive, perfectly swept and polished wood-floors and empty hallways, rather lonely—but often echoing with my uncle's laughter. But his face is pensive now. For a brief instant, I see Dad, his older brother.

"You know how a photo negative looks—black and white and reversed?"

"Yes," I replied.

"Well that is what they [ghosts] look like," said Ron.

I caught a chill. It's strange when someone validates a paranormal experience. To learn someone else has seen the same thing.

Uncle Ron was exactly right. Have you ever wondered why there is so much consistency in how spirits are portrayed in movies and pictures? It is because that is pretty much how apparitions really look, as I found out first-hand in the following, scary encounter.

The Lady in the Bonnet

A "white lady" apparition is a kind of ghost sighting widely reported in many places around the world. Common to these appearances are themes of family loss, as in a husband, fiancé, or child.[115] Of course, I knew nothing about these sightings, until I had my own experience with one. This happened back when I lived across from El Nido Park in Redondo Beach, by Pacific Crest Cemetery.

I was reclining on my couch one night, drifting in and out of sleep. Like I mentioned earlier, that's when you're most open to seeing into the spiritual realm.

It was during such a moment when I saw the figure of a woman standing in my dining area across from the living room.

Although I could not make out her face, I got the impression of a young woman. She wore a turn-of-the-century dress and apron, something you might see a maid or farm girl wear, and she had an old-fashioned bonnet on her head.

Her appearance was translucent and white. The lady was turned away from me, staring at an old family photo I had hanging on the dining room wall. It was a 1950s black-and-white photo of a large group—a family reunion on my dad's side. My great-grandpa Oscar Lewis sat sternly in the front on the left. Aunt Beverly was in the front on the other side. While my dad stood all the way in the back row and on the very end on the left—a young teenager, nervously holding a finger to his face. Dad barely resembled the brawny, confident guy I would know later. Now here's the weird part:

The ghost was brushing off the picture of my family with a feather-duster!

Why was this woman dusting off my family photo? Was she someone from the picture or a distant ancestor perhaps? According to *The Nuttall Encyclopedia*, these spirits were thought to be the ghosts of deceased ancestors.[116]

This brings up another thought. Years ago I had a reading from world renowned psychic Atira Hatton. Readers of my Book I will recall Atira and I both attended Doreen Virtue's Angel Therapy Practitioner Course together back in 2003.

Atira told me I have "an old lady" watching over me as a guiding spirit. She said the woman is an ancestor. She said the lady told her, "He doesn't know me." I have no idea if it is true or not, but I found the idea a little creepy.

Or maybe this ghost in my dining room was simply looking, as the legends say, for her own lost family members and happened to stop along the way to check out mine.

Just then, the white lady turned to look at me.

But there was no face.

I startled awake, and the woman vanished.

I sank back into the couch again and drifted off to sleep.

I was jolted awake an instant later, terrified.

There, right in front of my face, hanging in mid-air was a small stuffed doll! It was a "Stewie" figure from the *Family Guy* cartoon. My youngest son Preston gave it to me.

The Stewie doll naturally has a cross look on his face, which added a creepy, unsettling vibe to this encounter. What was really disturbing, though, was the *way* an unseen hand *dangled* the doll in front of my face, *waving it back and forth!*

I gasped in terror, reeling back on the couch. The Stewie doll was back in the cup on my coffee table where it normally rested.

To this day, I have no idea who the lady was I saw that night. I never saw her ghost again—but I did catch glimpses down the hallway of a hazy mist lingering there—and my wife reported seeing a misty form moving across the hallway from bedroom to bedroom at night.

The Girl Watching

In another case, I awoke to the specter of a girl in a nightgown, standing over the loveseat couch where my stepdaughter Yuni liked to lounge at night. The ghost-girl had her ethereal arms stretched out, resting on the arm of the couch while leaning over it, staring straight down at Yuni's face as she slept.

As with the Lady in the Bonnet, I could not see the ghost-child's face as it was turned away from me. And also like the Lady, the child disappeared as I awoke fully, still staring at the loveseat. Another time, I saw my stepdaughter sleeping on that couch...

But her spirit was sitting up.

Yuni tells me she sometimes hears a voice whispering her name when she is alone outside. She said one time she could even feel the breath on her ear. Perhaps it was just her guardian angel.

The first week of September 2018, we brought Yuni home from Miller Children's Hospital in Long Beach, California, following scoliosis correction surgery. She was two months away from turning 14. This was a major operation involving spinal fusion, cadaver bone grafts, and a blood transfusion from her mother. Yuni took it like a champ and was released two days early. Those first few days at home were the hardest for her to cope, with pain and discomfort, but she tried not to let it affect her mood. Still, those kinds of moments in life are a real test.

Realizing she was being cranky early one morning when Janet woke her up, Yuni apologized to her mom, but in so doing, said something unexpected.

"I'm sorry, Mommie. I have six people inside me."

That was a bit unsettling, but perhaps just an effect of sleepiness and pain medication.

Yuni was baptized years ago and completed confirmation in June, 2019. She continues growing in her faith.

And thankfully, we are not having paranormal activity anymore. All of that calmed down before we moved to our Gardena home. But years ago, when I lived alone in Redondo Beach, it was a whole different story.

I would often come home to find items like my Saint Michael candle had mysteriously moved from one end of the dresser to the other, even though no one had entered my apartment. I would also discover objects moved to strange, unexpected places. I even found my bathroom sink full of pennies when I returned home from work and turned on the lights.

Remember in Book I when I mentioned "pennies from heaven?" Well this did not seem to be the gentle prodding of an angel—these signs seemed mocking and scary. They were eerie and unsettling things to come home to.

I also returned home at night to find the cabinets in the kitchen hanging open, which is quite startling to see when you first turn on the lights.

There were other frightening phenomena, like feeling my bed or even my body shaking at night. This is alarming, as shaking and convulsions can be markers for demonic attack (Mark 9:20).[117]

The nighttime attacks were the worst.

Chapter 16

Christ the Conqueror

The most severe demon attack I ever experienced was from a powerful succubus that came calling one night in 2014 around 3:00 a.m.—the "witching hour," when I was still living alone in my apartment in Redondo Beach. As was common with these attacks, I experienced *The Swarming* while I slept, accompanied by sleep paralysis and being caught in a whirlpool of pulsating, electric energy. I felt myself surrounded in this vortex, being compelled to surrender to the entity. My late Uncle Jerry had experienced these attacks too. He called it, "The Swirling."

"It's that demon spirit, Richard, it's trying to possess you. You can't let it."

I didn't. Instead, I forced myself back to consciousness.

Awake now, and sitting up in bed, the room was quiet and dark. But I could still feel the demon on me, its prickly energy stinging and raising the hairs on my arms. I began praying. Psalms and spiritual songs are very powerful against demon attacks. Psalms, 22, 23, 27, 31, 91 and 118 are effective, as is the Lord's Prayer found in Matthew 6:9-13.

Psalm 23 and the Lord's Prayer are two of my favorites to speak aloud, as I can recite them without having to look them up and read them.

I got up and went to the bathroom. It is said that spirits have trouble crossing over water and that water can dispel them. Some dispute this, saying spirits are in no way bound by water. Of course, Holy Water is well-known for being effective in fighting unclean spirits, but even crossing the water lines running under the bathroom floor keeps the unclean spirits off. I have never had one of these attacking entities follow me in there. The only exception was the "toilet devil," which came upon me years ago when my spiritual awakening first began, a story I relayed in Chapter 22 of Book I. For the sake of new readers, and those of you who would like a refresh, I will briefly recount it.

The First Swarm

It was a Sunday night, August 10, 2003. I had experienced a profound psychic awakening while reading Doreen Virtue's 1999 book, *Divine Guidance*. I was experiencing shifts in my perception and senses. I would go on to have visions and other experiences, which continue to this day. A floodgate had opened that would require me to learn discernment and psychic self-defense methods to protect myself.

That night, I was continuing to read *Divine Guidance*, now on the toilet, of all places. As I was reading, I fell into an almost trance-like state. My eyes defocused, and it was like the text was magnified, floating off the pages somehow. I experienced tunnel vision as I looked at the copy, and the pages seemed to get brighter. Suddenly, I experienced a piercing ringing in my ears. Then I felt an entity, starting at my leg, making its way up to my head, as I was engulfed in pulsating, electric-energy—*The Swarming*.

I call it *the swarming* because that is what it feels like: you are literally swarmed in an oscillating whirlpool of dark energy. You are tingling all over with electric energy, the hairs on your body stand on end. But it is *not* good.

Back then, I thought it was an angel manifesting to me—perhaps I was being called to some great mission. So, I surrendered to the experience and allowed myself to bathe in *the swarming*. This is not good. Later, I figured out this was a succubus spirit. I suffered many such attacks afterward. But the entity simply left me alone once I said no more and willed the experience to stop. And the waking attacks did stop, but the nighttime attacks were worse, especially the final one in 2014.

The "toilet devil" in 2003 is the only spirit that ever attacked me in the bathroom. I have heard spirits can latch onto you and "hitch a ride," therefore crossing the water by you. Maybe that is what happened back in 2003. In all others instances, they seem to have been prevented from crossing the water lines, including that final attack in 2014.

Deliverance

The chilling thing is, although the incubus/succubus could not follow me into the bathroom, it stayed in the bedroom *waiting for me*.

I poured a cup of water and raised it into the air, praying –

"Dear Lord, make this [water] Holy Water, pure and true, fit to dispel unclean spirits." Then I brought the cup down to chest level and marked it with the sign of the cross.

"In the name of the Father, the Son, and the Holy Spirit. Amen."

I took a several gulps of the water. I then dipped my finger into the water and drew the sign of the cross on my forehead. Then I dipped my fingertips back into the cup and sprinkled the water all over my face, shirt, and arms.

Christians have been making use of Holy Water since the days of the early church. Bishop Serapion of Thmuis' Pontifical from about the year AD 400 contains the blessing of Holy Water, and church tradition traces its use all the way back to the apostle Saint Matthew, who some believe adopted it to win over Jewish converts as they would be familiar with the rite.[118] Many say only a priest can bless the water—and I agree. But the Bible teaches that all Christians are priests with direct access to God, through Jesus our great High Priest (Hebrews 4:14). "But you are a chosen people, a royal priesthood, a holy nation, God's special possession, that you may declare the praises of him who called you out of darkness into his wonderful light" (1 Peter 2:9, NIV (See also Revelation 5:10, 20:6)). So, any Christian with believing faith can call on God to bless the water and make it Holy.

There is real power in the water, but the power comes from our faith. It is similar to how we ask God to bless our food and drink before we eat. I do not think anything physical happens to the water in the material world, it does not change on a molecular level or anything, of course; but in the spiritual world, that water becomes a weapon against evil.

As Saint Teresa of Avila said, "I know by frequent experience that there is nothing which puts the devils to flight like Holy water."[119] Holy Water really works, but it also evaporates quickly, which is why oil and salt are also used in deliverance sessions because they remain intact longer.

Some Christians do not support the use of divine elements. Perhaps they think it is just superstitious nonsense. But the Scripture says,

> Is anyone among you suffering? Let him pray. Is anyone cheerful? Let him sing praise. Is anyone among you sick? Let him call for the elders of the church, and let them pray over him, anointing him with oil in the name of the Lord. (James 5:13-14, ESV)

I walked back out into the room and began sprinkling the Holy Water all around, on the bed, the pillows, the headboard, etc.

"Unclean spirit, I cast you out in the name of Jesus Christ," I said, as I sprinkled the water. "I command you to leave and never return." I repeated this prayer a number of times, but I could sense the demon was still there, so I turned on the lights. Light has power too. It may keep you awake—but you really do not want to go back to sleep right away with an incubus in your room. If you do go back to sleep again too soon, the demon will just attack you again.

Prayer is the most effective weapon against demons, as is regular church attendance, partaking of the sacraments, living a holy life, and surrounding yourself with blessed and holy objects around your home and on your person.[120]

The most important thing is to rely on Jesus as the moral and spiritual center of your life. He is the ultimate authority over demons and all the powers of darkness (Ephesians 1:20-23).

But there are also some common-sense "housekeeping" things you can do to keep your home space clear. Light is an effective deterrent against negative entities, and so is sound and a fresh breeze. This is why stale, dark attics and unoccupied rooms become breeding grounds for paranormal activity. It is important to allow sunshine to cleanse every room in your house. In the same way ultraviolet rays break down a skunk's noxious odor, sunlight also cleanses away foul and unclean spirits. So, let the sunshine and sound and joy in, and keep things clean and clutter free.[121]

Exorcists will often place a Bible on the head or chest of someone suffering from demonic oppression. I have also found this to be very effective. Following an attack, and at other times during those periods of testing—when I anticipated a potential attack was coming—I have often gone to sleep hugging a Bible to my chest. I have NEVER experienced a demon that could climb up on your chest with the Holy Bible there.

I AM HERE

With the lights on, now sitting up in bed, my Bible open in my hands, I began to read aloud Psalm 91. The Scriptures are perhaps the most potent weapon of all against the evil one.

"If you make the Lord your refuge, if you make the Most High your shelter, no evil will conquer you…"

The Holy Water was all around the bed, and my Bible was on my chest, so the dark spirit was kept at bay at the foot of the bed. But still it would not go.

"For he will order his angels to protect you wherever you go…"

I felt a sharp pain go through my left, big toe. The demon was biting me!

So, I prayed and continued making my way through the verses, reading them aloud. The Psalms are powerful. The demon was apparently becoming agitated. To my surprise, the bed *started shaking* as I read.

"You will trample upon lions and cobras; you will crush fierce lions and serpents under your feet!"

The shaking intensified.

The Lord says, "I will rescue those who love me. I will protect those who trust in my name."

The lights in the room began to buzz and flicker, almost shutting off.

This was very chilling. Bed shaking, lights flickering low—but I was not afraid. At this moment, I knew my fate was in God's hands, and I trusted him no matter what was going to happen. I kept reading, raising my voice as the bed shook under me.

"When they call on me, I will answer; I will be with them in trouble. I will rescue and honor them. I will reward them with a long life and give them my salvation."

The bed stopped shaking and the lights stopped flickering. Somehow I had randomly flipped to Matthew 14:27. My eyes landed on this verse:

"Take courage. I am here."

As I was looking at the Bible text, behind it I could see a form was standing there. I looked up to see the Lord Jesus standing over me! He was big and smiling and radiating power. The thing that surprised me most was how He was dressed. I would have expected Jesus to appear in the classic flowing white robes and sandals. Here He was clothed as a warrior!

Although He wore a warrior's garb, it still looked ancient, with leathers and straps, rather than metal armor. I did not understand it at the time; but it became clear to me why He was dressed this way—this was the warrior Christ, the Lion of Judah!

Jesus' presence eradicated all darkness. The demon was gone instantly.

If it was destroyed or sent away, I do not know. All I know is it could not occupy any space with the Lord there.

I diverted my eyes from Him. I could feel my sins were before me, and I felt ashamed. The Lord said nothing in words, but I could feel His presence, reassuring me, and comforting me. He did not excuse my sins—He forgave them. I knew at that moment I would have victory over the demons that had been plaguing me. When I lifted my head, the manifestation was gone. The room was left bright and clean, filled up with the warm light from my bedside lamp.

Some will not believe this story. I would doubt it too had I not seen Him with my own open eyes and felt His love and forgiveness.

But I had experienced lesser visions of Christ before.

Real Presence

It happened several times during Communion, prior to receiving the Host, as well as during confession, when my head was bowed. I would see the Lord placing His hand upon my head. I felt pressure on the back of my neck as my head hung down. In the foreground, I would see an image of Christ in front of me. He always appeared powerful and majestic, wearing flowing white robes.

Mystics also say we have an area of spiritual "sight" at the top of our heads. Some call it the Sahasrara, or "Crown Chakra." If true, perhaps this could explain why we so often have visions when we bow our heads to pray.

> The Crown Chakra is our connection with Divinity. It is the portal through which the life energy enters our body… By balancing and strengthening the Seventh Chakra, we can connect with the Higher Power…which can then be shared with those around us…A person with a closed Crown Chakra gets no guidance from the Supreme Power…[122]

These are esoteric concepts, unconventional if not taboo to many Christians, and I understand that. I am not saying they are true. But they could be.

It could simply be the way God created us.

All I know is I often saw Jesus in those moments when my head was bowed. One thing though: those visions of Christ were never as clear as the manifestation in my bedroom, where He appeared in vivid color to my open eyes!

Christ the Conqueror

I continue to marvel at how His likeness in that manifestation was not at all as I would have imagined it. I would normally expect to see Jesus clothed in white robes, not as a general. Jesus wearing the garb of an ancient warrior, with leather armor and a strap across His shoulder, was unexpected. I had never pictured Christ arrayed in quite that manner before.

In my first book, I shared the story of my friend Alan, who Pastor Jon Reed of Hilltop Church of Christ, in El Segundo, CA, had encouraged me to speak to. Alan, also of Hilltop, had previously worked as a deliverance minister. I relayed how he helped deliver a girl who came out of Satanism. Although a Christian now, the girl still had a demon attachment.

Alan told the girl to call on Jesus, inviting Him into the room. Although Alan could not see Jesus himself, the girl, who could see into the spirit world due to her involvement with the occult, actually saw Christ arrive. She reported the demon was gone instantly!

When Alan told me that story I believed him, but I guess I had never thought of Christ in that way. I normally imagined Jesus as a loving shepherd, which He is. But He is also the Lion of Judah! (Revelation 5:5). And He arrived to me the night of the attack as a warrior prince! Now I better appreciated the majesty of Jesus Christ, by whom all things were made (Colossians 1:16). Of course, evil spirits cannot abide in His presence!

> He is the image of the invisible God, the firstborn of all creation. For by him all things were created, in heaven and on earth, visible and invisible, whether thrones or dominions

or rulers or authorities—all things were created through him and for him. And he is before all things, and in him all things hold together. (Colossians 1:15-17, ESV)

I have often pondered why the Lord would reveal himself to me. But remember before He departed, Jesus told His disciples, "I will not leave you as orphans; I will come to you. Yet a little while and the world will see me no more, but you will see me" (John 14:18-19, ESV).

Jesus also said, "And he who loves me will be loved by my Father, and I will love him and manifest myself to him" (John 14:21, ESV).

Having a bed shaking under me, then shaking more furiously *in response* as I read the Psalms aloud in prayer was quite unsettling. Still, during a moment like that, even as the bed was shaking and the lights were flickering down low, I found the fear departed. Because especially at those times, no matter what the outcome may be—I know who I am in Christ Jesus (Ephesians 1:7; Romans 8:1; Revelation 2:10; 1 Corinthians 15:57). I know that my redeemer lives (Job 19:25). I remember that He is with me always until the end of the age (Matthew 28:20). I trust Jesus all the way!

Over the years, my family and I have grown ever stronger in our prayer life and fellowship at church and have strived to make our house into a sanctuary for the Lord. Thankfully, the poltergeist activity in my home has ceased.

But I did see a UFO.

Figure 16.1: *Battesimo di Cristo* (Baptism of Christ) by Aert de Gelder, 1710 (public domain). This enigmatic work is currently housed at The Fitzwilliam Museum, Cambridge, England.[123]

As I looked, behold, a stormy wind came out of the north,
and a great cloud, with brightness around it,
and fire flashing forth continually,
and in the midst of the fire, as it were gleaming metal.
And from the midst of it came the likeness
of four living creatures.
And this was their appearance: they had a human likeness…
Ezekiel 1:4-5
Holy Bible, English Standard Version (ESV)

Chapter 17

UFOs: The Cosmic Conundrum

Although the term UFO, or unidentified flying object, was coined by the Air Force in the 1950s, sightings of unknown aerial phenomena have been going on since antiquity. If an airborne object is spotted, and unknown, that makes it a UFO to the observer. It should be noted that the vast majority of UFOs turn out to be explainable. In her excellent 2010 book *UFOs: Generals, Pilots, and Government Officials Go on the Record*, journalist Leslie Kean says 90 to 95% of UFO sightings can be explained.[124]

UAP, or unidentified aerial phenomena, is a term that has become more en vogue in recent years, especially for aviators and investigators who want to separate themselves from the sensationalism and fringe elements in the UFO enthusiast and research communities.

In some cases, the term UAP is more accurate, as a sighting may indeed be a phenomenon rather than an object—if you saw the Northern Lights, for example, and didn't know what they were. I consider the terms to be interchangeable, but for the sake of simplicity, I will use the classical term UFO in most cases unless UAP is absolutely demanded because that is what the source calls it or because the nature of the phenomena is truly unknown. In the case of an unknown something that appears on radar and seems to be under intelligent control, we will call it a UFO.

Again, most of the purported UFOs turn out to be explainable, such as aircraft, terrestrial spacecraft, weather phenomenon, and astronomical objects like bright planets or meteors, and a small amount are hoaxes. While only a small percentage of sightings remain unexplained, some sources say between five percent and up to 20% of reported sightings remain unexplained and can therefore be classified as unidentified.[125]

UFO does not mean extraterrestrial or alien. It means unidentified. Something unknown is unknown, until understood. So, there really should be no stigma attached to someone by virtue of their claiming to have seen an unidentified flying object, because that simply means they saw something they can't explain.

A great recent example is the American Airlines pilot who called in what sounds to me like a classic "cigar-shaped" UFO, which flew over his plane. American Airlines confirmed the radio recording February 21 is authentic. AA Flight 2292 was traveling over New Mexico, going from Cincinnati to Phoenix. The plane was flying at an altitude of 36,000 feet going 460 miles per hour. "It...looked like a long cylindrical object," the pilot said. "It went right over the top of us." The Federal Aviation Administration (FAA) says air traffic controllers didn't spot any object in the area on their radars. The FBI is reportedly investigating the incident.[126]

So, that is a textbook example of a UFO. It could have been a missile test, an unknown military aircraft or who knows what—but it remains unidentified until it is explained: a UFO.

What about aliens?

I believe there should be a line drawn between UFO sightings and alien visitations, especially abduction experiences. As far as alien encounters and abduction experiences go, I would propose most, if not all, of the alleged encounters are probably psychospiritual in nature (and also many sightings of allegedly physical craft are likely psychospiritual too). I realize there are many people who have had strange, often frightening encounters and experiences where they believe they have been abducted, but it is unlikely such events truly involve extraterrestrial biological entities. The distance between stars is just too great.

Our nearest stellar neighbor, Proxima Centauri, is 4.244 light-years away from earth—which is a whopping 24.95 trillion miles away![127]

If something like our Voyager 1 spacecraft, launched in 1977, were to travel to the star next door, it would take over 73,000 years to arrive! If we could travel at the speed of light, an impossibility, scientists say, due to Special Relativity, it would still take 4.22 years to arrive at Proxima Centauri![128] Here in our own "little" solar system, it takes Pluto 248 earth years just to make one trip around the sun.[129] The dwarf planet has yet to make a complete rotation since its discovery in 1930![130]

But even if the mysterious alien encounters do not really involve true biological entities, that does not mean such meetings are not extraterrestrial in nature. Consider this: angels and demons are not of this world; so, by definition that makes them extraterrestrial. What if *they* are the ones visiting earth from the heavenly dimensions?

Although I do not rule out the possibility of other sentient lifeforms in the universe, it is not a given. Life itself is a miracle. The law of biogenesis states that life arises only from other life, *Omne vivum ex vivo*, "all life [is] from life" as French chemist Louis Pasteur, the father of microbiology, put it.[131]

Since living matter has never been known to spontaneously generate from non-living matter—as Pasteur proved—quite simply, we should not be here if materialism were true. To the contrary, the law of biogenesis is in perfect harmony with the creation account in the book of Genesis, where God said, "Let the earth bring forth living creatures according to their kinds—livestock and creeping things and beasts of the earth according to their kinds." And it was so (Genesis 1:24, ESV).

Many contemporary UFO researchers assume since we are here, it follows they—those extraterrestrials, however rare statistically—should be there also. But it is also possible, when God decided to do the impossible and create man for His own pleasure and good purposes, it may have been a solo act. Even though non-living matter transitioning to complex living organisms like us is nigh impossible, here we are. I say it is because God guided it. But just because life flourished here does not necessarily mean it will succeed elsewhere without help from a guiding intelligence. At this point, Earth remains the only known place in the universe to harbor life, certainly intelligent life like us.[132]

But the universe is so big! Well, what if the vastness of the cosmos is needed for some unknown reason we do not fully understand? Atoms are mostly empty space, and everything we know of is made up of atoms. That is not wasted space. What is true at the atomic is true on a galactic scale.

The universe contains everything and yet is made up of mostly nothing. Some estimates make that one could travel through the galaxy from end-to-end 15,000 times and you are likely to never hit anything![133]

On another level, perhaps our expanding, beautiful universe is simply there for God's good pleasure. Maybe He likes looking at it. I am sure the vibrant, magnificent universe is also there for our enjoyment as well. What a marvel the billions of cascading galaxies filled with trillions of shimmering stars, along with the vast, multi-colored nebulae, hidden, waiting for billions of years until we humans could build such devices as the Hubble Space Telescope to finally bring these gigantic, colorful expanses into proper view!

Figure 17.1: *HH 901 and HH 902 in the Carina Nebula,* captured by the Hubble Space Telescope February 1-2, 2010 (public domain). This image, dubbed Mystic Mountain, was released in 2010 to commemorate Hubble's 20th anniversary in space. Traveling at the speed of light, 186,000 miles per second, it would take over three years just to make it from top to bottom across this enormous cosmic column of gas and dust. The universe is truly vast![134]

Scientific laws and principals, such as the conservation of mass, mass-energy equivalence, and biogenesis, preclude life arising by accident; while the law of conservation of energy, the first law of thermodynamics, validates the existence of our spiritual self—as energy in a closed-system cannot be created or destroyed, it can only be transformed.[135] Note, there is no known exception to this law under any circumstances.[136] The implications of this are sublime. This means that not only are we physical beings, we are also sentient, physical-*spirit*, life forms.

The energy that animates us, the spark that is your consciousness continues on after death because it can't be destroyed. This is *law*. Perhaps we on earth are the only such creatures in the universe. We really don't know.

In his masterful 2021 book *Return of the God Hypothesis*, Stephen C. Meyer argues that evidence from physics shows that from the beginning the universe has been finely tuned to allow for the possibility of life.[137] But there are so many conditions on earth that are just right for life to exist here. We simply do not know if the same can be said for other planets.

Yet, despite all of that, I actually do believe there is probably other sentient life out there. But that is just a personal feeling. I am willing to accept it may not be so. Still, it seems like God would not leave the expansive universe void of life, even if not with beings like us. Given the enormity of the cosmos, the diaspora of life on our planet, and the nature of God—it just seems hard to believe He would leave all the billions of galaxies and exo-planets out there vacant of life. Again, that is just a philosophical, perhaps even wishful thought. It is not a given. And really, if they are there—intelligent beings like us—could they even get here?

If God did choose to create intelligent life on other worlds, they would have to 1) overcome the limits of physics and 2) harness the right kinds of energy to 3) conquer the incredible vastness of the universe to reach us.

Still, wormholes may be the answer, especially if alien travelers have found areas where such things exist, and perhaps even the incredible technologies to traverse or even open up such portals in space-time. Although we do not yet possess such technology, perhaps an advanced alien civilization could have already discovered it.

But this also begs the question: do we really want those alien beings to gain access to us? Judging by our own experiences on this planet, maybe not. Just look at the European conquest of the Americas and the devastation visited upon the indigenous peoples who lived here.

Stephen Hawking

Renowned cosmologist, the late Stephen Hawking, was probably the most famous voice in the scientific community to make that argument. He sent shockwaves to ET enthusiasts everywhere when he shared his concern about alien contact, publicly in 2010.

> We only have to look at ourselves to see how intelligent life might develop into something we wouldn't want to meet… If aliens ever visit us, I think the outcome would be much as when Christopher Columbus first landed in America, which didn't turn out very well for the Native Americans.[138]

Of course, there are those who believe in the altruistic nature of alleged extraterrestrials. They argue beings advanced enough to overcome the limitations of the vastness of the universe to reach us would be saviors, heralding a new age of hope and unity for mankind. A nice thought perhaps, but such thinking could play right into a demonic agenda to hide behind an extraterrestrial alien façade, as some believe.

At any rate, I think professor Hawking made a good point. Stephen Hawking's worldview did not include a belief in the paranormal, by the way. A noted atheist, Dr. Hawking went on record to denounce belief in God or the afterlife.

> Before we understand science, it is natural to believe that God created the universe. But now science offers a more convincing explanation. What I meant by "we would know the mind of God" is, we would know everything that God would know, if there were a God, which there isn't.[139]

Hawking said heaven is "a fairy story for people afraid of the dark," and that our brains simply shut down at death like a failed computer.[140]

What a sad thought to me, especially when one considers how the cosmologist's life and career were truly great examples of God's anointing and providence. For instance, early on as a doctoral student, Hawking was supervised by Dennis William Sciama, one of the founders of modern cosmology. This was initially disappointing to Hawking, as he wanted to be assigned to eminent Yorkshire astronomer Fred Hoyle who formulated the theory of stellar nucleosynthesis and famously rejected the Big Bang theory. Not only did Sciama influence Hawking's thinking, but he also encouraged the young scholar to continue his work, even after Hawking was diagnosed with motor neuron disease in 1963 and given only two years to live.[141]

Hawking would go on to challenge the work of the great Fred Hoyle and become a popular figure and legend in the field of theoretical cosmology, communicating, lecturing, and authoring books with nothing but the use of a single hand, and later on, only his cheek muscles—fired on by his towering intellect and unquenchable spirit. He also supervised 39 successful PhD students.

One of the greatest scientific minds of our time, Dr. Hawking occupied the venerated chair at Cambridge previously held by none other than Sir Isaac Newton himself! He continued on as Director of Research at the Centre for Theoretical Cosmology at Cambridge and was a prolific writer, despite his severe physical disabilities. Hawking was widely considered the most brilliant theoretical physicist since Einstein.

Stephen Hawking died March 14, 2018, outliving his death sentence by over 50 years. But I also wonder if Dr. Hawking secretly harbored anger against God, perhaps without even realizing it? I am sure the man endured untold suffering due to his physical limitations. Still, the professor lived on for decades. Not only did his work re-write science, but he would also go on to increase awareness and advocacy and ultimately inspire people with disabilities around the world. I would say Stephen Hawking's life and career were a miracle from God.

Dr. Hawking did occasionally speak of God in his writings, for example stating, "If the universe has no boundaries but is self-contained... then God would not have had any freedom to choose how the universe began."[142] He later clarified himself to be speaking in metaphor. As he told *Time Magazine*, "God is the name people give to the reason we are here," he said. "But I think that reason is the laws of physics rather than someone with whom one can have a personal relationship. An impersonal God."[143]

There are many like Hawking who argue for a completely naturalistic explanation as to why biological life-forms like us exist. It's the old, outdated materialist argument.

Miller-Urey Experiment

Dr. Stanley Miller along with Dr. Harold Urey, sent shockwaves through scientific and religious circles with their famous 1952 University of Chicago Miller-Urey experiment, which proved that electricity applied to a chemical mix could produce amino acids, the building blocks of life.[144]

Biogenesis and its insistence on "all life from life" seemed in jeopardy, as now there was concrete proof the primordial soup or "warm little pond" that Darwin imagined on early Earth could produce life via random lightning strikes. Now, the origin of life itself could be explained by natural means without the need of an intelligent cause. That's the materialist viewpoint of the experiment's results. But is it true?

The experiment was a resounding success, even better than Stanley Miller understood, based on the equipment available to the scientist prior to his death. He reported five amino acids created. As it turned out, there were at least 25 amino acids identified, and scientists estimate 30 or 40 more could possibly be isolated as a result of the experiment—an extraordinary achievement.[145]

Still, despite the success of Miller's experiment, its results should not be overstated. While the findings demonstrated organic matter could be produced from non-living matter, amino acids are still only the building blocks of life. That is a long way from explaining the complex processes needed for such crude matter to organize itself into living cells able to replicate—not to mention how information-rich DNA arose and so on.

Also, the amino acids created in the Miller-Urey experiment were not all capable of producing life. Miller's experiment, and any subsequent attempt to synthesis amino acids—the building blocks of proteins—has produced molecules with left-handed chirality about 50 percent of the time, whereas all living things (other than diseased tissue) are made up of amino acids that exhibit left-handedness, or homochirality. Scientists are at a loss to explain why this is, and they have been unable to replicate it.[146] Also, later studies have shown that the reducing atmosphere as replicated by Miller and Urey could not have prevailed on primitive Earth.[147]

Then, of course, there is also the obvious fact that the experiment was a controlled, carefully orchestrated event. It was planned and thought out—intelligently designed. How could such a thing therefore ever explain away intelligent design? Further, and most compelling, scientists have moved away from the chemical evolution explanation anyway.

Oxygen on Early Earth

Results published in the journal *Nature* in 2011 in an article titled, "The Oxidation State of Hadean Magmas and Implications for Early Earth's Atmosphere" found the composition of early Earth's atmosphere not to be the noxious chemical soup originally imagined, but instead was comparable to what we have today. This is astounding! Early Earth had an oxygen-rich environment. This finding on the development of our atmosphere seems to echo Genesis.

> Then God said, "Let there be a space between the waters, to separate the waters of the heavens from the waters of the earth." And that is what happened. God made this space to separate the waters of the earth from the waters of the heavens. God called the space "sky." (Genesis 1:6-8, NLT)

This discovery is very perplexing to materialists because an oxygen-rich environment is not considered ideal for evolving life. In fact, chemical evolution would be largely inhibited by oxygen. So, now many scientists favor life's building blocks coming to earth via meteor strikes, comets, and asteroids, an idea popularized by Sir Fred Hoyle and others known as panspermia.[148]

Still, despite all the excitement at the idea of life riding to earth on space rocks, even if it turns out to be true, it still fails to explain how life got on those rocks in the first place. So, like it or not, science cannot escape the need for God. That is, unless you believe those cosmic seeds were sent to us by space aliens, but then again you would still need God, because who created the aliens?

And while life itself has not been found on meteorites, complex organic molecules have apparently been found, hosted by meteorites.

Zag and Monahans

In January 2018, in a study published in the journal *Science Advances* titled, "Organic matter in extraterrestrial water-bearing salt crystals," scientists reported they found the building blocks for life in water containing salt crystals embedded in meteorites that separately crashed to Earth, one in Texas (Monahans) and the other near Zag, Morroco, in 1998.

> Direct evidence of complex prebiotic chemistry from a water-rich world in the outer solar system is provided by the 4.5-billion-year-old halite crystals hosted in the Zag and Monahans (1998) meteorites... Associated with these trapped brines are organic compounds exhibiting wide chemical variations representing organic precursors, intermediates, and reaction products that make up life's precursor molecules such as amino acids.[149]

This lends support to the idea of "soft panspermia," a concept that says the organic molecules or building blocks of life fell to earth and later developed into life.

But even if that is true, what started it all?

Who set off the Big Bang?

Chapter 18

Intelligent Design

Not only is the beauty of the cosmos on display for our enjoyment and appreciation, it also serves as a reminder of God's majestic, creative power. Consider how the size, distance, and relation of our earth-sun-moon system are such that the moon fits perfectly in front of the sun to block it out completely; so we can experience viewing the sun's corona in total eclipse and study the event. That in and of itself, is a miracle! As the Scriptures say, "The heavens declare the Glory of God" (Psalm 19:1, ESV).

Naturalistic science has long argued we are on an average planet, orbiting an average star, occupying a minor spiral arm of an average galaxy—one of billions. Nothing special. But more and more, science is showing that is simply not true. Our planet, sun, moon, arrangement of the outer planets, and even the laws of physics are finely tuned for life, perfectly designed for us.

In his book, *The Intelligent Universe*, famed astronomer Fred Hoyle, argued the complexity of life is such; the idea of it arising by chance is so slim it can be completely ruled out.[150] And he equated the proteins needed for life assembling by chance about as likely as a blindfolded person solving a Rubik's Cube.

It is interesting to note, Hoyle was not a Christian—and while he received much derision for his alignment with steady-state theory as opposed to the big bang—he was obviously a brilliant thinker, scientist, and philosopher. It is little wonder he was knighted in 1972 for his contributions to science.

Author of the 2014 book, *God's Planet*, professor emeritus of astronomy at Harvard, and a senior astronomer emeritus at the Smithsonian Astrophysical Observatory, Owen Gingerich, said, "Fred Hoyle and I differ on lots of questions, but on this we agree: a common sense and satisfying interpretation of our world suggests the designing hand of a superintelligence."[151]

In her outstanding 1998 *Newsweek* article, titled "Science Finds God," Sharon Begely, along with Marian Westley, argue that for a growing number of scientists, instead of pushing God further out of the equation, the latest scientific discoveries actually support spirituality and even hint at the very nature of God.

> Physicists have stumbled on signs that the cosmos is custom-made for life and consciousness. It turns out that if the constants of nature—unchanging numbers like the strength of gravity, the charge of an electron and the mass of a proton—were the tiniest bit different, then atoms would not hold together, stars would not burn and life would never have made an appearance.[152]

Begley and Westley quote John Polkinghorne, a former physicist at Cambridge University, who became an Anglican priest in 1982.

"When you realize that the laws of nature must be incredibly finely tuned to produce the universe we see," said Polkinghorne, "that conspires to plant the idea that the universe did not just happen, but that there must be a purpose behind it."[153]

And as the aforementioned Stephen Meyer sums up in his 2021 book *Return of the God Hypothesis,* the recent scientific discoveries point not only to the purpose but reveal the mind behind the universe.

But not everyone agrees.

Neil deGrasse Tyson

Popular astrophysicist and consensus successor to the late Carl Sagan, Neil deGrasse Tyson, along with astronomy writer Donald Goldsmith, are among the many who argue for a completely naturalistic explanation for the evolution of the universe. They do so in lively fashion in their engaging 2004 book, *Origins: Fourteen Billion Years of Cosmic Evolution.*

Tyson, a self-described agnostic, is widely claimed by atheists, but says "I'm not trying to convert people [to atheism]. I don't care."[154]

But the scientist clearly does not believe in God.

"I remain unconvinced by any claims anyone has ever made about the existence or the power of a divine force operating in the universe," he said.[155]

Still, in *Origins*, Tyson's vivid descriptions sound like an endorsement of the Biblical account.

> At the time when the universe was just a fraction of a second old, a ferocious trillion degrees hot, and aglow with an unimaginable brilliance, its main agenda was expansion. With every passing moment the universe got bigger as more space came into existence from nothing (not easy to imagine, but here, evidence speaks louder than common sense).[156]

Eloquently put by Tyson and Goldsmith, but really, it is only adding exposition to the Genesis account. "And God said, "Let there be light," and there was light" (Genesis 1:3, ESV).

The idea that in the beginning, at the start of the Big Bang, the entire weight, mass, and energy of the universe fit into the space of a pinhead, not only stretches credulity, it is nigh unto madness unless one accepts the accompanying Biblical explanation. It actually takes more faith, I think, to believe it all just happened by chance.

Newton taught us that an object at rest, stays at rest, unless acted upon by an outside force.[157] And classical physics teaches us that an effect cannot occur before its cause.[158] Aristotle taught us that cause requires not only the matter and form, but also the agent acting to make the change and an end-state design.[159]

There is a point where we cannot go any further back between cause and effect, so there must have been an original cause. In the case of the origin of the universe, there is a literal point—that less than pinhead-size cosmic point, which contained all matter and energy before time—but that was the effect. Who or what affected the cause?

It was the one who said, "Let there be light."

And when that blinding light blazed, as Tyson points out, matter and antimatter would have continued to obliterate each other except for the fact that "symmetry between matter and anti-matter had been "broken" at the previous force splitting, which led to a slight excess of matter over anti-matter."[160]

It was an unbelievably slight difference.

For every one-billion antimatter particles, one-billion plus-one matter particles were born. Without that one-in-a-billion surviving particles of matter differential, over time, there would be no universe. The whole thing would have burned itself out. This is, as Tyson put it, "laboratory-confirmed physics" (p.26). So, we know it happened–but *why*? Why did this happen?

What caused this slight, infinitesimal difference?

"For reasons unknown," Tyson says.

I like Tyson. He makes complicated science topics fun and relatable; and, like Sagan, he knows how to captivate the public's imagination. But he also beats an old and misleading drum, when he speaks about our insignificant location in the galaxy, saying "We live on a cosmic speck of dust, orbiting a mediocre star, in the far suburbs of a common sort of galaxy…"[161] Tyson calls our place in the universe "cosmic unimportance." That couldn't be further from the truth.

Goldilocks Zone

Recent science is reversing the idea of cosmic unimportance. In 2018, scientists confirmed and Chelsea Gohd reported in an *Astronomy Magazine* online article posted October 31, 2018 that a supermassive black hole exists at the galactic core.[162] So, it turns out the center of our galaxy could be one of the worst places in the universe! We have a terrifying, giant cosmic killer at the heart of our galaxy, the super-massive black hole called Sagittarius A-Star, lurking there.[163] How fitting this cosmic killer was finally unmasked on Halloween!

Black holes blast out beams of supercharged, accelerated particles or cosmic rays—deadly to life, deadly to our cells. Thankfully, the heliosphere of our "unremarkable," yellow sun protects us—that and we are so far from the center of the galaxy. It's safer in the suburbs. And I say it is not by accident. And our modest little yellow dwarf star? It turns out our sun outshines over 90 percent of the stars in our galaxy by type! The others being mostly the dimmer orange, red, and white dwarf stars.[164]

Throughout the universe are amazing varieties of stars to marvel at, like the terrifying supergiants, with proportions of almost unbelievable scale. Canis Majoris, for example, is an enormous hypergiant, which would swallow up our solar system all the way to Saturn![165]

There are beautiful blue supergiants like Rigel in the constellation Orion and mysterious red supergiants like Betelgeuse. There are numerous binary stars, and even binary supergiants, like massive Antares, the orangish-red heart of Scorpius. There is also the supergiant Aldebaran, the bull's eye in Taurus. And of course, there are the tiny red and dim brown stars, not to mention the dangerous pulsars.

"Look up to the skies. Who created all these stars?...and calls all the stars by name. Because he is strong and powerful" (Isaiah 40:26, NCV). "He who made the Pleiades and Orion…the Lord is his name" (Amos 5:8, NIV).

The bottom line for life in very basic terms is this: a star in relation to a planet cannot be too big, burning too bright, or too small/too dim, burning too low. This all points out how singular and unique our star just so happens to be—a yellow dwarf, perfect for life here on earth.

So, it seems our average, middle-size yellow star is just right. And our location in, not only the galaxy but also our solar system, truly is the "Goldilocks Zone."[166]

Figure 18.1: *Galaxy NGC 4414,* a spiral galaxy about 55,000 light-years in diameter and approximately 60 million light-years from Earth. This magnificent image was taken by the Hubble telescope in 1995 and the final portrait you see here, rendered in 1999. NASA photo (public domain).[167]

Billions and Billions

According to the most recent estimates, including data obtained by NASA's New Horizons spacecraft, there are at least 100-200 billion galaxies in the observable universe, with 100 billion stars or more on average for each galaxy.[168]

New Horizons flew by Pluto in 2015 and is now some five billion miles from Earth, staring out at the inky blackness of outer space beyond our solar system.[169]

What we have learned is there are literally trillions of stars—some estimates making the number at "1,000,000,000,000,000,000,000,000 stars, or a "1" with 24 zeros after it—1 septillion in the American numbering system; 1 quadrillion in the European system."[170]

Recent research into exoplanets has found almost all stars in our galaxy have at least one planet in orbit around them. Many have planets orbiting in the star's own habitable zone.[171]

Scientists say 22 percent (more or less) of solar-type stars in the Milky Way have Earth-size planets in their Goldilocks zone. Researchers estimate in total that there could be billions of Earth-size planets orbiting in the habitable zones of Sun-like stars and red dwarfs in our Milky Way.[172]

But the habitable zone is just one marker for success. For beings like us to thrive on Earth, we have several other advantages, in addition to being in the right location in the right kind of galaxy in the right kind of solar system.

We benefit from an unusually large moon, which not only provides our tides, but stabilizes Earth's orbital axis, a condition that is likely very rare in the universe.[173]

We also enjoy the unique benefit of having a guardian planet, gas-giant Jupiter, which deflects or absorbs long-period comet strikes that would otherwise likely obliterate us.[174]

Scientists have found large gas giants like Jupiter and Saturn to be rare in the universe—and we are lucky enough to have not one but two of these guardian protectors![175] Not only do they balance out impact events in the solar system, but they also allowed major impacts to occur much earlier, before complex life began to appear on our planet. Without the protection of these guardian planets, life on earth might not even be possible at all.[176]

We also enjoy an atmosphere friendly to life, an abundance of water, benefit from plate tectonics, and have many other helpful conditions on our Earth and in our surrounding cosmic environment too numerous to mention here.[177]

Still, even if life in the universe is the rarest of occurrences as it seems, the idea that at least some of those other planets out there host living forms captures the imagination. And the notion that a few of them might even harbor intelligent life like us, while difficult to prove, is hard to resist.

Exopolitics and the Highways of Heaven

It is fantastic to imagine races of alien beings interacting with humans on a daily basis. Some say there are several alien races with relationships and treaties between their civilizations and our government. But I have no evidence of this and do not know anyone personally who will attest to it. I do know many people have seen UFOs and complained of tormenting abductions. Still, I think there are probably other explanations for the majority of UFO sightings, close encounters, and the abduction syndrome reported here on Earth.

Although I think there are likely many strange sightings that involve our own Top Secret technology, I believe most, if not all, face-to-face "close encounters" are of a spiritual nature.

Most ufologists do not want to give credence to the possibility that alien sightings and abduction experiences could be a kind of spiritual encounter, because that explanation does not fit their paradigm that these beings are extraterrestrial biological entities. While scientists and engineers naturally tend to look for nuts-and-bolts mechanical explanations for the craft reported buzzing through our skies and even seas, there is great deal of evidence for a paraphysical explanation behind much of that too.

The late John A. Keel's excellent 1970 book, *Operation Trojan Horse* (also re-issued in 1996 and 2013) is a thoroughly researched, exhaustive, breakthrough study of the UFO phenomena, through which the author makes a trenchant and decisive argument that alien encounters are paraphysical in nature, and simply a new façade for entities that have appeared historically as fairies, ghost ships, demons, and all manner of phantasma. Writes Keel:

> It is a world of illusion and hallucination where the unreal seems very real, and where reality itself is distorted by strange forces which can seemingly manipulate space, time and physical matter—forces that are almost entirely beyond our powers of comprehension.[178]

But the ultraterrestrial conclusion flies in the face of decades of belief about alien contact, which is thought to go back to ancient times, a notion popularized with the publication of Erich von Däniken's 1968 classic, *Chariots of the Gods*.

Däniken's ancient-astronaut theory is fun and compelling, and I do not rule out the possibility of our planet being visited by alien space travelers from other worlds, past or present. But the stories from the Bible, for example, of beings and wheels (as in Ezekiel Chapters 1 and 10 and Daniel 7:9-10) may simply be visions of angelic entities, even God Himself (Daniel 7:9) as the Bible says, and perhaps the stories of gods from our global folklores and mythologies are also recollections of encounters with celestial beings, not interplanetary alien visitors.

I also think the idea of a pre-Adamic race of our ancestors possessing advanced technology is an interesting possibility as well. But as to modern close encounters, there is another theory not given sufficient consideration by ufologists: what if celestial beings from the spirit realm—the gods, angels, and demons—use technology of some sort? Maybe the gods ride on lightships. This could be the answer to bridging the gap between what the ancient-astronaut people think and what the Scriptures relate.

Who can say there is no technology in heaven? Perhaps the spirit world is a tactile reality of a different kind (see 1 Corinthians 15:42-54).

Abductions

Now concerning the abduction syndrome, it is a little publicized fact in the UFO research community that calling on the name and authority of Jesus Christ causes abduction experiences to end.[179]

Why would trusting faith in calling on the name of Jesus Christ stop the attack of supposedly otherworldly ETs were there not a spiritual, most likely demonic, cause at work? And even if some of the abduction experiences really are being caused by extraterrestrial humanoids, it is still just as likely that demonic beings may be mimicking the abduction phenomena to deceive their victims.

> I am afraid that as the serpent deceived Eve by his cunning, your thoughts will be led astray from a sincere and pure devotion to Christ... Satan disguises himself as an angel of light... When he lies, he speaks his native language, for he is a liar and the father of lies. (2 Corinthians 11:3, 14, ESV, John 8:44, NIV)

The CE4 Research Group provides an interesting account of the effect that calling on the name of Jesus Christ is having on the abduction syndrome:

> The experience was shown to be able to be stopped or terminated by calling on the name and authority of Jesus Christ. Not as a magic word but by their allegiance to and personal relationship with Him. We also found that by sharing this with other experiencers we could help them also stop their experiences.[180]

We will return to the topic of close encounters a little later. For now, let's focus on UFOs and the government connection.

Chapter 19

Air Force, NASA, and the Pentagon

I have had a couple of UAP experiences myself, both of which I am at a loss to explain. The first one happened in Colorado many years ago. The last one occurred during a more recent skywatching trip to the desert of Borrego Springs, California. That one was a most remarkable sighting indeed—both surprising and mystifying. For a brief moment, it looked as though the very fabric of the starry night sky itself opened up (more to follow on that later).

And while two sightings may sound like a lot to some, I see it as very rare and unusual. As a lifelong astronomy enthusiast I have looked up at the night sky almost every day of my life. In my career with the Air Force I have seen the most advanced aircraft and spacecraft in flight, but there was nothing quite like the two unexplained sightings I did have.

I do not advocate an either-or explanation of aerial phenomena. I strive to keep an open mind about it. Of course, most aerial phenomena are explainable. But what about the small percentage that are not?

Again, it seems unlikely to me, given our current knowledge of the laws of physics, that alien visitors from other planets, if they do exist, could in fact reach us given the vast distances between stars. But I do not rule it out completely. In addition to the psycho-spiritual explanation for UFOs and natural explanations, like astronomical objects and weather phenomena, there is also the possibility of black budget classified aircraft and even secret spacecraft being the culprit to fool unwitting observers. According to the April 9, 2020 episode of the *Science* channel program *Black Files Declassified*, every year over $90 Billion is allocated to clandestine programs—the black budget.

There is a continuously growing body of evidence of what appears to be verifiable aerial phenomena supported by radar data and credible witnesses, the documentation of which goes way back. In his revealing 2017 book, *Unacknowledged: An Expose of the World's Greatest Secret*, Dr. Steven M. Greer quotes from former Air Force pilot and early UFO investigator, Lt. Col. Charles Brown:

> Some of the objects reported were tracked on radar. We had objects with four-way confirmation, ground visual, ground radar, airborne visual, airborne radar. And so far as I'm concerned, it doesn't get any better than that. You are not talking about someone's imagination.[181]

Gruff Chuck

At one time, humans believed it was impossible to break the sound barrier. Now, it is an everyday occurrence, thanks to Air Force know-how and the bravery of test pilots like the late, retired Brig. Gen. Chuck Yeager, who became the first person to break the sound barrier on October 14, 1947. The legendary Chuck Yeager passed away December 07, 2020 at the ripe age of 97.

I was privileged to interview General Yeager at an aircraft technology and flying demonstration at Edwards Air Force Base, California back in 2003. He was a big proponent of modern, stealth aircraft, and especially unmanned aerial vehicles. Chuck told me it is much better for pilots to fly remotely and not have to risk their lives. A poignant sentiment, as Yeager risked his own neck so many times during his flying career, first as a World War II combat ace and later as a test pilot. The late Yeager was blessed with keen, 20/10 vision, nerves of steel, and a brusque sense of humor.

He was an adorably crotchety old fellow when I met him. Chuck cracked wise often, claimed to have never seen a UFO, and apparently did not think much of pilots who say they have.

In a June 23, 2015 tweet, Yeager said, "I was asked again if I ever saw a UFO. My answer: No, I don't drink before I fly."[182]

Figure 19.1: *The Late Brig. Gen. Chuck Yeager (retired) kneels in front of a B-2 Stealth Bomber.*[183] General Yeager was responsive to the practical benefits of drone technology when I interviewed him at Edwards Air Force Base in 2003.

The Astronauts

But we can be sure alien beings *have* landed on other worlds. Our own Neil Armstrong and Edwin "Buzz" Aldrin touched down their Eagle spacecraft in the Moon's Sea of Tranquility, July 20, 1969, stepping out onto the lunar surface some six hours later on July 21.

Those aliens from another world conducted tests and set up scientific experiments, collected soil and rock samples, took photographs, and left footprints and earthly artifacts behind.

Figure 19.2: *Astronaut and lunar module pilot, Buzz Aldrin,* stands on the surface of the Moon, July 21, 1969. Photo by astronaut and mission commander, Neil Armstrong (public domain). This iconic image is on display at the Griffith Observatory in Los Angeles. Photo reproduction taken by the author at the museum during the transit of Venus across the Sun June 5, 2012.

I attempted to interview Buzz Aldrin for this book, to get his thoughts on Christianity and the supernatural, as well as aliens and UFOs. Buzz took Communion upon landing on the Moon, a story he relates in his excellent 2009 book, *Magnificent Desolation: The Long Journey Home from the Moon.* And of course, I was interested in any mysterious phenomena or encounters he may have witnessed or been privy to.

Aldrin, an elder in Webster Presbyterian Church near Houston at the time of the Moon landing, in retrospect seemed to question his decision to partake in a Christian rite on the Moon, as Apollo 11 had come in peace "for all mankind." But at the time, he says he knew no other way to add proper meaning to the moment than to give thanks to God in the way he understood. After reading those thoughts in his memoir, I wondered—did Buzz regret taking Holy Communion? Was he still a believer in Jesus Christ? A brilliant man, no doubt—Dr. Aldrin's work as an astronautical engineer literally made rendezvous docking in space possible, and his pioneering techniques for Earth and lunar orbit are still being used today. So, was there still room for almighty God in that intellectual mind so filled with knowledge and adventures?

For John Glenn, there was. Glenn, who passed away in December 2016 at age 95, was the first American to orbit the Earth in February 1962. He later returned to space in October 1998 aboard Space Shuttle Discovery, at the time becoming the oldest person ever to fly in space.[184] Glenn, a Presbyterian like Aldrin, seemed bolstered in his faith upon returning to Earth. "To look out at this kind of creation and not believe in God is to me impossible," Glenn told reporters after returning from his final trip to space at age 77. "It just strengthens my faith."[185]

Neil Armstrong, the first man to set foot on the Moon July 21, 1969 died on August 25, 2012 at age 82, due to complications following coronary bypass surgery on August 7. Raised in a Christian home, he was apparently quiet about his religious views. He once gave his religious affiliation as deist.[186] Upon his return from the Moon, Armstrong gave a speech in front of the U.S. Congress in which he thanked them for giving him the opportunity to see some of the "grandest views of the Creator."[187]

While he may have been private about his religious life, according to his son Mark, Aldrin did believe in extraterrestrial life. But his belief was apparently more from a logical point of view, as Aldrin said "it would be arrogant not to."[188]

As to Buzz, speaking through his publicist back in 2014 when I originally queried him, Dr. Aldrin seemed mildly interested in my Book I. But, by 2019, when I re-engaged, his spokeswoman said he was too busy on other projects.

I would love to hear Aldrin's opinions—not only on matters of faith, but also on more fringe topics, such as the possible existence of man-made structures on other worlds. Some people even claim the Apollo astronauts discovered alien technology on the Moon and were sworn to secrecy.

In his encyclopedic 2013 book on the supposed contact between aliens and humans since the 1930s, and the rumored corresponding cover-up by world governments, *Earth: An Alien Enterprise*, ufologist Timothy Good claims Buzz Aldrin, Michael Collins, and Neil Armstrong, aboard Apollo 11, saw a bell-shaped UFO flying alongside them on their way to the Moon. Also, Mr. Good says Armstrong admitted to a rumor that the astronauts discovered a giant spacecraft present when they landed on the lunar surface.[189]

If the fantastic story is true, I can appreciate why Dr. Aldrin might not want to (or be able to) talk about these things. Timothy Good went on to cite an off-the-record conversation Neil Armstrong supposedly had with a Professor Herbert Schwartz about the spaceships Good claims they saw on the Moon. "I can't go into details [Good purports to be quoting Armstrong here], except to say that their ships were far superior to ours, both in size and technology. Boy, were they big—and menacing."[190]

I am not sure how Mr. Good could have gotten access to such information. If there really were contact with ET intelligences, then or now, it is likely our government would keep that information to itself, not just for national security concerns but to avoid widespread panic. Personally, I am very skeptical about any rumors that our astronauts saw something alien on the Moon. I would have to see a lot more proof to be convinced otherwise.

Working through NASA, I also queried the following legendary astronauts: Retired Brig. Gen. James McDivitt (USAF), Retired Col. Frank Borman (USAF), and Retired Navy Capt. James Lovell (USN)—all living legends, all purported to have encountered UFOs during their NASA missions. Not one of them answered my query. NASA public affairs was pretty nonchalant about it, saying it was up to the astronauts if they wanted to respond.

July 8, 2014, Buzz Aldrin participated in a Reddit AMA, "ask me anything," where he corrected the record about the supposed UFO sighting aboard Apollo 11:

> On Apollo 11 in route to the Moon, I observed a light out the window that appeared to be moving alongside us. There were many explanations of what that could be, other than another spacecraft from another country or another world—it was either the rocket we had separated from, or the 4 panels that moved away when we extracted the lander from the rocket and we were nose to nose with the two spacecraft. So, in the close vicinity, moving away, were 4 panels. And I feel absolutely convinced that we were looking at the sun reflected off of one of these panels. Which one? I don't know. So technically, the definition could be "unidentified." We well understood exactly what that was.[191]

Dr. Aldrin says he was unaware the outside world was not informed of the sighting, when he talked about it in 2005 while being interviewed for a *Science* channel documentary, "First on the Moon: The Untold Story." The filmmakers omitted the crew's conclusion that what they saw was probably simply one of the four detached spacecraft adapter panels from the upper stage of the Saturn V rocket. According to Aldrin, his words had been taken out of context. He made a request to the *Science* channel to make a correction, but they refused.[192] Aldrin was again questioned about the incident when he appeared on the *Howard Stern Show* August 15, 2007. Aldrin confirmed there was no such sighting of anything deemed extraterrestrial:

> It was not an alien... There may be aliens in our Milky Way galaxy, and there are billions of other galaxies. The probability is almost CERTAIN that there is life somewhere in space. It was not that remarkable, that special, that unusual, that life here on earth evolved gradually, slowly, to where we are today. But the distances involved in where some evidence of life may be, they may be hundreds of light years away.[193]

The Brookings Report

In 1961, the Proposed Studies on the Implications of Peaceful Space Activities for Human Affairs, commissioned by NASA and carried out by the Brookings Institute, commonly referred to as the "Brookings Report," was submitted to the 87th U.S. Congress. The 1960 report is notable for short excepts discussing the implications of a discovery of extraterrestrial life and examines potential impacts such a discovery might have on our societies. On page 30, for example, it speculates that evidence of intelligent extraterrestrial life might be found in artifacts left on the Moon or other planets.[194]

The report says the consequences of a discovery of intelligent extraterrestrial life on the values and attitudes of the general public are unpredictable, and would vary greatly in different cultures and between groups within complex societies. "[S]ocieties sure of their own place in the universe have disintegrated when confronted by a superior society, and others have survived even though changed."[195]

The report has a short section called, "The implications of a discovery of extraterrestrial life," which says, "The knowledge that life existed in other parts of the universe might lead to a greater unity of men on Earth, based on the 'oneness' of man or on the age-old assumption that any stranger is threatening."[196]

Although it does not recommend a cover-up, the report goes on to say, "Anthropological files contain many examples of societies, sure of their place in the universe, which have disintegrated when they had to associate with previously unfamiliar societies espousing different ideas and different life ways; others that survived such an experience usually did so by paying the price of changes in values and attitudes and behavior."[197]

The report also, once again, openly discusses the possibility that we might discover objects left behind by alien extraterrestrial life, stating "artifacts left at some point in time by these life forms might possibly be discovered through our space activities on the Moon, Mars, or Venus."[198]

Unexplained Photos

The Mars Global Surveyor mission took amazing close-up pictures of Phobos, one of the moons of Mars in 1998. On the surface of Phobos, there appears to be a monolithic structure, something like an obelisk. There are those who say such objects and other man-made structures can also be seen in NASA photographs of the Moon and Mars as well.

In his 2013 book, *MARS: The Alien Connection*, M.J. Craig offers up over a hundred NASA and European Space Agency photos of Mars and the Moon that appear to show what look like man-made structures. All the photos Craig shows have been released to the public.

I have seen many of those photos, and they are intriguing.

Figure 19.3: *NASA Image taken from Spirit Mars Rover Mission to Gusev Crater* (public domain).[199]

Take a look at the photo above. You will notice a creepy, skull-form near the bottom left of the frame. Maybe it is just a rock, or maybe not.

The latest Mars rover, *Perseverance*, touched down at Jezero Crater February 18, 2021. The vehicle offers unprecedented technology and capability, and the opportunity to provide even more revealing imagery of the Red Planet.[200] Hopefully, NASA will be forthcoming in releasing the imagery.

"We should visit the moon of Mars," said Dr. Buzz Aldrin in a C-SPAN interview. "There's a monolith there…When people find out about that they are going to say, who put that there? Who put that there?" During the interview Dr. Aldrin had been advocating further exploration and development of Earth's moon when he went on to say we should explore farther, "fly by the comets, visit asteroids."[201] Then he went on to talk about the monolith on Phobos.

I am sure Buzz has information that could further add to our understanding of these matters. Perhaps one day we will get his full answer on the extraterrestrial question and how it ties in with his faith and understanding of God.

Figure 19.4: *Astronaut Edwin E. "Buzz" Aldrin Jr.*, taken 16 April 1969. Image courtesy of NASA (public domain).[202]

Blue Book Part Deux?

December 16, 2017, the *New York Times* broke the story of the Department of Defense's latest UFO investigation program in an explosive article by Helene Cooper, Ralph Blumenthal, and Leslie Kean called, "Glowing Auras and 'Black Money': The Pentagon's Mysterious U.F.O. Program."[203]

The article disclosed the Advanced Aerospace Threat Identification Program (AATIP), which investigated UFO sightings:

> [T]he program produced documents that describe sightings of aircraft that seemed to move at very high velocities with no visible signs of propulsion, or that hovered with no apparent means of lift. Officials with the program have also studied videos of encounters between unknown objects and American military aircraft.[204]

Incredibly, Pentagon officials admitted to the existence of the program, which ran from 2007 at a cost of $22 million until funding was reportedly pulled in 2012; however, the *Times* reported the AATIP continues to investigate sightings and some of the program's findings still remain classified. The AATIP pursued such fantastical-sounding research titles as "Traversable Wormholes, Stargates, and Negative Energy," "Invisibility Cloaking," as well as "Warp Drive, Dark Energy, and the Manipulation of Extra Dimensions."[205]

In the January 28, 2019 edition of *Defense News*, Kelsey Atherton brought to light several of those topics of interest in an article titled, "On the Pentagon's Wish List: Warp Drives and Invisibility Cloaks."

> On Jan. 16, 2019, the Defense Intelligence Agency released a list of 38 research titles funded by the Advanced Aerospace Threat Identification Program, which includes the above title on warp drives, one on invisibility cloaking, and another about stargates...of note in the DIA's list of 38 studies are many others with some more immediate applications.

"Advanced Nuclear Propulsion for Manned Deep Space Missions" and "Positron Aerospace Propulsion" have both been studied in some form by NASA, and "Laser Lihtcraft Nanosatellites" is a technology explored by the Air Force research Laboratory...

The last study in the list appears twice: "State of the Art and Evolution of High Energy Laser Weapons" has both a classified secret/NOFORN (no foreign nationals) version and an unclassified, for-official-use-only version.[206]

There was reportedly another government investigation under the Pentagon umbrella going on called the Advanced Aerospace Weapon System Applications program, or AAWSAP, which was allegedly exploring paranormal phenomena and UAPs, while AATIP was strictly investigating military UAP encounters. The AAWSAP program is disclosed in a book released in October 2021 titled *Skinwalkers at the Pentagon: An Insiders' Account of the Secret Government UFO Program* by James T. Lacatski, D.Eng., Colm A. Kelleher, Ph.D., and George Knapp.

Some say AAWSAP and AATIP are part of the same, overarching program, and some use the terms interchangeably. I expect more information will be forthcoming on the nuance of these investigations. But to avoid confusion, I will just use AATIP for all of it, as that is largely what the media has latched onto, and the public has been made aware of.

One of the more remarkable incidents to emerge from AATIP was footage released by DoD taken during a November 14, 2004 encounter off the San Diego coast, where two Navy F/A-18 pilots from the aircraft carrier *Nimitz* chased a large, 40-foot-long, wingless object, which apparently was flying at incredible speeds with maneuvering ability beyond that of any aircraft currently known. One of the pilots described it to ABC News as "not from this world."[207]

For seasoned fighter pilots to be impressed that way is beyond sublime, as they themselves operate some of the fastest, most maneuverable aircraft currently known.

In 2015, Navy fighter pilots from the nuclear aircraft carrier USS *Theodore Roosevelt* had an incredible UFO engagement off the eastern seaboard, near the Florida coast where they apparently encountered a fleet of UFOs.[208]

Dubbed the "gimbal," the craft looks like a classic flying saucer. You can check out the amazing footage of the object captured by one of the F/A-18 onboard cameras for yourself. It's quite possibly the best footage ever captured of a UFO.[209]

More recently, leaked video taken from a Navy ship seems to show a UFO hovering over the water off of California before splashing down.[210]

The Navy sightings were characterized as unidentified, but they would not remain unexplained, or at least that was the goal of an upcoming Pentagon report on what our government agencies know about UAPs. The Pentagon formed a task force to investigate, which was to deliver its findings to Congress in June 2021.[211]

The report was the result of a provision in the $2.3 trillion coronavirus relief and appropriations bill signed into law in 2020. The stipulation called for a "detailed analysis of unidentified aerial phenomena data and intelligence" from the Office of Naval Intelligence, the Unidentified Aerial Phenomena Task Force and the FBI.[212]

Luis Elizondo, the former intelligence officer who led AATIP and the Unidentified Aerial Phenomena Task Force (or UAPTF), said "We're seeing these things [UAPs] on a daily basis. The longer we keep a lid on it, the more problematic it becomes. It actually works against our interests to keep a cork on this."[213]

Ahead of the report's release we learned the task force was unable to adequately explain the recent uptick in UFO sightings; what they are, or where they are from (see Chapter 21). After the report came out this did not change. To date, there is not a single shred of evidence that any of the sightings are extraterrestrial in nature. One possible explanation says they could be advanced aircraft developed by an adversary, which would be concerning. But another explanation that I agree with is they are our own Top Secret programs.

The F/A-18 encounters may have simply involved advanced classified military aircraft at a higher level of secrecy and deeper in the black budget than AATIP's. At only $22 million, the program barely scraped the surface of the over $700 billion or so annual U.S. defense budget,[214] and those are just the openly disclosed funds we know of. But one way or the other, we do seem to be getting closer than ever to uncovering the real UFO story.

AlienCon 2019

By this cloudy Friday afternoon in Los Angeles, June 21, 2019, the AATIP story and the connection between UFOs and the U.S. Navy had only deepened. The evening session of AlienCon featured an advanced screening of the latest episode of the History channel's new show, *Unidentified*, and the electrifying videos of Navy F-18 encounters with strange craft that were capturing the public's imagination.

Active duty pilot Lt. Ryan Graves had come forth expressing concerns that at least 50, up to 100 military members had witnessed these events, and thinking the Department of Defense was doing nothing about it. These videos show craft ranging from a "tic-tac" shape (USS *Nimitz*, 2004), a cube shape (USS *Roosevelt*, 2015), and the enigmatic "gimbal" craft (USS *Roosevelt*, 2015), which looks like a flying saucer. The gimbal video also shows an area of cold air around the vehicle, which experts say means it must not be using conventional propulsion, especially as the craft displays advanced maneuvering capability unknown to modern airplanes, which human pilots could not tolerate without some kind of technology to dampen the g-force effects.

Bob Lazar

The gimbal craft lends credibility to the theories of Bob Lazar, a controversial figure in the UFO community, who said flying saucers proceed in a tilted position, belly forward, not horizontally as they always appear in science-fiction films.[215] The gimbal seems to proceed just as Lazar described. It rotates into a belly forward position, and possibly employs advanced anti-gravity technology, as Lazar had said. Perhaps Bob Lazar was right all along.[216]

Lazar rose to prominence following a TV interview in 1989 with paranormal researcher George Knapp. Lazar claims to have been hired in the late 1980s to reverse-engineer extraterrestrial technology at a purportedly secret site called "S-4," a subsidiary installation located several kilometers south of Area 51. Lazar claims he examined an alien craft that ran on an antimatter reactor powered by element 115, an unknown element at the time, which was actually synthesized in 2003, lending more weight to Lazar's account.

Lazar was interviewed more recently for the 2018 documentary film *Bob Lazar: Area 51 & Flying Saucers*.[217]

His drawing and explanation of the vehicle's propulsion mechanism seem not only compelling but rational and logical. But here's one thing about Lazar that no one seems to have considered: What if Bob Lazar really did work on engine propulsion for these craft at S-4, not reverse-engineering alien UFOs, but instead working on our own, advanced technology? This is pure conjecture, but he could have made up the alien part, or even been tricked into believing it was alien technology as a cover story to mask the real truth. When scientists work on projects of that magnitude of secrecy, no matter what their clearance, they are only told the minimum of what they "need to know." For example, to people working on the atom bomb during World War II, the project was so secret that many participants involved were kept in the dark about what it was they were doing.[218] Now back to the Navy encounters.

Unidentified

The UFOs appeared in formation and were said to be harassing and following Carrier Strike Group 12 in its 2015 fleet deployment led by the USS *Theodore Roosevelt*, a nuclear-powered aircraft carrier. One of the cube-shaped craft reportedly caused two of the F-18s flying in formation to have to peel off from each other to avoid colliding with the strange object.

UFOs reportedly followed the battle group all the way from the East Coast off Florida to reappear in the Persian Gulf. "No one seemed to really care," said Graves. Fellow active duty pilot Lt. Danny Aucoin, agrees. "You tell your skipper and it ends there."

While it is thrilling and a bit scary to imagine those apparent machines as exotic, extraterrestrial craft, the indifference of Navy officials leads me to believe these unusual events could actually be planned encounters with our own technology, perhaps drones, known to the government at the highest levels, and probably of our own making. The skipper or captain of the fleet would be read in on these activities, perhaps tests of Top Secret technology, whereas a pilot or radar operator might not be made aware, especially if the intent were to test their reactions.

But what if it is true that alien spacecraft are buzzing about unfettered on our planet? Could intergalactic alien societies have discovered fantastic technologies to create or harness shortcuts in space-time? Would ETs then make it their mission to irritate and harass hapless young Navy fighter pilots? That seems unlikely. Again, I think it more probable to be our own government testing out advanced aircraft. And what better testbed to try out new secret technology than our own high-tech military resources, equipment, and people?

Still, the Navy came up with new protocols and guidelines for reporting UFOs in direct response to the uptick in sightings and complaints from pilots.[219] That alone is enough to make one wonder, "what if?"

We will go more in depth on the government's official findings from the UAP Task Force in Chapter 21. For now, let's look at the actual plausibility of UFOs being from extraplanetary sources in the universe.

It would take incredible feats of scientific innovation to overcome the limitations of physics to make intergalactic space travel practical, let alone plausible. Although science teaches us that faster-than-light-speed travel is impossible, according to Einstein and Rosen, there may be another way.

Chapter 20

The Great Endeavor

Follow the Wormhole

Wormholes are scientifically feasible within the known laws of physics. The idea of wormholes arose as a possible solution to the limits of Einstein's general relativity. Wormholes provide for a theoretical passageway through space-time. Such a construct could possibly be used to create shortcuts for impossibly long journeys across the universe.[220]

In 1916, Austrian physicist Ludwig Flamm imagined white holes as the theoretical time reversal of black holes. Entrances to both black and white holes could be connected by a space-time conduit. While black holes were posited from Einstein's theory of general relativity over 80 years ago, they have since been observed.[221] Both white holes and wormholes remain theoretical.

In 1935, Einstein continued to build upon Flamm and others including himself, using his own theory of special relativity, and along with physicist Nathan Rosen, they came up with the idea of "bridges" in space-time, which is how the modern concept of the wormhole, also known as the Einstein-Rosen Bridge, came to be.[222]

Wormholes while theoretical, not only make interstellar space travel faster, therefore practical, wormholes would actually make space travel instantaneous, like folding two points on a piece of paper together. The concept was well illustrated in the fantastic 2014 space film, *Interstellar*. The fastest way to get from point A to point B is not a straight line. It is to bring both points together at once, either by navigating known wormholes mapped and navigated, or by using technology—yet unknown to us, capable of safely creating a wormhole—assuming that wormhole travel itself would even be safe.[223]

At least one scientist authored a study said to have proven wormholes really can exist, but his findings showed travel through them would actually be slower than going directly.[224] But let's assume for a moment that wormhole travel would be faster as is commonly believed.

Technology-driven wormhole creation is similar to how characters in science fiction get from point A to B. Star Wars uses "hyperdrive" engines on spaceships like Han Solo's *Millennium Falcon* to travel in "hyperspace," a parallel universe they jump in and out of to get around the galaxy and the limits of physics. In *Star Trek,* they use "warp drive" technology, where Capt. Kirk and crew go faster than light via "warp bubbles," bending space-time around their starship.[225]

Perhaps the most realistic portrayal and closest to Einstein-Rosen's is the concept of "jump drives" in *Battlestar Galactica*, which actually folds space, providing instantaneous jumps from point A to B within the known galaxy.[226]

Science fiction aside, wormholes, while hypothetical, are believed to be a viable possibility.[227]

And I must admit, certain UFO cases are so remarkable, they make one wonder if we really are being visited by physical ETs. Perhaps some alien race already cracked the Einstein-Rosen code. Then again, the paraphysical ultraterrestrial theory has merit also.

UFO Sightings

Tony's UFO

The first time I thought about taking UFOs seriously was hearing about my Uncle Tony's reported encounter when I was a kid. An unexpected paradox to the pragmatic nature of Uncle Tony was his lifelong insistence about a strange UFO encounter he claimed he had one night in the mid-1980s after leaving Franklin Market in Greensboro, North Carolina. Tony recounted that he saw the craft descend toward his vehicle and said it followed him all the way from Franklin Boulevard down Eastland Avenue to his house.

The flying saucer reportedly hovered over the home with colorful lights flashing. Tony said he got out of his car to get a closer look. He was not a bit afraid and apparently tried to communicate with the visitors. But the UFO just disappeared into the night. As I recall, Tony did not seem particularly interested in the UFO topic or science fiction, but as to this story, he relayed it as matter-of-factly as you might expect someone reporting spotting a deer on the way home.

I was staying with Uncle Tony and Aunt Beverly that weekend when Tony walked in and told us what happened. Cousin Ron and I ran outside to try and get a glimpse of the UFO, but Tony told us it was already gone. I remember going out and staring up into the starry sky and imagining what that UFO would have looked like, hovering over the house with colorful lights flashing, but there was nothing there.

None of us really believed him back then, but Tony stuck to that story the rest of his life, and his story never changed.

Tony did have one witness who corroborated his story, my cousin Krystal Steiner, his daughter, who was along for the ride to the store that evening.

> Yes, I believe in them. So did my dad. We saw one when we lived in the old house on Eastland Ave… It was a night I will never forget. I remember being scared. We even stopped at

the little store on Franklin Boulevard. Dad needed beer [smiley emoticon] and the "UFO" seemed to stop and hover and the lights reverse going the other way... It followed us coming down Franklin Blvd. Dad and I saw it hovering over the house. Lights were all around it... I also believe there is life out in space. I think we should leave it alone.[228]

David's UFO

As hard to believe as Tony's UFO was, I heard an almost identical story that reportedly occurred in the mid-1980s also, this one witnessed by my brother-in-law David and several of his siblings when they were kids growing up in Central Mexico at the time.

David and company were walking home from the market one night when they claimed to encounter a craft with colorful lights flashing all around. When they got home, David ran inside and told his mother, asking if he could use the polaroid and take a few pictures of the vehicle. His mom strictly forbid him from going back outside in pursuit of pictures, and the moment passed.

Ron's UFO

My paranormal Uncle Ron, whose ghostly stories I shared in Chapter 15, also had a UFO sighting. It happened one morning many years ago over the skies of Greensboro, North Carolina. It was dawn, and Ron was just leaving for work. He saw a formation of UFOs, which appeared for a short while and then disappeared. He has no idea what they were.

Anecdotal stories are interesting, but cases with multiple reported sightings over a region are most compelling. Again, most UAPs and UFOs are explainable, such as lights produced by weather, aircraft, or other man-made devices like the pulsing emanations from a lighthouse or radio tower. Even the moon or a bright planet like Venus can be mistaken for a UFO. Still, some of these phenomena resist our best efforts to explain them away.

The UAP flaps that especially sparked my imagination were the Gulf Breeze Sightings, the Phoenix Lights, and the Belgian UFO Wave. And after many years pondering these mysteries, I finally saw something myself.

Red Light over Academy Boulevard

I saw my first UAP as the 1980s were coming to a close. I was driving home one night when I lived in base housing at the Air Force Academy, in Colorado Springs, Colorado. As I made my way north up the winding Academy Boulevard to the south entrance of the base, I noticed a small, luminous red ball at the 10 o'clock position outside my driver's window. It looked just like those glowing red lights you see on radio towers except this one was not in a fixed position.

The fiery ball was moving around, generally going northward also but zig-zagging up and down. I noticed the traffic slowing as other drivers were observing the phenomenon too. They had curious, smiling faces and puzzled looks, eyes peering and brows furrowed, staring at the glowing scarlet ball of light. Some drivers had even pulled their cars over and were standing beside the road looking on.

The Air Force Academy is tucked into the foothills on the east side of the Rampart Range of the Rocky Mountains. It spans 18,000 miles of green and woods, quite lovely and very dark at night. Once I made it through the open front gate and shade of night on the Academy grounds, the phenomena was gone. I have no idea what I saw that night. I told my wife about it and tuned to the late news, but there was nothing on about it. I never saw any reports in the papers or on the news about that sighting.

Although I only saw a glowing red light, I was intrigued. And while nowhere near as dramatic as witnessing a strange, flying craft, I was later encouraged to learn that others have also reported seeing a similar glowing red ball of light floating in the night sky.

Gulf Breeze Mystery

The Gulf Breeze Sightings is a 1990 book by Ed and Francis Walters, which documents their alleged personal and harrowing experiences during a wave of UFO sightings in Gulf Breeze, Florida in the late 1980s. Although the book is considered by many to be a hoax, there might in fact have been something strange going on in the skies over Gulf Breeze.

Consider the following account by Kevin Seeger, submitted to Amazon.com on April 25, 2004 in reference to Ed and Francis Walters' controversial story:

> I read this book many years ago and revisited it when I returned to Gulf Breeze last summer. As a former resident of Gulf Breeze, I can say with certainty that there were strange things in the skies in the early '90s. I never saw the exact craft that Ed had taken umpteen photos of, but I saw my share of fighter jets chasing glowing orbs, and I had a real good daylight sighting of a pulsating reddish-orange sphere at treetop level.[229]

I found that remark by Mr. Seeger to be particularly interesting, as his "reddish-orange sphere" sounds so much like what I had seen over Academy Blvd. It was most fascinating to learn his observations correlated to what I saw in Colorado around that time, which was not long after the Gulf Breeze sightings supposedly took place. I never made the connection between my red orb and the red sphere reported in the Gulf Breeze incident until I read Seeger's comments in the Amazon review all these years later. My only recollections of the Gulf Breeze sightings were of Ed Walters' funky-looking crown-shaped UFO photos that were allegedly faked.

Although many have cast aspersions on Ed Walters' account, hundreds of other witnesses reported seeing UFOs over Gulf Breeze over a three-year period. Perhaps it was all a reaction to Walters, but there were others who came forward with videos and photos.

For example, Gulf Breeze resident Garland Bland Pugh is credited for an impressive 1993 photo over Gulf Breeze, which featured a dark, saucer-shaped craft with a glowing reddish-orange ball of light or orb under it. Mr. Pugh, originally from Alabama, was a Christian and an Air Force veteran who passed away May 31, 2015. His was apparently not a silent voice on the UFO topic. Speaking about Pugh, Jeff Ritzmann of Joppa, Maryland, said the following in a March 9, 2017 on-line post:

> I was shocked to discover Bland's passing. I had just emailed him and when the email bounced back, I got a bad feeling. Bland and I had a great discussion of Gulf Breeze and the UFO phenomena many years ago. He was so kind and generous with his time, and I will always remember our talk.[230]

Kenny and Tracy Cafasso of Wright, Florida said the following in a February 8, 2017 posting:

> Mr. Pugh I really admired you for the love of animals, to being a great Republican, and showing the light Bama was the team to cheer for. Thank you for welcoming me in your home. Love the UFO info you gave me. Rest in Peace and Always ROLLTIDE!![231]

So, perhaps there is more to the Gulf Breeze UFO story and the mystery of Ed Walters than skeptics care to admit. Back to Seeger's account:

> I came late to the Ed Walters story, as the events depicted in this book coincided exactly with my freshman year at FSU in Tallahassee. I moved back to Gulf Breeze in 1988 and heard the stories from a friend of mine who was a good friend to Ed's family. I was [t]old that my friend (Patrick Hanks in the book) was convinced of the authenticity of Ed's story. He offered strange tales from Ed's past that I would later read in Ed's second book. He seemed truly perplexed and never hint-

ed that the whole thing was a big joke. Later, he was visited in Chicago by "the authorities" and vowed never to talk about it again. There are many UFO abduction stories in print. What makes this story interesting, aside from the fact that it occurred in my home town, is the unprecedented siege laid upon Walters by the UFO. Most abductees see a light in the sky that descends on them, then the next thing they know they are in hypnotic regression therapy, spewing forth details of their abduction. Walters was literally under siege by the aliens. He would hear voices in his head telling him to step forward so that he could be brought aboard, but he consistently refused, dodging the blue beam, and incessantly snapping photos then ducking for cover. This went on for months; meanwhile everybody in town was seeing UFO's nightly. This was the first close encounter case in the annals of ufology that allowed for an investigation to take place while the sightings were still occurring. MUFON gave Walters a stereoscopic camera that used dual lenses to take photos so that the object in the picture could be triangulated to determine its size and distance from the camera. Walters managed to take some photos with this camera, which is foolproof to the double exposure techniques of which he has been accused. Walters was finally nabbed by the blue beam from Shoreline Park South in May 1988 and what he learned under hypnosis became his second book, which I read many years ago but have not revisited recently. I cannot be sure that this was not an elaborate hoax, but I am sure of UFO's in the Gulf Breeze skies, an increase of military presence in the Pensacola area airspace, many stories from friends and neighbors who saw odd things, took pictures and videos, and my own "missing time" experience, shared with a friend in 1992. There are so many tales of alien abduction. I once assumed they were all made up, but my Gulf Breeze experiences have shown me that people need not make up stories. There is something strange going on.[232]

So, what constitutes a UFO or UAP? As I mentioned earlier, the vast majority of sightings are something explainable: airplane, meteorite, lightning, or optical illusion, etc. But there is a small minority of unidentified aerial phenomena that remain unidentified.

Calling NORAD

Back when I lived and worked at the Air Force Academy, intrigued by my own sighting of the glowing red sphere and spurred on by my friend and co-worker Airman Scott Larsen, I made a call to nearby NORAD, the North American Aerospace Defense Command, located at Cheyenne Mountain Air Force Station, a short distance from Peterson Air Force Base in Colorado Springs, Colorado. NORAD is the joint U.S. and Canadian effort to keep our North American continent safe from enemy attack. The airmen there monitor our airspace at all times.

Years later, as an Air Force television director, I was privileged to tour the control rooms of NORAD as I was gathering documentary video footage of all the key sights in Air Force Space Command. To this day, you may still see the footage that my crew and I shot, appearing on such networks as the Discovery channel and History channel.

NORAD is burrowed deep inside the solid rock of Cheyenne Mountain. It is said that NORAD can withstand a nuclear blast. The Command Center is well within the safety of two, 20-ton steel doors, which the operators at the mountain open and close once a week as well as for exercises and, God forbid, a real world nuclear attack. NORAD controllers track all movement in our airspace, from an enemy missile, to (if such exist) an extraterrestrial mechanical vehicle.

That is why I first called them as a young Airman working at the Academy. I wanted to know if they were seeing UFOs. A kindly sergeant was put on the phone to talk to me. He chuckled politely at my inquiry, but told me no one had reported the object I described. Still, I wonder, could he or would he have told me if they had? The sergeant gave me the Air Force official position on UFOs, which is the service takes a reactive approach. That is to say, they assess our airspace for threats, but they are not expressly looking out for sightings of the ET variety. Apparently, the days of the Air Force investigating flying saucers was long over.

I reminded the sergeant about Project Blue Book, and he quickly agreed but said the Air Force stopped investigating UFO phenomena of that sort at the termination of Project Blue Book, which was ordered closed in 1969 and all activities under the project ceased by 1970.[233]

Project Blue Book

Blue Book was first helmed by Capt. Edward J. Ruppelt, a highly decorated airman from World War II who coined the phrase "unidentified flying object." Ruppelt also ran Blue Book's previous iteration, Project Grudge, and worked with the scientific advisor to Blue Book, noted astronomer Dr. J. Allen Hynek, who was the scientific consultant of the project, as he had been with predecessors Projects Sign and Grudge.[234]

In his 2017 book, *The Close Encounters Man*, Mark O'Connell says Hynek initially felt Ruppelt did not fully trust him, but that was during Hynek's debunking days. Ruppelt favored a level-headed approach and did not like investigators who leaned too much in either direction on the ET question. The captain apparently did regard Hynek favorably, as Ruppelt recommended the scientist stay on as advisor after Ruppelt retired.[235]

> Dr. Hynek was one of the most impressive scientists I met while working on the UFO project, and I met a good many. He didn't do two things that some of them did: give you the answer before he knew the question; or immediately begin to expound on his accomplishments in the field of science.[236]

In turn, Hynek recognized the challenge Ruppelt had in pleasing Pentagon generals who "don't like mysteries; they want hard, crisp answers."[237]

"He was trying to do the best job he could to debunk it," said

Hynek. "And yet he had this weird perception…something was going on that was beyond him."[238]

Hynek continued working for Project Blue Book past the Ruppelt years up to its termination and initially created the categorizations of Close Encounters of the First, Second, and Third Kind.[239]

A Close Encounter of the First Kind or CE-1 involves seeing an object within 500 feet or so—close enough to make out detail. A CE-2 involves the craft having a physical effect on the environment. CE-3 involves a witness seeing beings in or around a UFO that appear to be associated with the craft either as pilots or passengers.

Hynek's scale has been extended today to include CE 4-5, and some ufologists add 6-7.[240] Although initially skeptical, Hynek seemed to have softened in his views of the phenomena due to a small number of cases that were truly puzzling as well as the caliber of witnesses who began to emerge, those with significant credibility, such as military pilots.[241]

Some say both Blue Book and Grudge were ordered to commence due to the Pentagon's displeasure with Project Sign, led by Capt. Robert R. Sneider. They say Sign investigators had apparently come to the astounding conclusion the flying disc phenomenon was the result of extraterrestrial vehicles. In his study, *Project Sign: and the Estimate of the Situation*, Michael D. Swords reports, "Sign investigated the phenomenon for seven months and decided that it was best explained by the extraterrestrial (spacecraft) hypothesis (ETH). An Estimate was produced for the Pentagon giving reasons for this."[242]

But after Blue Book, the Air Force ceased its investigative efforts, claiming satisfaction the UFO phenomena posed no threat to national security, and asserting there was no credible evidence the sightings were the result of extraterrestrial encounters. The Air Force Fact Sheet titled *Unidentified Flying Objects and Air Force Project Blue Book* says the following:

> (1) no UFO reported, investigated and evaluated by the Air Force was ever an indication of threat to our national secu-

rity; (2) there was no evidence submitted to or discovered by the Air Force that sightings categorized as "unidentified" represented technological developments or principles beyond the range of modem scientific knowledge; and (3) there was no evidence indicating that sightings categorized as "unidentified" were extraterrestrial vehicles.[243]

My NORAD sergeant admitted the Air Force does still track UFOs until they are identified but basically said they get identified. As far as answering any "are they out there" questions, the official Air Force explanation was, "We don't know."

I remember being disappointed with that answer. But again: Do you think the sergeant would have told me if he really knew? And what are the chances a public relations NCO at NORAD would even know the answer in the first place? Perhaps he was simply reading off the talking points from the Air Force fact sheet.

Space Command Adventures

In 2000, I traveled to all the major bases in Air Force Space Command, as the video director of the command's over-arching mission briefing "The Future is Space." The video was shot on location at the various sites and the post-production editing took place at the TV center at Hill Air Force Base, Utah.

It was a thrill touring the control centers and operational areas at such places as Beale Air Force Base, Falcon (now called Schriever), F.E. Warren, Cape Canaveral Air Force Station, NORAD, and Vandenberg. Over the years, in my role as an Air Force journalist and producer-director, I have been privileged to see rocket launches at Vandenberg Air Force Base, as well as Wallops Island, Virginia. I even reported on the last Space Shuttle launch, which took place July 8, 2011 at Cape Canaveral Air Force Station, Florida. My video feature on that historic launch can be seen here: https://www.youtube.com/watch?v=1Kn73spglIA.[244]

Wallops Epiphany

But the most memorable launch for me so far was watching ORS-1 lift-off on the Minotaur I rocket, blasting into space from the Mid-Atlantic Regional Spaceport, Wallops Island, Virginia, the evening of June 29, 2011.

The amazing thing to me was being so relatively close to the rocket launch, compared to when I witnessed the first Delta IV launch at Vandenberg in June, 2006, or the last Shuttle, launched at the Cape. They keep the press back a safe distance away from launches, and even further away with the larger vehicles. The Minotaur rocket handles small to medium payloads, so I was closer.

Also, Wallops Island is in the middle of a swampy grassland area by the ocean where there are no city lights polluting the night sky. It is the sky of our ancestors: inky black and clear, with every star blazing on full display. That was the backdrop I enjoyed, as I watched the Minotaur I rocket send ORS-1 into space. The Minotaur's burners were glowing blue as it pushed away into the starfield. That black, starry sky, glowing afterburner, and churning sound seemed like something straight out of *Star Wars*.

Space Trekkers

I was proud to meet the fine men and women of Air Force Space Command. One of the more fascinating technical specialties belonged to the airmen who worked in Space Operations, which now falls to the U.S. Space Force. Their job is to track objects in space. The technology is mind-blowing.

In the past, our airmen and now the Space Force currently tracks all objects in orbit the size of a softball or larger. I have seen the control screens and watched the objects being tracked. If our military forces can follow targets in space the size of a softball, do you not think they could also detect actual alien spacecraft entering our atmosphere? Of course they could.

If such craft were conventional in nature.

But if the spacecraft had some kind of unknown cloaking technology, which hides them from us—or the UFOs are of an interdimensional, paraphysical, or outright spiritual nature—that might be a different story.

And there is always the possibility that NASA, the U.S. government, and even the governments of other nations do see and track extraterrestrial spacecraft movements, or that of our own secret spacecraft—activities they are aware of but refuse to tell us.

If that were true, it would mean government officials at the highest levels really do know what is going on with the UFO phenomena but are keeping it a lid on it.

Chapter 21

Nocturnal Lights and Area 51

Borrego Springs is an unincorporated area of northeast San Diego County, California, set in the midst of Anza-Borrego Desert State Park. One of our last remaining "dark sky" areas, the region attracts people to stargazing events at the park visitor's center and other locations year-round. January 19, 2018, Anza-Borrego Desert State Park was certified as an International Dark Sky Park by the International Dark-Sky Association, and it is easy to understand why. Each time I go there I am as amazed at the stark beauty and burning heat of the desert landscape, as I am at the blazing stars burning brightly in the clear, night sky.

On April 15, 2016, I traveled to Borrego with my eldest son Matthew for an impromptu night of stargazing. After an exhausting drive through the Los Angeles traffic that Friday night, Matt and I checked into our hotel, grabbed up binoculars and a star map, and headed outside to take in the heavenly spectacle.

We walked along for a while, flashlights in hand, sand and rocks crunching under our shoes. Finally, we found a nice, level spot, and lay down on the ground to stare at stars, constellations, and planets.

Since I was a child, I have lain horizontal on my back to stargaze.

I highly recommend it. It is truly the best way to take in the stars. You look upward into the heavens without the distraction of your head moving or strain on your neck from looking up.

That position is how I spotted my first meteor—lying prone, while riding home one summer night in the bed of my uncle's truck, with a girl I liked, as we stared up at the starry sky. Since that time, I have seen many meteors streaking across the night sky and have even seen a few meteoroids flare up into a blue-green fireball, with a sonic boom and sizzling sound as it streaked to Earth. My wife and I saw one together like that, staring out over our balcony at the night sky over El Nido Park in Redondo Beach, and it brought an audible gasp from both of us.

Matt and I saw a few meteors that night in Borrego. They were beautiful. I have seen many meteors since that evening ride in the back of my uncle's truck. But I had never seen anything like what I was about to see in the desert sky over Borrego Springs.

UAP over Borrego

I was gazing up and to the left, when to my surprise, a large glowing light appeared in the midst of the blackness of space. It emerged for only a moment, perhaps only one but no more than three seconds in duration, and made no sound. The radiant light was white with a tint of yellow, soft—glowing off-white—much like an old-fashioned incandescent indoor lightbulb.

It was intensely bright, oval in shape, like an eye, with the appearance in mass of perhaps two or three full moons. Almost as soon as it appeared, the phenomenon disappeared. It wiped to darkness as if the fabric of space closed over it. In the manner of an eyelid closing, the light shut off.

"Did you see that?!" I said, turning to Matt.

"See what, Dad?" he replied, turning his head from the other direction. He missed it.

I have no idea what I saw, but it was incredible, and I can think of no natural phenomena to explain it. It was almost like the fabric of space opened with an oval light behind it, and then winked shut.

The experience lasted only a moment, and it was over. Again, I have no idea what I saw, but it was amazing! In that brief moment of time, I felt as though I was being shown something bigger than myself—like something of a process, something hidden, something special—now revealed. Could it have been a portal opening? I don't know. But I had a feeling I was being shown a glimpse behind the Wizard's curtain somehow.

Later, I did some research to find out if anyone else had spotted the UAP I saw. Although there were no other reports on file for that particular night, I found many strange UFO sightings that have occurred nearby. As the *San Diego Reader* reported, "The area around Borrego has long been a hotbed of inexplicable airborne activity."[245]

There have been many sightings there in recent years, and I found one that was very similar to mine. This sighting occurred on June 6, 2017 and was reported to UFO-hunters.com:

> [S]eries of lights in California desert. While driving east on S22 in San Diego county, passing by the Borrego Valley Airport, myself and another party in our vehicle witness[ed] a series of perhaps six to eight lights appear in the sky ahead of us…The lights were as bright as headlights and white in color. (The other witness thought they were "yellowish.") …The lights faded, blinked out, or shut off in a few seconds…I have seen many, many military flare drops. At first, I thought this was possible but the sighting was too short of duration for flares. Flares last many minutes. The lights appeared before us on the highway and disappeared in three to five seconds…I observe the sky nightly and have become accustomed to what aircraft, with their landing lights and position lights look like. This was not that.[246]

A February 17, 2018, sighting in Borrego Springs involved bright lights that hovered and faded out. It was reported to UFO newshub.com.

> We observed two bright, white, star-like objects that faded out during a camping trip. This happened at the southern end of Clark Dry Lake off Rockhouse Canyon Road due west of Borrego Springs. The sighting took place in the southern sky near Sirius around 8pm. Sirius was equidistant from the two objects and Orion.
>
> She noted how bright they were, the word she used was "piercing." I said, "Yes, they are definitely too bright to be stars, keep watching them. I was fumbling for my phone and she yelled, "One just disappeared!" I stopped fumbling for my phone and wanted to witness this for myself. About six seconds later, the second object "faded out."[247]

Those are just a few of the many sightings that have been reported over that desert landscape. Clearly, something strange is going on over the skies of Borrego Springs, California.

I have been around military hardware and aircraft since I was 18. I have filmed many fighter jets and cargo planes in daytime and nighttime, and know very well what they look like. Also, I have witnessed and filmed rocket launches both day and night as well. I am also used to seeing helicopters, searchlights, radio tower lights and lighthouse beacons. And I have been an astronomy enthusiast and avid starwatcher since I was a little kid.

I have seen meteors, comets, planets, the Andromeda Galaxy, the aurora borealis, lunar eclipses, bright stars, and spotted the International Space Station in orbit, all with the naked eye. But this sighting over Borrego Springs was unlike anything I had seen before or since.

The nearest thing I can compare it to is the oval-shaped orb of light illustrated at the top-center on the cover of Steven M. Greer's 2017 book, *Unacknowledged: An Expose of the World's Greatest Secret*, a title that came out after my Borrego experience. I also noticed those same oval orb flashes on the cover of Frank Joseph's 2018 book, *Military Encounters with Extraterrestrials*. Those are the closest likeness to the UAP I saw. Perhaps these kinds of lights are a known part of the UFO paradox—the "nocturnal lights" so often reported to Blue Book. I know not what they are, but I know what they are not: They are not flares or plumes from any conventional jet or rocket technology.

In his classic and definitive 1972 treatise on the UFO phenomenon, *The UFO Experience: A Scientific Inquiry*, Dr. J. Allen Hynek set forth the modern definitions for unidentified flying object witness reporting, still applicable today. Hynek said the average UFO reporter is a rational person, a productive contributor to society, and one not given to fancy. Time and again he found the witnesses first tried to explain away what they saw by every other possible means until finally admitting to the fact that what they experienced was unlike anything they had ever seen.

Hynek drew a distinction, however, with contactees—people who claimed to be in telepathic communication with aliens. Those individuals, he felt, were less reliable on account of having been influenced by psychology perhaps, but definitely outside the realm of real scientific inquiry. His opinion fits well with my own idea that those individuals, who truly experience abduction encounters not the product of psychosis, are probably the victim of a spiritual attack.

I also found parity in Hynek's lowest but most commonly reported spectrum of nocturnal lights and daylight discs when compared to my own sighting in the desert. In *The UFO Experience*, Hynek said a nocturnal light could well be a daylight disc if seen in the day.[248] He says daylight discs are usually dome or oval shaped, often white, which my sighting was certainly oval shaped, like an eye, and white.[249] He also said the light is usually not accompanied by sound or no loud sound, and might hover, both of which were true in my case.[250] And in Hynek's reports I even found a link to the yellowish hue I detected in the white light that night—which is apparently is being reported in other sightings at Borrego and elsewhere.

"It was much brighter than Venus. It appeared as an intense

white-maybe with a slight yellowish tint."[251]

E-1 Encounters

In review, the two distinct UAP sightings I personally experienced, many years apart, were 1) the warbling, glowing red ball of light in Colorado Springs, and 2) the white, oval light that appeared in Borrego Springs. They were two very rare and unusual sightings, but both would fall at the bottom of Hynek's scale.

Before arriving at Close Encounters, CE 1-3, there are three preceding levels. I suggest they be designated "E" for simply "Encounters." So then, by Hynek's scale, the levels would follow as such: E-1 nocturnal lights, E-2 daylight discs, and E-3 radar-visual. Following these are the famous CE or Close Encounters.

Area 51

I believe most, if not all, CE-1 and CE-2 UFO sightings are probably advanced human technology, operated by our own people, or the peoples of other governments. Black technology is perhaps decades, maybe even 50 or more years beyond anything we see fielded today. Satellite photos clearly show a military base in the middle of the Nevada desert at a salt flat known as Groom Lake, better known as "Area 51." It is a remote detachment of Edwards Air Force Base, within the Nevada Test and Training Range.[252] The facility is a real place and still has one of the world's longest runways in operation today.

The Top Secret U2 spy plane was developed and flown there in the 1950s. Featuring unprecedented altitude capabilities not know in the civil sector, a sleek, all-black exterior, and dragon-like appearance, it was surely responsible for many UFO sightings.

Retired Air Force photographer, Jose "Lou" Hernandez, a veteran of over 40 years of combined military and civil service, believes in UFOs. "Oh yeah, they're real. I saw one in Palmdale near the 'Skunk Works'" (J. Hernandez, personal communication, June 1, 2019).

Skunk Works is an official pseudonym for Lockheed Martin's secretive Advanced Development Programs (ADP) responsible for designing the U-2, the Lockheed SR-71 Blackbird, the Lockheed F-117 Nighthawk, as well as the Lockheed Martin F-22 Raptor, and the Lockheed Martin F-35 Lightning II.[253]

The F-117A Nighthawk "Stealth Fighter" (a misnomer, it is actually a ground attack/bomber), was a black project developed at Groom Lake. I saw the F-117 on display at Edwards Air Force Base in 2003. To look that gnarly beast in the face is to see what would easily be taken as an alien craft right out of science fiction.

Top Secret research and development continues at Groom Lake to this day, although Bob Lazar claimed more advanced research now takes place at an alleged subsidiary facility adjacent to Papoose Lake, located south of the main Area 51 base.[254]

B-2 Bomber

Speaking of stealth, there is none stealthier than the majestic B-2 Spirit or Stealth Bomber, which I have been privileged to see up close, and I have observed in flight. The aircraft seems otherworldly as it swoops quietly over the horizon like a large, dark shadow.

Not only is the special black coating designed for "stealth," the vehicle thins to a fingernail on the horizon as it approaches; and it makes very little noise. Quite unsettling to observe, it is everything you expect a UFO to be. That reaction is even more apparent as no doubt some unsuspecting witnesses must have seen it in flight back when it was still a classified black project, unknown to the public at large decades ago.

The B-2 Spirit was developed during the Carter administration.[255] Although its maiden flight from Palmdale, California to Edwards Air Force Base took place in 1989,[256] it is easy to imagine earlier test flights of the B-2 and/or preliminary designs being mistaken for ET spacecraft.

Flying Wings Are Not New

The "flying wing" design goes way back, to the very start of aircraft development, beginning in the early 1900s, with the first sustained flight of a flying wing in 1910, all the way to legendary aircraft designer and industrialist Jack Northrop's impressive flying wing designs of the 1940s, to the futuristic designs of today.²⁵⁷

Despite the long history of flying wings, they would be a rarity in the skies of the 1940s and were, no doubt, responsible for mistaken UFO sightings at the time. A December 2016 *Air Force Magazine* article, "Jack Northrop and the Flying Wing" states: "Seen head-on, the Flying Wing looked like a flying saucer and was sometimes mistaken for one in UFO sighting reports."²⁵⁸

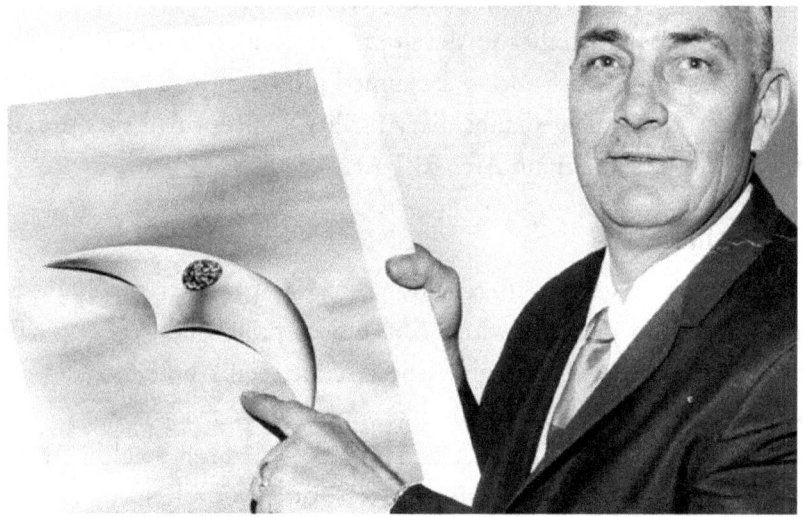

Figure 21.1: *Kenneth Arnold with a drawing of the UFO he claimed to have seen.*²⁵⁹ Notice how the drawing looks very much like "flying wing" aircraft, unknown to many in the public, but already flying back then.

Kenneth Arnold

Pilot Kenneth Arnold launched the modern UFO craze with his reported sighting of "nine unusual objects" flying in tandem, June 24, 1947 near Mount Rainier, Washington. Arnold compared the objects' movement to a saucer being skipped across water, and described their shape as "saucer-like." It was from that description that we got the mid-century terms "flying saucer" or "flying disc."²⁶⁰

But if one delves further into Arnold's descriptions, i.e., "flat like a pie pan," "shaped like a pie plate," "half-moon shaped, oval in front and convex in the rear," "something like a pie plate that was cut in half with a sort of a convex triangle in the rear," a more complete picture forms—he seems to be describing crescent-shaped flying wings, which were already flown by then! I believe the aircraft Mr. Arnold saw were simply our own flying wings.²⁶¹

Figure 21.2: *Northrop YB-49 Flying Wing.* U.S. Air Force photo taken in 1972 (pub-

lic domain). These huge, UFO-like aircraft were flying in 1947.²⁶²

William Rhodes

July 7, 1947, some two weeks after the first reports of the Kenneth Arnold sighting were making news, a man named William Rhodes reportedly saw an object circling above his Phoenix home. He took two photographs, which are some of the first and most famous UFO pictures ever taken.²⁶³

William Rhodes told the story of his sighting to the Phoenix publication, the *Arizona Republic* newspaper, which published Rhodes› story and pictures. Just one day after the Rhodes sighting, the Roswell, New Mexico incident happened on July 8, 1947.

The Rhodes photos were among the first investigated by Project Sign, the predecessor of Blue Book. The negatives underwent technical analysis at Wright Field, Ohio.

February 19, 1948, Lewis C. Gust, Chief of Technical Projects Office, gave the verdict on Rhodes' photos. "Reference is made to the films taken by Mr. Rhodes… It is concluded that the image is of true photographic nature…"[264]

The not yet legendary Dr. J. Allen Hynek of Ohio State University was brought in to review 223 incidents for possible astronomical explanations, the Rhodes photos among them. Here is what Hynek said. "No astronomical explanation seems possible for the unusual object cited in this incident. This case is especially important because of the photographic evidence and because of the similarity of these photographs to the drawings by Kenneth Arnold…"[265]

Rhodes reportedly took his plain Brownie box camera and quickly rushed outside after he heard a noise from inside his house. Once outside, he claimed to have seen a strangely-shaped object "like the heel of a man's shoe," moving away toward the southwest. He was able to get off two shots before the object was gone. He estimated the UFO to be 20-30 feet in diameter, traveling at speed of 100 mph, altitude 1,000-2,000 feet.

Rhodes claimed that after his photo was published in the *Arizona Republic*, government officials borrowed the imagery "for assessment," but when Rhodes asked for it back, he was told that would not be possible.[266]

As Hynek said, it is worth noting the similarity in the Rhodes UFO and the craft drawn by Kenneth Arnold, especially when considering the proximity in time of the sightings. I think it is likely Rhodes saw a flying wing, like Arnold, if he truly saw anything at all. Many researchers believe the Rhodes photos were simply a hoax.[267]

Hoaxes aside, I believe most if not all of the UFOs observed flying over our skies in the 1940s and 1950s to the present day, could likely be attributed to our own, man-made aircraft.

Figure 21.3: *William Rhodes UFO photo*. Taken July 7, 1947 by Mr. Rhodes, this is one of the earliest and best known UFO photos. There is a noticeable similarity to this image and the Kenneth Arnold description.[268]

Figure 21.4: *B-2 silhouette*. USAF image released to the public domain.[269]

The Belgian UFO Wave

Perhaps the most substantiated of all UFO flaps to date was the *Belgian Wave*, which occurred over the skies of Belgium from November 1989 through April 1990, and involved radar data and numerous eyewitness accounts, including many from the law enforcement, military, and aviation communities. These craft were reported to be triangular in shape. The weight of eyewitness testimony, especially expert witness testimony in addition to verification on radar, is impressive enough to suggest that something very real was flying over the skies of Belgium.

The reports detailed a large object of a flat, triangular shape with lights underneath, flying at low altitude. The vehicle reportedly moved slowly and silently across the landscape of Belgium (much like the B-2, slow and silent). Witness accounts tracked the craft as it moved from the town of Liege to the border of the Netherlands and Germany.[270]

Since the Belgian sightings were witnessed by so many people, it seems there would be more photos (albeit, that era was prior to smart phones or even flip phones). The photographic evidence is scant, with only one picture possibly being authentic, the Wallonia photo, supposedly taken June 15, 1990, in Wallonia, Belgium. The other photo is confirmed to be a fake. The Petit-Rechain photo claimed taken on April 4, 1990 has been confirmed to be a forgery created by a clever teenager named Patrick, and his friends.[271]

More and more triangle UFOs are showing up in photos these days. Beth Johnson of Guilford County, North Carolina spotted a triangle UFO flying over the trees lining highway 150 in Oak Ridge, near the Union Grove Church. She saw the craft while driving home around 11:30 p.m. July 22, 2021. Johnson stopped to take a photo. It was late at night in a rural area so there was no traffic. She rolled down her window and snapped the pic.

"It was large in size. Moving slowly. Not making any sound," said

Johnson. "What is crazy is I could see the large craft but the lights were all that came out in the photo. It was silent. It seemed to glide."[272]

Note, Ms. Johnson's description sounds almost identical to the Belgian UFOs: large, triangular shape with lights underneath, flying at low altitude, moving slowly and silently.

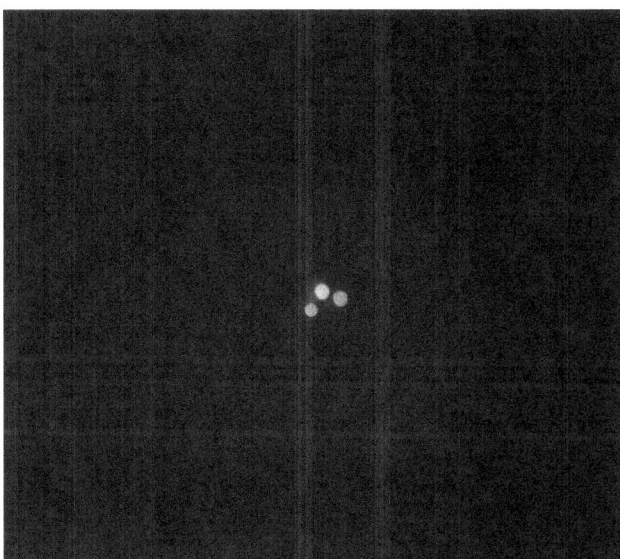

Figure 21.5: *Triangle UFO flying over Highway 150, Oak Ridge, North Carolina*. This photo by Beth Johnson was taken around 11:30 p.m. July 22, 2021. Used by permission of Ms. Johnson.

I think these reports of triangular-shaped aircraft fit nicely as the next generation of vehicles descended from the likes of the aforementioned B-2 or the Air Force's F-117A Nighthawk mentioned earlier.

The Shadowy Nighthawk

Designed in the 1970s at Area 51 by Skunk Works and fielded in the early 1980s, the F-117A Nighthawk, was a well-kept Top Secret, virtually unknown to Pentagon officials until being unveiled publicly in 1988, after the aircraft had been operational for many years. Following that, the F-117 first went into action in Panama in 1989 and went on to take a starring role for the U.S. in the First Gulf War in 1991.[273]

Figure 21.6: *F-117A Nighthawk "Stealth Fighter."* This alien-looking aircraft flies over Nellis Air Force Base, Nevada, August 6, 2002 during the joint service experimentation process dubbed Millennium Challenge 2002. Air Force photo by Staff Sgt. Aaron Allmon II (public domain).[274]

I got a look at the F-117 on display at the U.S. Air Force Museum in Dayton, Ohio. I have also seen the enigmatic aircraft in flight, at Edwards Air Force Base during a civic leader's tour that I covered in the early 2000s. I also got a particularly close-up view of an F-117 on display in a hangar there during the show. The Air Force allowed me to take photos. Although I was not able to touch it, I did get within inches to eyeball the famous "Wobblin' Goblin."

The aircraft definitely looks exotic, and it is easy to see how someone in the early 1980s could have mistaken it as something not of this world.

The F-117 was retired in April 2008, due to the fielding of next generation stealth aircraft like the amazing F-22A Raptor, but the original Stealth Fighter is still reportedly being spotted in flight![275]

Aurora Program

One can only imagine the secret projects being developed behind the scenes that we do not know about. Back in 1990, *Aviation Week &*

Space Technology mentioned the mysterious "Aurora" aircraft had been a line item in the U.S. defense budget in 1986, and some speculate Aurora funding reached billions of dollars.[276]

A line of secret Aurora aircraft could explain a lot, although the program was called a myth by Ben Rich of Skunk Works and others, and the government has never acknowledged such craft were ever in development.[277]

According to Rich, the "Aurora" name was arbitrarily assigned to the funding for the B-2 bomber design competition by a colonel working at the Pentagon, and somehow the name got leaked to the media.[278]

But then again, if there really were a secret Aurora program out there, the government would likely not acknowledge it, and an insider like Rich would be obliged to deny it, too. At any rate, there are many who believe the Aurora program or something like it was developed, and has been operating for years.[279]

It is reasonable to expect that there is much going on in air and space that we are not privy too. For example, the Space Force's mysterious X-37B space plane has been in operation for years. Although publicly acknowledged, we really do not know much about what it does, other than the fact that it can carry payloads and experiments into orbit and return them, along with demonstrating and testing reusable space flight technology.[280]

I tried to do a video feature on the X-37B back when it was first being developed, but the Air Force declined my request. The service has historically been reticent to comment on the capabilities of the X-37B and what it does during its extended time in space. But we do know the spacecraft has achieved notable successes, such as proving that it can operate in orbit non-stop for over two years![281]

Just imagine how much more could be accomplished by a program completely shrouded in secrecy, something like the fabled Aurora, which could explain the elusive triangle aircraft people have been spotting for quite some time, such as the sightings over Belgium.

In his 2015 book, *Insiders Reveal Secret Space Programs & Extraterrestrial Alliances*, Dr. Michael E. Salla discloses what he claims is the design of the pinnacle Aurora aircraft, the tactical-reconnaissance TR-3B, code-named "Astra." This alleged Top-Secret plane is said to be nuclear-powered, incorporates antigravity technology, and has engines built by Rockwell. Dr. Salla says he got this information from a whistleblower named Edgar Fouche, who supposedly spent 30 years working on classified projects with the Air Force and aerospace industry.[282]

The illustration credited to Fouche, and appearing in Salla's book, offers top view, bottom view, and front view. The Astra design looks exactly like the flying triangle craft as reported over Belgium from November 1989 to April 1990, and elsewhere. I think it is possible the TR-3B is a real aircraft.

There is at least one triangle UFO we can validate, recorded from the deck of the USS *Russell* off the coast of San Diego in July 2019. The Pentagon confirmed the UFO encounter, which appears to show several unidentified flying triangles "flashing" in the clouds. The brief video appears greenish as it was shot through a night-vision camera. Having watched the clip several times, I see no reason to doubt this is no more or no less than our own secret aircraft.[283]

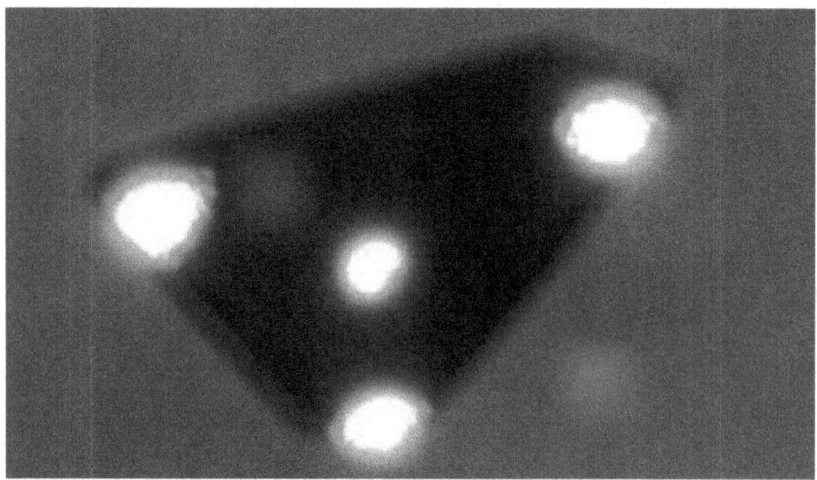

Figure 21.7: *Alleged photo of flying triangle from The Belgian Wave* taken by J.S. Henrardi on June 15, 1990, Wallonia, Belgium. Mr. Henrardi has released this image to the public domain. Could this be the Top Secret TR-3B "Astra"?[284]

Nocturnal Lights and Area 51

Figure 21.8: *A flashing, triangular-shaped UFO* is shown through a night-vision camera over the USS *Russell* in 2019, in footage leaked to filmmaker Jeremy Corbell. The Pentagon confirmed the triangular UFO video is real.[285]

While the Air Force closed the covers of Project Blue Book, the final phase of its official investigation into UFOs in 1970, the phenomena continued being observed and reported. UFO sightings over skies around the world have persisted seemingly nonstop ever since, too numerous to list here. But I must point out a notable contemporary sighting involving our commercial airlines.

Chicago O'Hare UFO

November 7, 2006, about 4:15 p.m., a remarkable sighting occurred over Chicago O'Hare International Airport, with too many witnesses to deny. Aviation experts and others spotted a large UFO hovering over gate C-17. At least 12 employees saw it. Airport employees were allegedly told not to talk about it.

Reporter Jon Hilkevitch broke the story in a January 1, 2007 *Chicago Tribune* article titled, "In the sky! A bird? A plane? A ... UFO?"

[The phenomena] was first seen by a United ramp worker who was directing back a United plane at Gate C17, according to an account the worker provided to the National UFO Reporting Center. The sighting occurred during daylight, about 4:30 p.m., just before sunset. All the witnesses said the object was dark gray and well defined in the overcast skies.[286]

The craft was apparently fairly large, according to witnesses, with estimates by different accounts to be 6-24 feet in diameter. Also, the vehicle did not display any lights.

The object, estimated to be hovering 1,500 feet above the ground, was seen to suddenly accelerate straight up through the solid overcast skies, which the FAA reported had 1,900-foot cloud ceilings at the time. "It was like somebody punched a hole in the sky," said one United employee. It left behind an open hole of clear air in the cloud layer, the witnesses said.[287]

Mr. Hilkevitch's sleuthing forced the government to disclose the incident. Both United Airlines and the Federal Aviation Administration (FAA) initially denied that they had any information on the O'Hare UFO sighting until the *Tribune* filed a Freedom of Information Act (FOIA) request. The FAA then ordered an internal review of air-traffic communications tapes to comply with the newspaper's FOIA request, which uncovered a call by the United supervisor to an FAA manager in the airport tower referencing the UFO sighting.[288]

Concerning the photo evidence of the Chicago O'Hare sighting, it clearly looks like a large, triangular-shaped aircraft, leading me to believe, yet again, it is simply one of our own, furtive craft, not extraterrestrial at all, and likely tracing its lineage all the way back to the flying wings of the late 1940s.

Figure 21.9: *UFO over Chicago O'Hare.* This image is a passenger photo, shot from inside the terminal. Although fuzzy, the UFO clearly has the classic triangle shape of a flying wing like the B-2 Spirit.[289]

In December 2017 we learned UFO investigations by DoD had continued since Bluebook with the Advanced Aerospace Threat Identification Program (AATIP) from 2007 to at least 2012—and U.S. government programs to investigate UFOs have endured. This was confirmed in June 2020 with the acknowledgement of the Pentagon's Unidentified Aerial Phenomenon Task Force, which would deliver its findings to Congress June 25, 2021.[290]

Results of the UAP Report

Ahead of the highly anticipated report by intelligence officials, on June 3, 2021, we learned the results coming out from the report would likely raise more questions than answers. First off, it found no evidence of alien technology in the strange UFO encounters investigated, in a déjà vu very similar to the Air Force findings of Blue Book. But, on the other hand, it does not rule out the extraterrestrial hypothesis either, as much of the phenomena remains difficult to explain, such as the speed, acceleration, and ability to change direction with some of these craft. Some of them supposedly have even been seen to submerge.[291]

Such reports are given added weight by former President Barack Obama, who said, "There is footage and records of objects in the skies that we don't know exactly what they are."[292]

One of the sightings mentioned, surely referencing the gimbal craft, was described "like a spinning top moving against the wind" and appearing almost daily from the summer of 2014 to March 2015.[293]

But if it is true the perplexing objects encountered are not our own, that presents a threat even more terrifying than alien ETs—the possibility that our primary adversaries, Russia and China, have outpaced the U.S. in developing highly advanced hypersonic military technology. This is a real concern to some in our defense and intelligence communities.[294]

Still, I find it unlikely that China and Russia could be so far ahead of the U.S. And I also doubt the ability of the AATIP and its follow-on task force to truly penetrate the dark web of secrecy behind the real nature of our Top Secret black projects. If you recall, the whole AATIP was largely funded at the request of the late Harry Reid, the Nevada Democrat who was the Senate majority leader at the time.[295] After that, the reigns of AATIP and the follow-on task force were handed over to front man, Mr. Luis Elizondo.

I am pretty sure our larger "military-industrial complex" is able to duck a few curious senators and well-meaning intelligence officials with a meager $22 million research budget for UAPs. To put that in perspective, the Air Force spends $80 million dollars for a single F-35 jet, nearly four times the budget of the entire AATIP program![296] And the newest carrier in the Navy, the Ford class, costs $12.8 billion each, and that doesn't even include the cost of the aircraft, upgrades, and personnel and operations costs.[297] Put in context of our over $700 billion (disclosed) defense budget,[298] this latest UAP study and report, while interesting, amounts to little more than a curiosity. Ultimately, it was not able to penetrate the true nature of the ever enigmatic UFO mystery.

President Dwight D. Eisenhower in his farewell address to the nation January 17, 1961, famously said "we must guard against the acquisition of unwarranted influence, whether sought or unsought, by the military–industrial complex. The potential for the disastrous rise of misplaced power exists, and will persist."[299] As a former WWII general and chief of staff of the Army following the war and later Supreme Allied Commander of NATO,[300] Eisenhower well knew what he was talking about.

They made a nuclear bomb and kept the secret. They developed stealth aircraft and kept it a secret. We have landed spacecraft on planets, moons and asteroids, and have sent probes to the farthest reaches of the solar system and beyond. Our secret military programs have likely made unimaginable advances developing further technology, perhaps with the help of engineers like Bob Lazar and others.

Also, remember in the Navy incidents how the skippers would be non-plussed by these encounters? It was always the young, junior-officer pilots who were getting worked up about it. Maybe the high-ranking Navy brass really knew what was going on, and were in on it all along.

I believe these UFOs are our own, secret stuff. Otherwise they are either 1) our adversaries, or 2) actual extraterrestrial aliens, neither of which is a very comforting alternative.

Bottom line from the UAP study is this: They found no evidence the craft originate from an extraterrestrial source. And while the report does not rule out adversary nations or non-governmental sources, it clearly states, "Some UAP observations could be attributable to developments and classified programs by U.S. entities."[301] That's what I think they are.

As to the Air Force, it seems the service's glory days at the leading edge of the UFO mystery are long past, having become a distant, Cold War memory. Still, Air Force Instruction 10-206, *Operational Reporting* October 2008 edition, actually had a protocol for reporting UFOs:

> 5.6.3. Report the following specific sightings: 5.6.3.1. Hostile or unidentified aircraft, which appears directed against

the United States, Canada, or their forces. 5.6.3.2. Missiles. 5.6.3.3. *Unidentified flying objects* [emphasis added].

For unidentified objects the instruction says to follow its Figure 5.1. *Communications Instructions Reporting Vital Intelligence Sightings (CIRVIS)* guidance to gather and report specific sighting details. "For unidentifiable objects give a description including shape, size (compared to a known object e.g., pea, silver dollar, baseball, basketball, fighter aircraft, or C-5), number and formation, any discernible features or details (e.g., color, trail or exhaust, sound)."[302]

The Air Force must have received a fairly significant number of UFO reports to have had an official protocol for dealing with them. Interestingly, though, that part on UFO reporting does not appear in subsequent editions of AFI 10-206. Writer Lee Speigel claims the rules disappeared due to a *Huffington Post* inquiry into UFO reporting. "The military deleted a passage about unidentified flying objects from a 2008 Air Force personnel manual just days after the Huffington Post asked Pentagon officials about the purpose of the UFO section."[303]

Maybe the Air Force just got tired of dealing with the UFO question after so many years.

Figure 21.10: *Image of an alleged UFO, Passoria, New Jersey.* This photo was taken by George Stock in July 1952 (public domain).[304]

Chapter 22

Classic and Ancient Encounters

Following are a couple of notable classic encounters. An excellent series of five UFO photos was taken by amateur photographer George Stock in July 1952 from his backyard in Passoria, New Jersey. Mr. Stock allegedly encountered the UFO flying over his house, also witnessed by his neighbor who was outside with him. The image above appears on the CIA's public website[305, 306] The date shown on the CIA site is 31 July 1952, although I found varying accounts saying the incident occurred either 28 or 29 July.[307]

Stock's series of pictures is unique among early UFO photography in that the imagery of the craft is clear and in sharp focus. The Passoria incident took place during a wave of UFO reports flooding intelligence channels and news outlets in 1952. The U.S. Air Force claimed the photo was a fake, saying the object pictured is only about the size of a lady's sun hat. But according to David Hatcher Childress and Bill Clendenon in their 2002 book, *Atlantis and the Power System of the Gods,* the Air Force analyzed newspaper reprints, rather than the original.[308]

Figure 22.1: *Image of an alleged UFO, Passoria, New Jersey.* This photo was taken by George Stock in July 1952.[309]

The incident is also reported in a 2010 article by Wendelle Stevens posted on the Open Minds website where it says the *Morning Call*, the newspaper that carried the images, had the photographs analyzed and "received a report that a fairly large object was actually photographed at about the estimated distance from the camera."[310]

The George Stock pictures were popular successors to the famous McMinnville UFO photos taken on Paul and Evelyn Trent's farm, near McMinnville, Oregon, May 11, 1950.[311]

The Trent farm was actually just outside Sheridan, Oregon, approximately nine miles southwest of McMinnville, the nearest large town.[312]

As the story goes, Evelyn first spotted the craft and called out to her husband, who was inside the house. Paul managed to snap two photos of the vehicle, which was also supposedly seen by Paul Trent's dad before it zoomed off to the west. The photos were well publicized, including being published in the June 26, 1950 edition of *Life Magazine*.[313]

And like William Rhodes mentioned earlier, the Trents didn't get their imagery back either, at least not right away. *Life* told the couple they had misplaced the negatives.[314]

Unbeknownst to the Trents, their photos were apparently passed around and studied. They went from the files of the United Press International (UPI), and then loaned to Dr. William K. Hartmann, an astronomer and investigator for the Condon Committee.[315]

In 1975, the negatives were found in the files of the *News-Register*, a local McMinnville, Oregon newspaper that published the story way back on June 8, 1950. They were found by Dr. Bruce Maccabee, a former optical physicist for the U.S. Navy and a ufologist. After completing his own study of the photos, Maccabee ensured that the original negatives were finally returned to the Trents, who apparently never asked for money for their photos nor did they seek any notoriety.[316]

Skeptics have claimed the photos are hoax; although the Trents, who died in the late-1990s, maintained the veracity of the story for the rest of their lives.[317] Ufologists such as Dr. Maccabee say the photos were not faked, and show a real, physical object in the sky above the Trent farm.[318]

Figure 22.2: *One of the McMinnville UFO photographs* taken May 11, 1950 by Paul Trent. This is the first of two pictures taken of an alleged UFO by Mr. Trent in McMinnville, Oregon, 1950.[319]

Ancient Encounters

Exciting though they were, the classic encounters of the 1950s echo a strange resemblance to the ancient past. What we would recognize as modern flying saucers and other contemporary UFO phenomena are purported to show up in ancient artifacts, ruins, parietal art, petroglyphs, hieroglyphs, along with oral traditions, written accounts, drawings and paintings.

Our ancestors around the world report encounters with beings, flying vehicles, and/or beings in flying vehicles, centuries before humans had mastered heavier-than-air flight. The weight of testimony and eyewitness accounts leads one to conclude there must be something to it. The only question remaining is just what were our ancestors experiencing? I propose three possible explanations for those ancient encounters:

1. They were spiritual in nature—i.e., angels, demons, etc.—which would easily accommodate the Biblical worldview (although 2 and 3 below do not discount the Bible either).

2. The visitors were really us—recollections of advanced pre-historic people, or future, advanced humans time traveling back to the past. Or –

3. Maybe there really were Ancient Aliens visiting planet Earth, beings who advanced beyond the challenges of intergalactic space travel offered by the laws of physics. But there really is no proof of this, and no reason not to take the Biblical accounts of angelic encounters at face value.

Consider No 2. Perhaps there was a pre-Adamic race on planet earth that developed into a modern society, much like today (or even more advanced). These people could have suffered a cataclysmic devastation, where all their accomplishments were wiped away.

Is it so hard to imagine? Keep in mind, most people do not remember earlier than their grandparent's generation. Think about Rome, now a mere shadow of itself; yet the Romans accomplished things, which are astonishing even by today's standards. The Roman aqueducts are legendary, and still in use today in some places some 2,000 years later![320]

Roman concrete is a technology lost to time. It is far superior to modern cement, and contemporary builders and geologists have been unable to unlock the secrets of how the Romans mixed their amazing concrete.[321] It remains lost to history, at least for now.

Greek fire is another forgotten technology lost to the ages. An incendiary weapon used in ancient times, Greek fire was employed in catapulted bombs and sprayed under pressure to launch flames at enemy ships and fortifications. Credited to the Christian Greek Kallinikos in the 7th century, flammable liquids were used in Greek and Roman warfare—but nothing was as lethal as Greek Fire, which is said to have burned even on water.[322]

There are many mysteries such as these. And they are just a couple of known examples. What of the ancient civilizations long forgotten?

I would propose that if our current world were ravaged by a nuclear holocaust, if we were to be bombed back to "the stone age," as they say, within a few generations our histories would be lost, our memories long forgotten, save for a legend or two, and maybe the occasional perplexing artifact that our descendants might uncover. It would be like starting over again.

Figure 22.3: *The hieroglyphs in Temple of Seti I.* This enigmatic image features hieroglyphs that show seemingly modern aircraft and vehicles depicted on a riser in a temple in Abydos Egypt. Photo reproduction taken July 15, 2009 (public domain).

Egyptologists say the "helicopter" image is the result of carved stone being re-used over time creating overlapping hieroglyphs, seemingly depicting modern technology machines. There are also some who believe that the photographic image of the carvings may have been retouched.[323] Still, even the raw, apparently untouched photos are provocative, although the Egyptologists' explanation of overlapping carvings seems sufficient to explain away the coincidence.[324]

The Ancient Ones

Perhaps there was a pre-Adamic race of people judged and wiped out by God prior to the rise of our current civilization. Maybe they were flying around in the ancient sky and timeless space. Could their disembodied spirits even be the voices of angry apparitions roaming the earth plane today?

There is something incongruous about the activity reported of demons, especially when you remember they supposedly used to be angels. How could angels, even fallen ones, act in the depraved nature so often attributed to demons? Does a creature change its nature so completely?

Also, consider the Scriptures, which declare the fallen angels are currently being held in chains until judgment. "And the angels who did not keep their positions of authority but abandoned their proper dwelling—these he has kept in darkness, bound with everlasting chains for judgment on the great Day" (Jude 6, NIV).

"For if God did not spare angels when they sinned, but sent them to hell, putting them in chains of darkness to be held for judgment…" (2 Peter 2:4, NIV). If the fallen angels are being held in chains, restrained until judgment, then who are the "unclean spirits" reported all throughout the New Testament and still plaguing us today?

Some scholars say the above verses are referring to the ultimate state of the fallen angels—while they may be roaming free now, their ultimate fate is already sealed. Others say some of them are being held in chains, while others are still free, for now. Many think the fallen ones already in chains are the "sons of God," the Nephilim from Genesis 6 who intermingled with human flesh and were judged by the

Great Flood. Those He has already bound in judgment. Still others say "chains" refers to the restraint God places upon the evil ones—while they may oppress people, God does not allow them to unleash their full power against us (Job 1:12, 2:6).

While I agree with the traditional church teaching that the demons are fallen angels, who became evil by their own doing, it is an intriguing idea that at least some of them are actually angry spirits of a pre-Adamic race of men wiped out by an earlier judgment from God, natural disaster, or their own misdeeds.

Genesis 1:1-2 says, "In the beginning, God created the heavens and the earth. The earth was without form and void, and darkness was over the face of the deep. And the Spirit of God was hovering over the face of the waters" (ESV). Some biblical scholars say the original language here implies the state of planet Earth at creation was one of destruction.

> "It should be noted in this connection that the verb *was* in Genesis 1:2 may quite possibly be rendered 'became' and be construed to mean: 'And the earth became formless and void.' Only a cosmic catastrophe could account for the introduction of chaotic confusion into the original perfection of God's creation."[325]

More and more, the discoveries of archeology are ever pushing back the accepted dates for advanced civilizations.[326]

A growing, albeit controversial, body of evidence suggests there may have existed ancient Earth civilizations far more advanced than mainstream science acknowledges, while some say the existence of an advanced civilization like ours, if such a civilization ever existed, would be extremely difficult to detect.[327] Some suggest the antediluvian past hides forgotten histories, perhaps even nuclear cataclysms—both here on Earth and maybe even on Mars.[328] To that end, scientists have found high concentrations of the gas isotope xenon-129 in the atmosphere of Mars.

In a September 2016 Jet Propulsion Laboratory/NASA article, Elizabeth Zubritsky reported on recent findings from the Mars Curiosity rover: "The atmospheres of Earth and Mars exhibit very different patterns of xenon and krypton isotopes, particularly for xenon-129. Mars has much more of it in the atmosphere than does Earth."[329]

NASA claims the xenon could be there as a result of impact events. "These isotopes could have been released into the atmosphere by impacts on the surface and by gas escaping from the regolith, which is the soil and broken rocks of the surface."[330]

But the only known way to produce xenon-129 is by nuclear reaction. The Red Planet also has an excess of uranium and thorium; so the implication is that there was a giant nuclear explosion on Mars in the ancient past.

This theory was first propagated by Dr. John E. Brandenburg, a plasma physicist and Pentecostal Christian, who started arguing for it at least as far back as 2011. At first, he proposed it was a natural nuclear explosion, an event that is known to geology. And he pointed to Earth's own geological past, as the Oklo, Gabon region of Africa has uranium-coated sediments from a nuclear reaction that supposedly occurred there two billion years ago.[331]

In a 2011 *Fox News* article called, "Was There a Natural Nuclear Blast on Mars?" Dr. Brandenburg spoke about the Martian event. He said it was equivalent to one million one-megaton hydrogen bombs and occurred in the northern Mare Acidalium region.

"This explosion filled the Martian atmosphere with radio-isotopes as well, which are seen in recent gamma ray spectrometry data taken by NASA."[332]

The idea of ancient nuclear explosions on Earth and Mars is, pardon my saying, a bombshell. But what if those nuclear events were not due to natural causes? That is apparently what Dr. Brandenburg started thinking. He sent shockwaves through the scientific world with his controversial article published November 20, 2014 in the *Journal of Cosmology* titled, "Evidence of a Massive Thermonuclear Explosion on Mars in the Past, The Cydonian Hypothesis, and Fermi's Paradox."

> A signature feature of Mars atmosphere is the predominance of two noble gas isotopes: 129 Xe and 40 Ar over their other isotopes (Mahaffey et al. 2013) (Fig.2) relative to Earth and other inventories (Hunten, 1987). Both these gases are recognized as radiogenic, being due to nuclear reactions in a planetary environment… This pattern of phenomenon can be explained as due to two large anomalous nuclear explosions on Mars.[333]

Could there have been an ancient race on Mars, perhaps cousins to us? Maybe our ancestors on Earth, that pre-Adamic race who evolved to space travel, eventually colonized Mars—much as we are about to do again today.[334] There are even those who belive our ancestors came from Mars.

All of this may simply be a repeat of what already occurred in the primordial past, prior to the state of destruction at the start of the Genesis account, "In the beginning God created the heavens and the earth. And the earth was a formless and desolate emptiness" (Genesis 1:1-2, NASB).

Vexing archeological finds which contradict mainstream science, theories of advanced civilizations in prehistoric America, or even the ubiquitous legends of Atlantis, make a lot more sense under such an ancient-ancestor model. Perhaps our Martian ancestors or cousins were destroyed in an ancient cataclysm.

Dr. Brandenburg did not limit his speculation to isotopes—he went on to blow the lid off several Mars conspiracies related to mysterious structures imaged on the Red Planet by modern technology, such as the infamous "Face on Mars."

> The new images of the Face at Cydonia Mensa confirm eyes, nose, mouth, helmet structure with additional detail of nostrils and helmet ornaments being clearly seen…and new high resolution images show evidence of collapsed brickwork.[335]

Brandenburg believes there was an ancient civilization, primitive and indigenous to Mars.

Adherents to the ancient astronaut theory believe it was flesh-and-blood, biological aliens who visited our planet. They believe it was those ancient aliens who nuked Mars. Perhaps there really were beings who found a way to overcome relativity to bend the fabric of space or harness already existent portals in space-time. Maybe that is the answer. Perhaps they really did come here and are still visiting us today. But what if there is a very different kind of extraterrestrial warping to Earth?

Revisiting the Cosmic Destruction of Sodom and Gomorrah

If you believe in angels who can operate outside the time-space construct of our physical universe, perhaps it is not too much of a stretch to imagine such beings having the capacity to make adjustments to that construct—tweak the "matrix," if you will. The possibility might be something akin to a computer operator changing lines of code. Perhaps they can manipulate energy and matter, atoms and molecules. It is easy to imagine beings such as that could set off a nuclear explosion.

$E = mc^2$ simply means the amount of energy in mass is mass times the speed of light, squared.[336] But this insight by Mr. Einstein is actually mind-blowing, when you think about it. The speed of light, 186,000 miles per second, is so incredible, and is why so much energy is released in a nuclear event. With a nuclear blast, a chain reaction is set off. Exploding atoms spread out and cause others to explode, each time setting off this massive, exponential release of energy. With each split or crashing together of the atoms, a violent, volatile ripping apart of the subatomic stuff of our reality occurs!

So, was the destruction of Sodom and Gomorrah a nuclear event? Possibly. But to me, the Biblical account sounds much more like a devastating series of meteorite strikes, which—believe it or not—could actually be just as bad or even worse than a thermonuclear event!

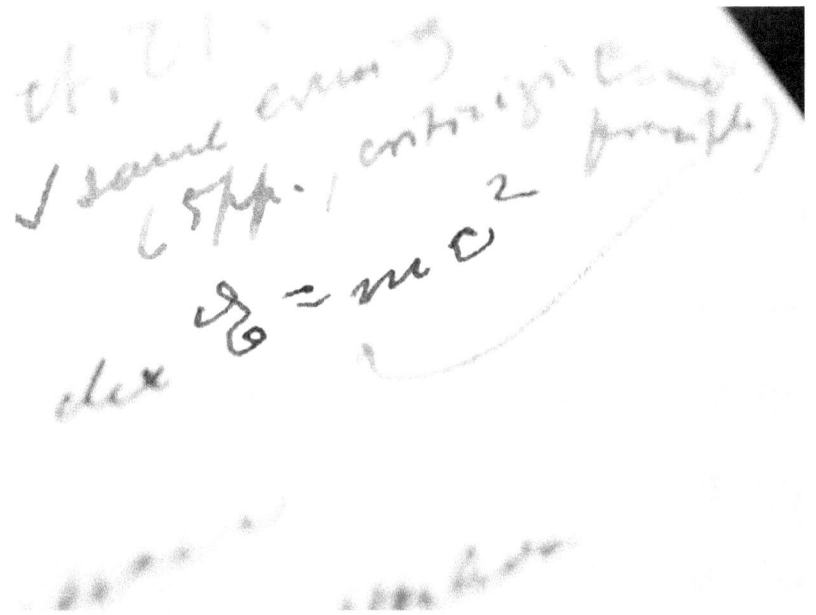

Figure 22.4: $E = mc2$. This undated photograph, provided by Boston-based RR Auction, shows a letter written by Albert Einstein, in which he wrote out his famous "E = mc2" equation. The letter sold at auction for more than $1.2 million.[337]

The sun had risen on the earth when Lot came to Zoar. Then the LORD rained on Sodom and Gomorrah sulfur and fire from the LORD out of heaven. And he overthrew those cities, and all the valley, and all the inhabitants of the cities, and what grew on the ground. But Lot's wife, behind him, looked back, and she became a pillar of salt.

And Abraham went early in the morning to the place where he had stood before the LORD. And he looked down toward Sodom and Gomorrah and toward all the land of the valley, and he looked and, behold, the smoke of the land went up like the smoke of a furnace. So it was that, when God destroyed the cities of the valley, God remembered Abraham and sent Lot out of the midst of the overthrow when he overthrew the cities in which Lot had lived. (Genesis 19:23-29, ESV)

In "Scientists Admit Biblical Account of Sodom is Accurate," a November 23, 2018 article by Adam Eliyahu Berkowitz, reports archaeologists have proven a heavenly cataclysm indeed descended upon the cities of the valley—advancing the theory that it happened by a meteoritic airburst event. Berkowitz says the remains of 120 small settlements in the region showed signs of extreme heat and wind.

> Pottery was discovered to have been exposed to heat so intense that it melted into glass… The event was so catastrophic that the area remained unpopulated for 600 years.[338]

Scientists likened the event to a meteoric airburst that leveled more than 770 square miles of forest in Tunguska, a sparsely populated area of Siberia Russia, June 30, 1908. "The [Tunguska] burst equaled that of a 15-megaton nuclear explosion, or 1,000 times more powerful than the first nuclear bomb ever made that was dropped on Hiroshima 37 years later."[339]

Modern research suggests the ancient cities of Sodom and Gomorrah may have resided under what today is the northern basin of the Dead Sea.

In late 1999, Michael Sanders and an international team of researchers, after several weeks of diving in a mini-submarine, discovered what appears to be salt embedded in the remains of ancient settlements on the seabed.[340]

This idea is explored in an April 1, 2014 online article by Xavier Séguin titled, "The Nuke Bomb of Yahveh."[341]

> [T]he Dead Sea could well reflect a radioactive destruction. Effectively, the very high salt content of this fossil sea could be the consequence of a nuclear explosion.[342]

Of course, salt deposits are also linked with meteorite strikes. And one cannot help but recall how Lot's wife looked back and became a pillar of salt. Here's more from Séguin.

"What the Bible does not tell, is that the inland sea that adjoined Sodom and Gomorrah, has also been transformed into salt...Since then, it is a dead sea..."[343]

That discovery could mean the Biblical destruction of Sodom and Gomorrah literally created the Dead Sea! I think all of the above supports an explosive meteoric airburst event hypothesis involving a devastating series of meteorite strikes, which is in accord with both science and the narrative of Genesis.[344]

Chapter 23

UFOs and Religion

Celestial Craft

Minus the secret aircraft buzzing about our planet under the control of earthly pilots, what if angels and demons are also arriving to us in aerial vehicles from the heavenly realms? Imagine if the flying saucers were actually operated by celestial beings from another dimension.

That idea may not be the most popular among mainstream ufologists, but it makes perfect sense if the ultraterrestrial, paraphysical theory on CE-2 and higher UFO encounters, especially abduction scenarios, is true. Perhaps it is a psychospiritual experience involving the mystical.

Or maybe it is simply the science of a sort unknown. Ancient astronaut theorists think that could only mean one thing: flesh and blood extraterrestrials, not angels. But what if it really were angels all along? It is often said the spiritual world is more real than this one. Who can say of what substance the angels are made?

Of course it could all be an illusion created by those beings, but consider the idea that the angels and demons our Bible tells us about may actually use some type of interdimensional craft in their travel to the earth plane. The possibility may be more plausible than most people realize.

As discussed in Chapter 7 on NDEs, and well known throughout the literature, there are numerous accounts of people near-death who report traversing a tunnel leading to a bright light. Could that tunnel be the wormhole, or Einstein-Rosen Bridge, that physics tells us is more than feasible?

The Highways of Heaven

Perhaps the famed tunnel of light—now almost a cliché thanks to its ubiquity in decades of NDE reporting—is nothing less than a dimensional portal used for transportation. If true, this would be something that opens up and allows entities passage to and from our world to other areas of time and space, including from here to the heavenlies and back. Maybe that is how we enter paradise. Maybe angels and demons zoom their flying saucers through these portals.

I am not saying angelic beings *have* to use celestial craft to travel to and from heaven, but apparently, sometimes they do.

For what reason, I cannot say.

Wheels in the Sky

It is a fascinating concept to imagine angels using flying craft to enter our world. That likelihood certainly seemed to be on display during the prophet Ezekiel's mysterious encounter with heavenly creatures piloting what, according to the account, sounds like mechanical wheels.

> In my thirtieth year, in the fourth month on the fifth day, while I was among the exiles by the Kebar River, the heavens were opened and I saw visions of God… I looked, and I saw a windstorm coming out of the north—an immense cloud with flashing lightning and surrounded by brilliant light. The center of the fire looked like glowing metal, and in the fire was what looked like four living creatures. In ap-

pearance their form was human, but each of them had four faces and four wings… As I looked at the living creatures, I saw a wheel on the ground beside each creature with its four faces. This was the appearance and structure of the wheels: They sparkled like topaz, and all four looked alike. Each appeared to be made like a wheel intersecting a wheel. As they moved, they would go in any one of the four directions the creatures faced; the wheels did not change direction as the creatures went. Their rims were high and awesome, and all four rims were full of eyes all around.

When the living creatures moved, the wheels beside them moved; and when the living creatures rose from the ground, the wheels also rose. Wherever the spirit would go, they would go, and the wheels would rise along with them, because <u>the spirit of the living creatures was in the wheels</u> [emphasis added]. (Ezekiel 1:1, 4-6, 15-20, NIV)

Now, of course, the account was a vision, so it could all be chalked up as simply a spiritual experience. Indeed, this narrative was the prelude to the Lord calling Ezekiel to be a prophet. But there seems to be something very literal and real coming across in the telling.

The heavens are opened with electricity and fire in the clouds, much like a rocket or other aircraft roaring in for a landing. And when the prophet describes the wheels, they definitely sound metallic. Note how they "sparkled like topaz." Also, the "rims were high and awesome, and all four rims were full of eyes all around." Eyes all around sounds a lot like windows to me.

Of course, if these vehicles are celestial craft from the heavenly dimension, perhaps they are not truly mechanical in the ordinary sense. In a dream, you are able to touch and feel things, even though you are not physically touching anything. Then again, perhaps there really is technology in heaven. Again, maybe the spiritual world is more real than the physical, yet different somehow. Rather than Erich von Däniken's *Chariots of the Gods* (1968) which says these were encounters with ancient aliens, maybe the gods really do have chariots of fire.

Recall for a moment Jesus' body after the Resurrection. He was able to touch and be touched, break bread, and He even ate fish with His disciples. Yet He also moved through walls, appeared and disappeared, and finally ascended into the clouds and was gone (Luke 24, John 20-21, Acts 1). Perhaps the physics of heaven may be something altogether different (1 Corinthians 15:42-55).

Elijah's Whirlwind

Another interesting example, which sounds a lot like a UFO encounter, is the story of Elijah's journey as he is taken up into heaven.

> When they had crossed, Elijah said to Elisha, "Ask what I shall do for you, before I am taken from you." And Elisha said, "Please let there be a double portion of your spirit on me." And he said, "You have asked a hard thing; yet, if you see me as I am being taken from you, it shall be so for you, but if you do not see me, it shall not be so." And as they still went on and talked, behold, chariots of fire and horses of fire separated the two of them. And Elijah went up by a whirlwind into heaven. And Elisha saw it and he cried, "My father, my father! The chariots of Israel and its horsemen!" And he saw him no more.
>
> Then he took hold of his own clothes and tore them in two pieces. And he took up the cloak of Elijah that had fallen from him and went back and stood on the bank of the Jordan. (2 Kings 2:9-13, ESV)

Elisha called them the "chariots of Israel." In other words, chariots of God. Elisha understood the chariots were from God. Earlier in verse one it says, "the LORD was about to take Elijah up to heaven." So, we know it was from God.

Figure 23.1: *Ezekiel's Vision* by Raphael, 1518. Oil on panel (public domain). Currently housed in the Palatine Gallery of Palazzo Pitti, Florence, Italy.[345]

At the same time, Elijah being taken up into a whirlwind, by vessels of fire (or perhaps breathing fire), does sounds a lot like some kind of airship, spaceship, or lightship. The prophet's knowledge that the chariots were of God is sound—but his understanding of flying ships of any kind would have no bearing back in the 9th century BC, when a human would have no context except to describe the sighting as flying chariots.

So again, it seems these chariots are simply vehicles by which angels travel to our dimension. Angels would, of course, be classified as extraterrestrial—and it very well could be that angels and demons are the ETs steering lightships.

On the other hand, if these were simply flesh-and-blood beings from another world whom the ancestors encountered, it would mean our ancient peoples deified advanced beings whose technological airships or spaceships they did not understand. If that is the case, it throws the account of the prophets into question.

And I am not saying biological, alien extraterrestrials don't exist. They may very well. And I am not saying it would be impossible for them to have made contact with our people here on Earth—I'm just saying it's highly unlikely.

Again, any other flesh-and-blood beings in our galaxy, if they exist, would somehow have to figure out how to overcome the constraints of physics to get here. We ourselves have achieved interplanetary flight within our own solar system—but true interstellar spaceflight is a lot more challenging to achieve than most people understand.

For an interesting examination of the mind-bending physics of intergalactic spaceflight, I highly recommend Christopher Nolan's weighty space epic, *Interstellar* (2014). That film is one of the few interplanetary cinema fictions which honestly tries to wrestle with Einstein's theory of special relativity, inconvenient to the warp speed of popcorn space opera though it may be.

As to UFOs, no matter what one makes of their possible nature or origin, it seems they have been making appearances in our world far longer than many people realize. They apparently even show up in classical art.

UFOs in Paintings

In addition to written accounts such as the biblical examples cited herein, there also appear to be UFOs showing up in ancient drawings and paintings around the world, long before humans had achieved heavier-than-air flight. These depictions usually correlate with important religious events as in the image below.

Figure 23.2: *The Madonna with Saint Giovannino,* 15th century. Oil on canvas (public domain). Attributed to Bastiano Mainardi and Arcangelo di Jacopo del Sellaio. Currently housed at Palazzo Vecchio, Florence, Italy.[346]

The Madonna with Saint Giovannino shows what appears to be a UFO hovering over Mother Mary's left shoulder in the background. There is no doubt the artist placed this flying object as an intentional element in the sky, but why? What does it mean?

If you look closely, a little further down in the frame is the figure of a man standing on a ledge who appears to be observing the aerial phenomena. Again, this is just one of many examples of what appear to be UFOs depicted in paintings and other illustrations, creating a modern enigma for us to consider what our ancestors were trying to represent in these images.

Deliver Me from ET

If certain UFO phenomena could be linked to a spiritual cause, then even more so the alien abduction experience. Again, I believe most, if not all, such encounters are probably spiritual in nature. As I mentioned earlier, it has been reported that calling on God for deliverance, especially by invoking the power of the name of Jesus Christ, and doing so with belief, will free the sufferer from this particular form of what can only be a demonic attack.

This aspect of the abduction syndrome may be a vexing anomaly to most UFO investigators, but it should come as no surprise to the Christian.

> Therefore, God has highly exalted him and bestowed on him the name that is above every name, so that at the name of Jesus every knee should bow, in heaven and on earth and under the earth, and every tongue confess that Jesus Christ is Lord, to the glory of God the Father. (Philippians 2:9-11, ESV)

The problem with modern UFO researchers is the circular reasoning by which most of them conduct their investigations and postulate theories. They proceed from an assumption that UFOs and abduction encounters must involve flesh-and-blood extraterrestrial travelers from another planet. But what if the abduction encounters really are demonic attacks?

The Bible is very clear on this point, and Jesus himself said that the devil is a liar. "He was a murderer from the beginning, not holding to the truth, for there is no truth in him. When he lies, he speaks his native language, for he is a liar and the father of lies" (John 8:44, NIV). And Paul: "The Spirit clearly says that in later times some will abandon the faith and follow deceiving spirits and things taught by demons" (1 Timothy 4:1, NIV).

So, we see the devil and his demons are liars. And it is interesting to note, the presumed aliens also lie to people. Thomas Horn and Cris Putnam mention this in their encyclopedic volume, *Exo-Vaticana*. "…[T]he messages coming from these entities are often contradictory and absurd. Contactees and channelers…are routinely betrayed and played for fools by the so-called space brothers."[347]

Further, as our knowledge of the universe has expanded and become more sophisticated, so apparently have the origin stories these entities tell us. At one point, they said they came from planets in our local solar system, like Venus.[348] Now they say they are from other regions in the galaxy or other galaxies.[349]

But others are apparently vague about where they come from.[350] They appear in dreamlike and contradictory fashion, with experiencers often reporting symptoms of sleep paralysis, contradictory and nonsensical information, deception, paranormal effects, with the aliens portraying non-physical attributes.[351]

The elusive, intangible manifestations in the abductee phenomena led researchers like Dr. Hynek to admit there were some "attributes of the psychic world" connected to the phenomena.[352]

Hynek's collaborator Dr. Jacques Vallee postulated that some UFOs may come from another dimension.[353] Now, things like interlocking universes and earth-bound interdimensional aliens were on the table.[354]

They were looking for a scientific explanation, whenever the metaphysical reality of abduction syndrome is really where the research was taking them, and remains a far more convincing explanation today.[355]

Abductees tell stories of beings called the Nordics, a human-like species, usually reported with blonde hair and blue or green eyes. These alleged aliens originally claimed to be from the planet Venus when they first began appearing to contactees in the 1950s. Later they changed their story to say they came from the Pleiades star cluster.[356]

Experiencers describe the Nordic beings as angelic in nature.[357] There are also mystical beings linked to Native American mythologies, such as the Hopi, who await the return of the "lost white brother," as the Maya awaited the return of their white-bearded Kukulkan who the Aztecs called Quetzalcoatl, the Feathered Serpent.[358]

From the serpent in the garden in Genesis 3, to the sons of God taking wives of earth women who bore children to them in Genesis 6, even to the stories of the Greek god Zeus appearing as a swan to seduce Aetolian princess Zeda and producing hybrid offspring—these tales of celestial beings intermingling with humans seem eerily similar to modern abduction accounts.

This is only scratching the surface of ancient mythologies and theories on alien anthropology, but it is quite easy to draw comparisons of these concepts of angelic beings contacting or abducting humans along with native cultures' mystical serpent beings and "star people," and realizing they are likely the Watchers, the fallen angels, the *nachash* or "shining ones" of the Bible (Genesis 3:1, 6:1-6; Numbers 13:33; Daniel 4:13, 17, 23).[359]

> Now the Shining One was more clever than any animal of the field that the Lord God had made. He asked the woman, "Did God actually say, 'You are not to eat from any tree of the garden'?" (Genesis 3:1, ISV).

Again, I'm not saying intelligent life existing on other worlds is impossible. I think the popular idea that we are not alone appeals to our collective consciousness. Like author and futurist Arthur C. Clarke joked, "The best proof that there's intelligent life in outer space is the fact that it hasn't come here."[360]

But even if we *are* alone, the Bible tells us we are never alone, "for the LORD your God goes with you; he will never leave you nor forsake you" (Deuteronomy 31:6, NIV). And as the Lord himself said, "lo, I am with you always, *even* to the end of the age" (Matthew 28:20, NKJV).

Alien Baptism?

Pope Francis made an interesting remark on May 12, 2014. While speaking to a group made up mostly of clergy, he spoke about the possibility of baptizing aliens! Francis said that 'Martians,' should they ever visit our planet, would be welcome to the sacrament of baptism. This comment, initially relayed by Vatican Radio, was widely reported.

> "If–for example–tomorrow an expedition of Martians came, and some of them came to us, here… Martians, right? Green, with that long nose and big ears, just like children paint them… And one says, 'But I want to be baptized!' What would happen? …Who are we to close doors?" he said.[361]

Those comments may have led some to wonder if Pope Francis and the Catholic Church know something that has not been disclosed to the public at large. But I think the point he was trying to get across is one of inclusiveness, in a humorous way. Still, such pontifications (ahem) make one stop and think. The concept of intelligent alien life in the universe brings up all kinds of interesting questions to the Christian worldview. How does the recompensing death of Christ relate to alien worlds inhabited by intelligent life, if such places exist?

If we really do have alien brothers and sisters out there, then they would have to be welcomed as brothers and sisters in Christ. The Lord said, "I have other sheep that are not of this fold. I must bring them also, and they will listen to my voice. So there will be one flock, one shepherd" (John 10:16, ESV). That principle would necessarily extend not only to the gentiles outside of Judaism at the time of Jesus, but to all other sentient beings in the cosmos.

If they are there.

So many people are afraid of the implications that alien disclosure would have on our faith and worldview, but the God of the universe is safe from our own limiting beliefs and dogmatic ponderings. The Christian faith stands the test of time, and remains unshaken, even if aliens were to land at the White House in Washington, D.C., Red Square in Moscow, or St. Peter's Square at the Vatican.

In Christianity, we believe Christ's atoning death on the cross saves all who believe. The Scripture says, "whoever believes in Him should not perish but have everlasting life" (John 3:16, NKJV). So Francis makes a good point. Should that offer of grace not extend to ETs as well?

But some with a more rigid view may say salvation is only for earthlings.

The passage in John 3:16 does say, "For God so loved *the* world [emphasis added] that He gave His only begotten Son..." The English translation is rendered world, not worlds. So does that mean redemption is singular to Earth? Not necessarily.

The original Greek translated to the English "world" is actually the word "*kosmos.*"[362] God so loved *the cosmos*!

So, while it does mean world, it also means all of the orderly arrangement of creation. To the ancient mind the world practically was the whole universe anyway, so there is no reason that the concept would not extend to other inhabitants of the cosmos, if such beings exist.

Still, if that is too much of a stretch for you, think about this:

Most theologians agree the passage applies to all people, so it could also read, "For God so loved all people that he gave His only begotten Son..." All people would presumably still extend even to sentient alien life on other worlds as well, if they exist.

"For the grace of God has appeared that offers salvation to all people" (Titus 2:11, NIV).

It would be amazing to learn that we really do have space brothers and sisters out there. And it is fascinating to consider how the Gospel of Jesus Christ would propagate to their worlds. Would Jesus appear to them? Would the Son of God manifest himself as one of their race to offer them salvation? Perhaps we would travel to their planets aboard ion engine starships—bringing them the gospel, like the explorers of old. Space evangelists.

These are forbidden concepts to many, especially those who have a closed-minded view of the Bible, but I think it is interesting to speculate.

As so many in the scientific and UFO research communities agree, it would seem to be an incredible waste of space to have the vastness of the cosmos and the billions of planets out there but none of them inhabited by intelligent life. Is it promised? No. Is it possible? Why not?

As Jesus said, "What is impossible with man is possible with God" (Luke 18:27, ESV). But we really don't know.

At least not yet.

Chapter 24

Disclosure

No matter how you look at the UFO/UAP phenomena, the beliefs you hold, or explanations you accept, it seems clear something strange has been going on for a long time. It is high time the truth is revealed.

Boyd Bushman

One of the more intriguing alleged disclosures in recent years concerning aliens among us was the so-called deathbed confession video of the late Boyd Bushman, a self-described senior scientist for Lockheed Martin (retired), who had a reported 40-year career with the company.

His must have been a highly successful calling, if the assertions of Bushman are true. He claims to have been awarded 27 patents working in the aerospace industry. Bushman's credentials are said to have included work with defense contractors Hughes, General Dynamics, Texas Instruments, as well as Lockheed. The curious YouTube video of Bushman surfaced on October 24, 2014, following his death on August 7 of that same year.[363]

In the video, an apparently sincere Bushman talks about Area 51, reverse-engineering UFOs, antigravity technology, and alien ETs who look a lot like the classic grey aliens; but Bushman insists they have five fingers and toes. He also offered up some pictures of supposed UFOs and the purported aliens.

Bushman very casually discusses these bizarre topics and really does seem to believe what he is saying. After all, why would a man make up a bunch of silly stories before his death if he did not believe it himself? What would he have to gain by doing that? I invite you to watch the video and decide for yourself.

One of the things I found interesting from Mr. Bushman was concerning the manner by which the grey aliens supposedly communicate. "You have a question in your mind," said Bushman. "You walk in the room with a lot of them, and you hear the answer to your questions *by your own voice* [emphasis added], through telepathy."

The "by your own voice" part caught my attention, because that is the way many of us experience spiritual communication, commonly called clairaudience. There is a still, small voice, in your head (1 Kings 19:12). In my experience it sounds like your own voice—but it is not you talking.

Snopes.com has since gone on to try and debunk the Bushman video as false[364] and others have cast their doubts on his testimony as well.

RationalWiki points out the photos of the alien perfectly match a toy once sold at places like Walmart.[365] Also, the video interview was apparently taken in 2007, hardly a "deathbed confession."

As to Bushman, were his claims the ruminations of an over-active geriatric imagination? Or is there really a big cover-up going on? Some would write off this old codger as perhaps a well-intentioned true believer who got lost along the way. There is certainly cause to question at least some of his claims.

In the video, Bushman seems to say he was being fed the photos from insiders, which would make them second-hand at best. If so, perhaps those people were simply playing a cruel trick on him, as the Rational Wiki article suggested. On the other hand, as conspiracy theorists would say, perhaps it is all part of the disinformation agenda: make Bushman out to be a fool and throw everyone else off track of the real story, which Bushman was on to.

As to the creepy alien toy, in an interview with author and researcher David Wilcock, on "Cosmic Disclosure with David Wilcock," Season 7 Episode 21, from May 23, 2017, Corey Goode, the "insider's insider" and alleged whistleblower of the "secret space program," said the toy was put out in limited release to "preempt disclosure."[366]

Come to think of it, that could also redeem Ed Walters and the Gulf Breeze Sightings of 1987! What if the model found in Walters' residence was also a plant by those who want to discredit Ed's story and frustrate the disclosure of UFOs? So, the mystery continues.

Meanwhile, more and more credible witnesses in high places are going on the record.

Dennis Kucinich

On October 31, 2007, presidential candidate Rep. Dennis Kucinich made national headlines when he admitted seeing a UFO that his friend Shirley MacLaine had written about. This disclosure took place at the democratic primary debate at Drexel University in Philadelphia, Pennsylvania when event moderator, NBC's Tim Russert, had asked Kucinich about it. Kucinich confessed he saw something and said it was a UFO, unidentified. MacLaine wrote about the incident in her 2008 book *Sage-ing While Age-ing*.

As MacLaine described the sighting, it was a triangular craft, silent and hovering. MacLaine wrote Kucinich sighted the UFO over her home in Washington State. The stunning disclosure at the debate can be seen on YouTube.[367]

This matter was also detailed in a January 2, 2008 *Wall Street Journal* article by Michael M. Phillips "What Kucinich Saw: Witnesses Describe His Close Encounter."[368]

Apparently, Kucinich spotted not one but three triangular-shaped UFOs through a telescope he had gifted Ms. MacLaine, who was away at the time. The sighting occurred over her former home in Seattle, Washington, while he was staying there in 1982. MacLaine was in Canada performing in her one-woman stage show that weekend. Two other friends were there as well, who also witnessed the craft through the telescope when Kucinich alerted them.

MacLaine's former home in Seattle overlooked Mount Rainier, which is also the famous site where pilot Kenneth Arnold claimed to witness a string of nine, shiny UFOs skipping across the sky. Being that the craft Kucinich and his friends saw were reportedly triangular in shape, my guess is they were likely the government's purportedly secret TR-3B discussed earlier in Chapter 21, or some variant.

For Kucinich, this disclosure likely damaged his presidential hopes. But at least he stuck by the story.

Paul Hellyer and Shi-Li Sun

One of the most notable public voices to come out on the matter of disclosure was that of the late Paul Hellyer, former Canadian Minister of National Defense. Mr. Hellyer died August 8, 2021, two days after his 98th birthday.[369] During a Friday, December 18, 2018 re-broadcast of an *Ancient Aliens* episode, the program featured excerpts of Hellyer speaking at the *Citizen Hearing on Disclosure*, Washington D.C. A series of discussions, the 2013 event was also reported on by the *New York Times* in a May 3, 2013 article.[370]

Hellyer boldly stated UFOs are as real as the airplanes flying over our heads. "At least four species have been visiting Earth for thousands of years," Heller said. "They are different species and consequently may have different agendas."

Another prominent figure who spoke at the summit, former Chinese diplomat, Dr. Shi-Li Sun, now president of the Chinese UFO Research Organization (CURO), made the following surprising statement. "After years of research, a large number of Chinese UFO scholars, including myself, are convinced of the authenticity of UFOs and the existence of UFOs and aliens."[371]

Hellyer first created a stir in early September 2005, when he publicly announced he believes in UFOs. On September 25, 2005, as an invited speaker at an exopolitics conference in Toronto, he told those gathered that he first became open to the idea after he had seen a UFO one night with his late wife and some friends.[372]

Hellyer spoke out on the topic numerous times. In 2007, he reportedly linked the importance of disclosing alien technology to a possible means of solving climate change:

> I would like to see what (alien) technology there might be that could eliminate the burning of fossil fuels within a generation…that could be a way to save our planet…We need to persuade governments to come clean on what they know. Some of us suspect they know quite a lot.[373]

While Hellyer's past political credentials were impressive, he offered little except his own enthusiasm and apparent sincerity that aliens are visiting us, a belief apparently gleaned from the many accounts he heard from others, along with his own modest sighting, of which he said, "It just looks like a star."[374] Beyond that, he provided no proof the claims of alien visitation were true and little reason to believe them.

Still, it would be amazing to learn there really are other intelligent beings out there in the cosmos, not because there has to be, or because contactees and a few politicians say so; but because it is just like God to surprise us with the wonder and diversity of His creative genius.

Assuming for a moment that alien travelers from extraterrestrial civilizations are visiting us—are they really the ones abducting humans?

Chapter 25

The Fourth Kind

Closer Encounters

Those extraterrestrial brothers and sisters, if they do exist, are probably not the ones causing the abduction syndrome. Again, my take on alleged alien abductions based on evidence from the experiencers themselves, is it is most likely a spiritual phenomenon. Abductee James Bartley says:

> I have the maturity to recognize that what we are involved with is spiritual warfare on a cosmic multi-dimensional scale. The reader simply must be aware that the first line of defense for the dark gods is the so-called UFO research community itself.[375]

As we discussed in Book I, Christians can be and often are the victims of spiritual oppression and demonization, possession even. Abduction victims are sometimes Christians. Also, and this cannot be emphasized enough, it is becoming known among ufologists that invoking the name of Jesus Christ *ends* abduction scenarios.

This fact is mostly ignored by researchers because it does not fit their paradigm of extraterrestrials coming from other worlds in the universe. Also, there is probably fear of ridicule from fellow researchers, not to mention the implications of what it means to acknowledge Jesus Christ as Lord of the Cosmos!

Alien Resistance

Joe Jordan is the president and co-founder of the CE4 Research Group, an alien abduction investigation and research team based out of Florida. Jordan has been a Mutual UFO Network field investigator since 1992.[376]

The CE4 Research Group compiled data from over 350 alien abduction experiencers. The initial objective of the group's research was to confirm whether Christians were experiencing the abduction syndrome. They found some people professing Christian faith were indeed experiencing the phenomenon. But there was also a surprising outcome from the research.

"The experience was shown to be able to be stopped or terminated by calling on the name and authority of Jesus Christ. Not as a magic word but by their allegiance to and personal relationship with Him."[377]

They also found that by sharing this with other experiencers, even those not professing faith in Christ, calling on the name of Jesus helped them also stop their abduction experiences. This is something every abduction sufferer should know about, from the silent victims to the famous.

Barney and Betty Hill

The pattern for the modern UFO alien abduction was established by the famous Barney and Betty Hill account, which generated wide notoriety in articles and books and especially from the 1975 television movie *The UFO Incident* starring James Earl Jones as Barney Hill.

The couple was driving home to Portsmouth from Montreal, September 19, 1961 around 10:30 p.m. traveling just south of Lancaster, New Hampshire, when they spotted what Betty thought was a UFO but Barney thought (at least initially) was an airplane.

Betty claimed to have observed a bright point of light in the sky that moved from below the moon upward to the west of the moon. Barney was driving them along U.S. Route 3. Betty thought she was observing a falling star, but strangely, it moved upward. The object moved erratically and grew bigger and brighter, so Betty urged Barney to stop the car for a closer look. Barney stopped at a scenic picnic area just south of Twin Mountain.

Through binoculars, Barney observed what he thought was a commercial airplane, but he soon changed his mind, as the craft rapidly descended in his direction. The Hills say they continued driving on the isolated road, moving slowly through Franconia Notch in order to observe the object as it came closer.

Approximately one mile south of Indian Head, they said the object rapidly descended toward their vehicle, causing Barney to stop in the middle of the highway. The huge, silent craft hovered approximately 80-100 feet (24-30 m) above the Hill's 1957 Chevrolet Bel Air and filled the entire field of view in the windshield.

Barney had a recollection of observing humanoid forms wearing glossy black uniforms and black caps. As the story goes, red lights on what appeared to be bat-wing fins began to telescope out of the sides of the craft, and a long structure descended from the bottom of the craft. The silent craft approached to what Barney estimated was within 50-80 feet (15-24 meters) overhead and 300 feet (91 meters) away from him.[378]

As fantastic as the Hill's account sounds, there were UFO sightings in the area around the time of the alleged abduction.

Betty phoned her friend, Maj. Paul Henderson at nearby Pease Air Force Base, to report the sighting. Henderson found their story was corroborated by two separate UFO reports from radar data from two different nearby Air Force installations. All three reports are officially recorded in Project Blue Book.[379]

Mrs. Hill began having nightmares shortly after the event, which led the couple to be hypnotized. This is where much of the detail of their abduction experiences emerged.

While many enthusiasts still consider the Hill's account a notable chapter in UFO lore, most serious researchers find their story to be questionable at best, likely a fiction.

The event was almost completely debunked by Brian Dunning in his podcast "Betty and Barney Hill: The Original UFO Abduction, A critical look at the original UFO abduction story that so many people take for granted." This from the *Skeptoid Podcast #124* October 21, 2008.

> The Betty & Barney Hill abduction story has every indication of being merely an inventive tale from the mind of a lifelong UFO fanatic. Despite the best efforts of authors to bolster it with mischaracterized or exaggerated evidence, it is unsupported by any useful evidence, and is perfectly consistent with the purely natural explanation.[380]

I personally believe it's possible the Hill's may have actually seen something that night, perhaps astronomical but likely physical, maybe some advanced aviation technology unknown to them. Perhaps the sighting was some form of a flying wing or some other experimental aircraft that silently hovered over their car. The Air Force and NASA developed a slew of little-known, exotic test aircraft in the 1950s, such as the VZ-2, X-3, X-13, X-15 X-18, and XF-92A, all of which look like something out of science fiction.[381]

But based on the stories that would follow, we certainly cannot rule out the paraphysical, psycho-spiritual explanation for their sighting either. That certainly might explain the rest of the story.

The abduction narrative was largely driven by Mrs. Hill over the years. Following her husband's premature death of a cerebral hemorrhage in 1969, Betty became something of a cult figure in ufology throughout the rest of her life, until she died in 2004. However, her credibility had already come into question long before that. Mrs. Hill was reportedly booed of the stage by what at first was a friendly crowd at the National UFO Conference in New York City in 1980.[382]

The Demonic Kind

Perhaps the Hills, especially Mrs. Hill, were victims of an overactive imagination. But I think their abduction account easily fits into the ultraterrestrial interpretation. If true, they were likely victims of a spiritual attack, especially concerning the nightmares of Mrs. Hill and their hypnotized recollections. Some have linked Barney's account with a recently broadcast episode of *The Outer Limits*, or an earlier episode of *The Twilight Zone*, TV shows that he might have seen prior to the incident (which the Hills denied). Actually, I think his chilling description sounds a lot like a demonic attack.

Barney said things like, "Oh, those eyes. They're there in my brain" (from his first hypnosis session) and "I was told to close my eyes because I saw two eyes coming close to mine, and I felt like the eyes had pushed into my eyes" (from his second hypnosis session) and "All I see are these eyes... I'm not even afraid that they're not connected to a body. They're just there. They're just up close to me, pressing against my eyes."[383]

In episode 72 of the *History* channel show *Ancient Aliens: Declassified*, an installment from 2019 titled, "Extraterrestrial Abductions," the program featured paranormal investigator Linda Moulton Howe, who says abduction victims all report similar experiences, like seeing dark eyes staring over them in their beds, encountering an orb or orbs of light, and suffering paralysis. This is likely the same sleep paralysis as that experienced during the incubi/succubi attacks mentioned earlier, especially in Chapter 16. I also covered the subject thoroughly in Book I. The negative entities here simply wear an extraterrestrial alien façade, but we still get the same sleep paralysis, along with paranormal and poltergeist activities; flickering lights, objects going missing, and so on.[384] Many experiencers report entity attachments and paranormal activities following their encounters. This aspect of so-called alien abductions cannot be overlooked.

I thought the 2009 film *The Fourth Kind*, although panned by critics, was particularly terrifying. Something pretty much everyone missed is that the possessing spirits tormenting the residents of Nome, Alaska, were obviously demons, masquerading as alien abductors.

In real-life encounters, the "aliens" are often reported by abductees to literally walk through walls. How could flesh-and-blood extraterrestrials walk through walls? Also, it is worth noting that after the experiences, many victims report waking up safely in their beds.

Are we supposed to believe the same ETs who would capture people and perform savage medical torture and sexual experimentation on them, are then considerate enough to kindly tuck their victims back into bed? And how is it that among the neighbors, family members, friends, police, and first-responders, no one ever seems to witness saucers hovering over houses or aliens tiptoeing through yards and peeking in windows? No one ever witnesses these victims being taken.

I am not saying people do not experience horrible suffering in these ungodly encounters. I am quite convinced they do happen, but they are likely happening in the spiritual realm. From the terrifying flashbacks of Whitley Strieber, relayed in his classic 1987 book, *Communion: A True Story*—to the experiencers of today—it all matches the pattern of classic demonic attacks.[385]

Even in the supposed positive experiencer encounters, the pattern is the same.

Demi Lovato

Demi Lovato went on *The Kelly Clarkson* show Friday, October 1, 2021, to promote a new reality series, *Unidentified with Demi Lovato*. During the visit, Lovato told Clarkson about a strange encounter with three mysterious beings.

During a night while Lovato was dreaming, the singer claims to have been taken out of the bedroom at home and shown Earth along with the aliens' "pink and purple planet." Lovato was reticent to use the word "abduction" because that would imply it wasn't with consent, and the singer was all for it. This event, if true, fits the typical experiencer pattern that indicates an interdimensional, psychospiritual encounter.

So, what about the physical evidence occasionally reported by abductees and researchers? Well, aside from the many ways something like that can be hoaxed, some of it may indeed be real. Exorcists have long said preternatural spirit activities can produce physical signs.

Father Amorth

Father Gabriele Amorth, the former senior Exorcist of Rome, claimed to have performed some 160,000 exorcisms! Father Amorth died on Friday, September 16, 2016 at the age of 91, finally resting from his many battles with the devil after more than 60 years as a priest.[386]

Father Amorth reported he sometimes observed people coughing up nails and other disturbing items or finding such things materialized under pillows or mattresses following an exorcism, the aftermath of a black magic witchcraft spell having been placed on the oppressed.

"[W]e find the strangest objects, such as nails, pieces of glass, small wooden dolls, knotted strings, rolled wire, cotton thread of different colors, or blood clots. These objects may be expelled naturally, often by vomiting."[387]

Father Amorth also claimed the victim was never harmed when expelling these items and that sometimes items would materialize seemingly out of nowhere, like a person would feel stomach pain and a nail would suddenly be found on the floor, and the pain would disappear.[388] Amorth said his mentor, Father Candido Amantini, reported a similar observation. "I saw pieces of glass, iron, hair, and bone being vomited…"[389]

These strange, paranormal events defy explanation, especially as victims and their surroundings are examined prior to exorcism.

ET = Extraterrestrial or Evil Trickster?

So, even if abduction victims present with physical injuries to their bodies or even implanted devices, such occurrences do not rule out a spiritual cause. And again, why would abduction encounters stop when the victim calls on the name of Jesus for deliverance?

In the end, the Alien Greys, Reptilians, even the friendly Nordics, and all the rest, are likely none other than demonic entities. Otherwise, why do they stop in the name of Jesus?

That explanation of CE-III Close Encounter and higher contactee experiences seems to be the most satisfactory, reasonable, and complete.

Manifestations

One of the most potent arguments for the ET as demon trickster comes from the late Father Seraphim Rose (born Eugene Dennis Rose) via his insightfully forward-looking 1975 classic, *Orthodoxy and the Religion of the Future*:

> UFO encounters are but a contemporary form of an occult phenomenon which has existed throughout the centuries. Men have abandoned Christianity and look for "saviors" from outer space, and therefore the phenomenon supplies images of spacecraft and space beings... UFO phenomena are simply and precisely demonic in origin.[390]

Father Rose said modern investigators are finding the answers, but their lack of understanding of religious phenomena hinders them from understanding the significance of what they have found.[391]

Investigator Brad Steiger wrote, "We are dealing with a multidimensional paraphysical phenomenon, which is largely indigenous to planet Earth."[392]

Ankerberg and Weldon wrote, "the UFO phenomenon simply does not behave like extraterrestrial visitors."[393] And John Keel, who masterfully and decisively made the paraphysical case, wrote that the real UFO story is one "of ghosts and phantoms and strange mental aberrations; of an invisible world that surrounds us and occasionally engulfs us; of prophets and prophecies, and gods and demons."[394]

Clifford Wilson reported that in some cases people who contacted UFO beings have had those entities literally "possess" them and try to kill them when they resist.[395]

Christian literature offers many examples of demonic manifestations that neatly fit the UFO pattern: apparitions of beings and objects that suddenly materialize and dematerialize. These manifestations seek to awe and confuse people, and ultimately lead them astray.[396]

Touched by a Pleiadian

Some people claim to be able to conjure "lightships." For example, in the following video clips posted in July, 2017, "How to Summon a Pleiadian Lightship" and "How to Summon a Pleiadian," the author explains how positive intentions and a higher vibration increase your chances of making contact.

He says the Pleiadians (also known as Nordics) come from the higher realms and advocates cleansing yourself of lower vibrations by taking a shower prior to calling out for them to appear. You are instructed to lie perfectly still outside at night or in bed and not be alarmed if you see shadowy figures at your bedside, because you need the third eye active to effectively see them in all their glory. After 20-30 minutes of lying perfectly still, the author says you will enter a limbo state and may experience sleep paralysis—which he says is "normal and ideal."

At this point, you are invited to let their invisible fingers poke at you. You are able to then carry on a conversation where Pleiadians will answer yes/no questions depending on which hand they poke.[397] They will also appear as flashes of light, even in broad daylight, as the lightship clip allegedly shows.[398]

I think it is pretty clear that any beings summoned in this way would obviously not be flesh-and-blood extraterrestrials, nor their lightships, nuts-and-bolts spacecraft.

SUMMARY

When the Air Force closed Project Blue Book, out of the over 12,000 sightings investigated, only 701 or about five percent remained unexplained.[399] As I have stated many times, the majority of UFO/

UAPs are explainable as astronomical sightings, weather phenomena, or known manmade objects.

For the small percentage beyond that of actual flying craft not able to be explained or disclosed, those are probably Top Secret drones or other vehicles our government and/or the governments of the world are operating. Beyond that, there is an even smaller number that might be explained by the paraphysical theory.

Beyond that may exist a tiny fraction where the extraterrestrial alien visitors would dwell. But I think the interdimensional, spiritual explanation of close encounters is the best explanation for the strange encounters not otherwise explainable by natural means.

Still, I will grant that within that tiny percentile, there might indeed be strange visitors from another world. I hope there is. The God I know and love is too big to be limited by our constraints on His creative genius. If a populated universe is His intention, that is what we will have.

To those visitors—if you are here, there, or on the way—

And to all others who read this greeting –

I invite you to embrace our creator God, receive His Holy Spirit, and share in the glories of His Son, our Lord, Christ Jesus. Amen!

Come, all you who are thirsty,
come to the waters; Seek the Lord while he may be found call on him while he is near.
Let the wicked forsake their ways and the unrighteous their thoughts.
Let them turn to the Lord, and he will have mercy on them,
and to our God, for he will freely pardon.
Isaiah 55:1, 6-7
Holy Bible, New International Version (NIV)

Afterword

40 Days of Testing: A Reflection

It was a moment in time some years ago.

I thought it was going to be easy.

I went into the 40 Days of Purpose effort at my local church at the time with a hopeful attitude. I thought, *This is great! All I have to do is commit to the 40 Days study, maybe fast for 40 days from a thing or two and God will gladly reveal the* Purpose *of my life.*

Did God speak to me? Yes, definitely. Was it gentle? Not exactly.

I turned my attention to God and said, "Show me, Lord."

God through a feeling impressed upon my heart the following reply:

"So, you want to know what I have in mind for you. Do you *really* have any idea what I expect of you? Because you are not ready for it yet!"

Woah, wait a minute Lord, I thought nervously. *This is supposed to be easy (and fun)…*

Then, the Lord stopped speaking…

The Voice was gone.

Then life events started speaking volumes!

In his seminal 2002 book, *The Purpose Driven Life*, Pastor Rick Warren tells us life is a test and a trust. I started fasting, praying, and leading a small group, expecting God to acknowledge these meager efforts, as if they merited some kind of special treatment. It was as if I expected Him to say, "Oh wow, Richard! Good Job, I'm so impressed (snarky me, not God), now here let me reveal my plans for you…"

You see, before any of God's servants can fulfill His purpose, we must first be prepared. And the greater the purpose, the more challenging the expectation from the Lord, the more you must be equipped by testing and trials to become strong enough for what God has planned for you.

In Zechariah 13 the Lord says, "I will refine them like silver and test them like gold. They will call on my name and I will answer them; I will say, 'They are my people,' and they will say, 'The Lord is our God.'" And in Proverbs 17, "The crucible for silver and the furnace for gold, but the Lord tests the heart."

So, almost on cue, the *40 Days of Testing* began. Every area of my life felt besieged by challenges: personal, professional, and financial. I had to daily deal with difficult bosses, impossible situations, unrealistic deadlines, and seemingly unfair treatment. It was as if the floodgates of the underworld were opened, and the enemy just kept sending over volley after volley of very unfriendly fire. All the while, I also had to deal with a profoundly deep hurt in my personal life, which crushed my heart. So, whether I was at work or at home, I found no rest for my soul, day or night. It was that time of desolation spoken of so well by Dan Burke in his excellent 2020 guidebook, *Spiritual Warfare and The Discernment of Spirits*.

Meanwhile, although it felt like I was the one who needed help; the Lord kept placing people in my path who needed *my* help. It did not matter what I was going through, I was still expected to serve others. From intimate family and friends to complete strangers, people still needed me despite my own private misery.

Rick Warren also says, at times God will withdraw from you as a further test, to see how you handle it. For the first time in my life, I truly experienced that feeling. Oh, to be spurned by the Father is much more painful than any other pain of life. In a small way, I felt some meager semblance to the Psalmist who cried out, "My God, my God, why have you forsaken me?" (Psalm 22:1, NRSV).

I remember sitting in my office alone one day, tears streaming down my face, pleading with God, praying, "Lord, without you I am nothing. Return to me. I am lost without you. Oh, how I long for the days when I enjoyed being in your favor. All I need in this life is you, my God."

And in all of this turmoil I was reminded of what God told the Apostle Paul, "My grace is sufficient for you" (2 Corinthians 12:9, NABRE).

Then a couple of weeks later things started shifting. Even in my darkest hours, God still let me know He *was* present by saving me at the last moment in a situation, or simply providing a blessing or person that would lift a certain burden or another. The truth is, He was there all along!

A few days later, something really profound started happening: The tactics of Satan became transparent. Suddenly, I felt my strength and confidence were now fully shorn up. After going through those trials, I felt as though I could handle almost anything. I came to truly appreciate that no power or situation in heaven or on earth, not even death, can ever snatch me away from the love of God (Romans 8:38-39). I am His for all eternity.

For the first time in my life, I truly understood what James meant when he said, "Consider it pure joy, my brothers and sisters, whenever you face trials of many kinds, because you know that the testing of your faith produces perseverance" (James 1:2-3, NIV). It is one thing to hear and accept this truth on an intellectual level, but when you know and understand it in your heart—you receive a power the enemy can never extinguish.

Suddenly, I found myself facing difficult situations with a boldness of step, a smile beginning to form again and a gleam in my eye that said, "The LORD is my rock, my fortress and my deliverer" (Psalm 18:2, NIV). Then, the raging storm was finally lifted, and I was given blessed peace.

For a time…

There have been many other struggles, challenges, victories, and losses. The pangs of desolation will return. But so will the joys of consolation. We will experience lows and incredible highs. And there will be many more, as we continue along this journey of life.

Through it all, God is always in control. As Dr. Charles Stanley has said, "You better keep yourself tuned to *The Voice* of Almighty God."

Amen. Just trust Him.

GOD
I belong
JESUS
I'm worthy
HOLY SPIRIT
I'm competent
My cause is justified
I will be vindicated and rewarded
"I can do all things through Christ who strengthens me!"
FATHER
CHRIST
GOD
You love me!
I love you!

AUTHOR'S BIO

Richard D. Lewis is an author, journalist, and film critic. A graduate of the Defense Information School's writing, broadcast, and public affairs programs, Richard joined the Air Force in 1987 and spent 10 years as a Broadcast Producer stationed at Incirlik AB Turkey, Hill AFB Utah, and the Air Force Academy, Colorado. After separating in 1997, Richard began work in TV production in Salt Lake City, Utah. He was hired back as a civilian producer/director by the Air Force in 1999 and has since written about and documented Air Force mission activities at SMC Los Angeles, NORAD, Cape Canaveral AFS, Beale AFB,

Vandenberg AFB, March ARB, Schriever AFB, Peterson AFB, Grand Forks AFB, Van Nuys ANG Station, Edwards AFB, NASA Ames Research Center, and Wallops Island Flight Facility.

Richard has been featured in *Blackbelt Magazine, FILMINK,* Fangoria.com, *Rocket Magazine, Geek Monthly, P3 Production Update, Campus Circle, Astro News, Space Country Times,* Air Force.mil, BeyondHollywood.com, Veritas Radio, *The Paranormal Almanac, Realm of the Supernatural* and *The Other Side with Jim Harold,* along with The History Channel, Discovery Science Channel, AMC Theatres, KTLA 5, Los Angeles, Torrance Channel 3 TV, AFN TV, PBS, The Pentagon Channel, *Milsat Magazine, Santa Maria Times, and The Lompoc Record.*

Richard is a published songwriter on Aska's *Nine Tongues* LP (having written the acclaimed single "The Dream") and wrote screenplay treatments for Geoff Nicholls of Black Sabbath—which were pitched to the Horror Channel in England. Richard is also creator of the award-winning Pentagon Channel TV newsmagazine *Air Force Space Today.*

Upon completion of Doreen Virtue's Angel Therapy Practitioner Course in 2003, Richard became a certified spiritual counselor by the California Board of Hypnotherapy. He is also a communicant member of Ascension Lutheran Church in Torrance, California in good standing.

When Richard is not writing or geeking out over the latest Dodgers game or any other sport, he enjoys relaxing with his family in Gardena, California.

This is his second book.

List of Bible Versions and Acronyms

English Standard Version (ESV)
Holman Christian Standard Bible (HCSB)
International Standard Version (ISV)
King James Version (KJV)
New American Bible Revision Edition (NABRE)
New American Standard Bible (NASB)
New American Standard Bible 1995 (NASB 1995)
New Century Version (NCV)
New International Version (NIV)
New King James Version (NKJV)
New Living Translation (NLT)
New Revised Standard Version (NRSV)
Young's Literal Translation (YLT)

Endnotes

1. "Paradise Polled: Americans and the Afterlife." Roper Center. Accessed July 14, 2021. https://ropercenter.cornell.edu/paradise-polled-americans-and-afterlife .
2. Maggie Fox. "Fewer Americans Believe in God Still Believe in Afterlife." NBC News. Updated March 21, 2016. https://www.nbcnews.com/better/wellness/fewer-americans-believe-god-yet-they-still-believe-afterlife-n542966 .
3. 3Benjamin Mitchell-Yelling. "Dying to Tell a Good Story." *Psychology Today*. June 28, 2016. https://www.psychologytoday.com/us/blog/life-death-and-the-self/201606/dying-tell-good-story.
4. "Pam Reynolds case." Wikipedia. Accessed July 14, 2021. https://en.wikipedia.org/wiki/Pam_Reynolds_case .
5. Mario Beauregard. "Near death, explained." Salon. April 21, 2018. https://www.salon.com/2012/04/21/near_death_explained/.
6. Ibid.
7. Betty J. Eadie. *Embraced by the Light: The Most Profound and Complete Near-Death Experience Ever.* Bantam, 1994.
8. Lehman Strauss. "Man A Trinity (Spirit, Soul, Body)." Bible.org. June 14, 2004. https://bible.org/seriespage/2-man-trinity-spirit-soul-body.
9. Allen J. Wilcox et al. "Time of Implantation of the Conceptus and Loss of Pregnancy." The *New England Journal of Medicine*. June 10, 1999. https://www.nejm.org/doi/full/10.1056/NEJM199906103402304.

10 "Conception: How it Works." UCSF Health. Accessed July 14, 2021. https://www.ucsfhealth.org/education/conception-how-it-works.

11 Stanford University Medical Center. "Which fertilized eggs will become healthy human fetuses? Researchers predict with 93% accuracy." Science Daily. October 4, 2020. https://www.sciencedaily.com/releases/2010/10/101003205930.htm.

12 Ibid.

13 Ronald Bailey. "Is Heaven Populated Chiefly by the Souls of Embryos?" Reason. December 22, 2004. https://reason.com/2004/12/22/is-heaven-populated-chiefly-by/.

14 "The Declaration of Independence." US History.org. Accessed July 14, 2021. https://www.ushistory.org/documents/declaration.htm.

15 *The Matrix*, dir. Lily and Lana Wachowski. Warner Bros. 1999. 136 mins.

16 Michael Talbot, *The Holographic Universe* (New York: HarperCollins Publishers, 1991), 33-34.

17 "Psalm 90." Wikipedia. Accessed July 14, 2021. https://en.wikipedia.org/wiki/Psalm_90.

18 "Third Heaven." Wikipedia. Accessed July 14, 2021. https://en.wikipedia.org/wiki/Third_Heaven.

19 Don Piper. *90 Minutes in Heaven: A True Story of Death and Life*. Revell, 2004.

20 "North Wilkesboro and the Roots of NASCAR." NC Department of Natural and Cultural Resources. Accessed July 14, 2021. https://www.ncdcr.gov/blog/2013/05/18/north-wilkesboro-and-the-roots-of-nascar; "NASCAR Rooted in Prohibition." Prohibition: An Interactive History. Accessed July 14, 2021. https://prohibition.themobmuseum.org/the-history/prohibition-potpourri/nascar-and-prohibition/.

21 William Barrett. *Deathbed Visions*. White Crow Books, 2011.

22 Ibid.

23 Gary Rotstein. "They see dead people—apparently, lots of people do." The Morning Call. July 9, 2018. https://www.mcall.com/news/pennsylvania/mc-nws-pa-seeing-dead-people-20180707-story.html.

24 "Long Prairie Minnesota.jpg." Wikimedia Commons. Accessed July 14, 2021. https://commons.wikimedia.org/wiki/File:Long_Prairie_Minnesota.jpg.

25 Piper. *90 Minutes in Heaven*.

26 Kevin Williams. "P.M.H. Atwater's Near-Death Experience Research." Near-Death Experiences and the Afterlife. September 21, 2019. http://near-death.com/pmh-atwaters-nde-research/.

27 Eadie. *Embraced by the Light*.

28 Matt Perman. "Do We Receive Our Ressurection Bodies When We Die, or at the End of the Age?" Desiring God. January 23, 2006. https://www.desiringgod.org/articles/do-we-receive-our-resurrection-bodies-when-we-die-or-at-the-end-of-the-age#:~:text=The%20resurrection%20of%20the%20body%20will%20occur%20at,have%20now,%20except%20transformed%20into%20an%20immortal%20state.

29 "Chuck Smith: Verse by Verse Study on 2 Corinthians." Blue Letter Bible. Accessed July 14, 2021. https://www.blueletterbible.org/Comm/smith_chuck/c2000_2Cr/2Cr_005.cfm.

30 "Phantom limb." Wikipedia. Accessed July 14, 2021. https://en.wikipedia.org/wiki/Phantom_limb .

31 *Psycho*, dir. Alfred Hitchcock. Paramount Pictures. 1960. 109 mins.

32 "42 (number)." Wikipedia. Accessed July 14, 2021. https://en.wikipedia.org/wiki/42_(number) .

33 "Rainbow." Wikipedia. Accessed July 14, 2021. https://en.wikipedia.org/wiki/Rainbow .

34 "Conscious Development Program." International Academy of Consciousness. Accessed July 14, 2021. https://www.iacworld.org.

35 "The Catechism of the Catholic Church, No 1013." Vatican.va. Accessed September 11, 2021. http://www.vatican.va/archive/ENG0015/_P2I.HTM.

36 "Many Americans Mix Multiple Faiths." Pew Research Center. December 9, 2009. https://www.pewforum.org/2009/12/09/many-americans-mix-multiple-faiths/.

37 "Reincarnation." Wikipedia. Accessed September 2, 2021. https://en.wikipedia.org/wiki/Reincarnation

38 H. S. Schibli. *Pherekydes of Syros*. Claerondon Press, 1990.

39 Roger E. Oldon. *The Story of Christian Theology: Twenty Centuries of Traditional Reform*. IVP Academic, 1999.

40 Eusebius Pamphilus. *Eusebius' Ecclesiastical History*. Hendrickson Pub, 1998.
41 "*On the First Principles*." Wikipedia. Accessed July 14, 2021; "Origen." Wikipedia. Accessed July 14, 2021.
42 De Principiis (Book 1). New Advent. Accessed July 14, 2021. https://www.newadvent.org/fathers/04121.htm.
43 Dorothea Frede. "The Final Proof of the Immortality of the Soul in Plato's Phaedo 102a – 107a." *Phronesis* 23. 1978. https://www.jstor.org/stable/4182027.
44 Ronald E. Heine. "Origin: Scholarship in the Service of the Church" in *Christian Theology in Context*. Oxord University Press. 2012.
45 F. L. Cross and E. A. Livingstone. *The Oxford Dictionary of the Christian Church*. Oxford University Press. 2005.
46 "Letter 124." New Advent. https://www.newadvent.org/fathers/3001124.htm.
47 "What he Early Church Believed: Reincarnation." Catholic Answers. Accessed July 14, 2021. https://www.catholic.com/tract/reincarnation.
48 "Ante-Nicene Fathers/Volume IX/Origen on Matthew/Origen's Commentary on Matthew/Book XIII/Chapter 1." WikiSource. Accessed July 14, 2021. https://en.wikisource.org/wiki/Ante-Nicene_Fathers/Volume_IX/Origen_on_Matthew/Origen%27s_Commentary_on_Matthew/Book_XIII/Chapter_1.
49 Ibid.
50 "Reincarnation." Wikipedia. Accessed September 2, 2021. https://en.wikipedia.org/wiki/Reincarnation
51 "Jerome." Wikipedia. Accessed September 2, 2021. https://en.wikipedia.org/wiki/Jerome
52 "Vulgate." Wikipedia. Accessed September 2, 2021. https://en.wikipedia.org/wiki/Vulgate
53 "Letter 124." New Advent. https://www.newadvent.org/fathers/3001124.htm
54 De Principiis (Book 2). New Advent
55 De Principiis (Book 3). New Advent
56 Ibid.
57 Tara MacIsaac. "Fire Chief Investigates Past Life as Civil War General: Group Reincarnation? (+Video)." The Epoch Times. May 20, 2014. https://www.theepochtimes.com/fire-chief-investigates-past-life-as-civil-war-general-group-reincarnation-video_685737.html.

58 Stephen W. Sears. *Landscape Turned Red: The Battle of Antietam*. Mariner Books, 1993; Alann Schmidt. *September Mourn: The Dunker Church of Antietam Battlefield*. Sava Beattie, 2018.

59 Jeffrey J. Keene. *Someone Else's Yesterday: The Confederate General & Connecticut Yankee: A Past Life Revealed*. Blue Dolphin Publishing, 2003.

60 Jack D. Welsh. *Medical Histories of Confederate Generals*. The Kent State University Press, 1999; John B. Gordon. *Reminiscences of the Civil War: Major General of the Second Corps, Army of Virginia*. Epoch Texts, 2018.

61 Image: John B. Gordon and Jeff Keene. Reincarnation Research. https://reincarnationresearch.com/wp-content/uploads/2015/02/gordon-keene-past-life-reincarnation-semkiw-45l-2.jpg.

62 Dialogue with Trypho (Chapters 69-88). New Advent. Accessed July 14, 2021. https://www.newadvent.org/fathers/01286.htm.

63 James Johnson. Reconciling Isaiah 65:20 with "No more death." All Power to the Lamb. April 4, 2016. http://allpowertothelamb.com/2016/04/reconciling-isaiah/.

64 Concerning the Genuineness of "The Prophecy of Enoch." Bible Hub. Accessed July 14, 2021. https://biblehub.com/library/tertullian/on_the_apparel_of_women/chapter_iii_concerning_the_genuineness_of.htm.

65 16 Bible verses about Jesus As Son Of Man. Knowing Jesus. Accessed July 14, 2021. https://bible.knowing-jesus.com/topics/Jesus-As-Son-Of-Man.

66 Enoch The Prophet; R. H. Charles, trans. *The Book of Enoch*. Postomorrow Books, 2013 (originally 1912).

67 "What are the New Heavens and the New Earth?" Got Question. Accessed July 14, 2021. https://www.gotquestions.org/new-heavens-earth.html.

68 Carl Haub. Distilled Demographics: How Many People Have Ever Lived on Earth? Pipulation Reference Bureau (PRB). October 9, 2011. https://www.prb.org/resources/distilled-demographics-how-many-people-have-ever-lived-on-earth/.

69 Siege of Jerusalem. Wikipedia. Accessed July 14, 2021. https://en.wikipedia.org/wiki/Siege_of_Jerusalem

70 Flavius Josephus; Wiliam Whiston, ed. *The Wars of the Jews*. Project Gutenberg. Updated August 3, 2013. https://www.gutenberg.org/files/2850/2850-

h/2850-h.htm.

71 Siege of Jerusalem. Wikipedia.

72 Siege of Jerusalem. Wikipedia.

73 File: NinthAvStonesWesternWall.JPG. Wikimedia Commons. Accessed July 14, 2021. https://commons.wikimedia.org/wiki/File:NinthAvStonesWesternWall.JPG.

74 "Past life regression." Wikipedia. Accessed September 2, 2021. https://en.wikipedia.org/wiki/Past_life_regression

75 Michael Jawer. Children Who Seemingly Remember Past Lives. *Psychology Today*. December 13, 2014. https://www.psychologytoday.com/us/blog/feeling-too-much/201412/children-who-seemingly-remember-past-lives.

76 Ibid.

77 Bruce Leininger and Andrea Leininger with Ken Gross. *Soul Survivor: The Reincarnation of a World War II Fighter Pilot*. Self-published, 2009.

78 Ibid.

79 File: Last Judgement (Michelangelo).jpg. Wikimedia Commons. Accessed July 14, 2021. https://commons.wikimedia.org/wiki/File:Last_Judgement_(Michelangelo).jpg.

80 Americans' Belief in God, Miracles and Heaven Declines. The Harris Poll. December 16, 2013. https://theharrispoll.com/new-york-n-y-december-16-2013-a-new-harris-poll-finds-that-while-a-strong-majority-74-of-u-s-adults-do-believe-in-god-this-belief-is-in-decline-when-compared-to-previous-years-as-just-over/.

81 "Pneuma." Wikipedia. Accessed September 2, 2021. https://en.wikipedia.org/wiki/Pneuma

82 File: Po vodam.jpg. Wikimedia Commons. Accessed July 14, 2021. https://commons.wikimedia.org/wiki/File:Po_vodam.jpg.

83 Joe Nickell. Catching Ghosts. *Skeptical Inquirer* 18. June 1, 2008. https://skepticalinquirer.org/newsletter/catching-ghosts/; Terence Hines. *Pseudoscience and the Paranormal: A Critical Examination of the Evidence*. Prometheus Books, 1988.

84 Sabrina Stierwalt. 6 Possible Scientific Reasons for Ghosts. *Scientific American*. February 25, 2019. https://www.scientificamerican.com/article/6-possi-

ble-scientific-reasons-for-ghosts/; Benjamin Radford. *Investigating Ghosts: The Scientific Search for Spirits.* Rhombus Publishing. 2018.

85 Ghost. Wikipedia. Accessed July 14, 2021. https://en.wikipedia.org/wiki/Ghost.

86 Stephen Wagner. Theories and ExplanationAbout the Existence of Ghosts. Liveabout. Updated January 20, 2019. https://www.liveabout.com/what-are-ghosts-2594174.

87 John Blake. Do loved ones bid farewell from beyond the grave? CNN. September 23, 2011; Richard Lewis. *The Paranormal Christian: Bridging the Gap Between Unusual Experiences and the Biblical Worldview*. Zoran Press. 2020.

88 Marilyn A. Mendoza. The Healing Effects of After-Death Communications. *Psychology Today*. July 4, 2017. https://www.psychologytoday.com/us/blog/understanding-grief/201707/the-healing-effects-after-death-communications.

89 A. L. Barry. What About… Death and Dying. The Lutheran Church. 1998. https://files.lcms.org/wl/?id=4C9b1IpSFPRy18M2tCdDXhzJXAEw1Azd.

90 Brent Swancer. What is the Nature of Ghosts? Some Alternative Theories. Mysterious Universe. October 13, 2018. https://mysteriousuniverse.org/2018/10/what-is-the-nature-of-ghosts-some-alternative-theories/; 11 Signs A Ghost Is In Your Room. Paranormal School. Accessed July 14, 2021. https://paranormalschool.com/11-signs-a-ghost-is-in-your-room/.

91 Linda S. Watts. *Encyclopedia of American Folklore.* Facts on File, 2007. https://www.amazon.com/Encyclopedia-American-Folklore-Library-Literature/dp/0816056994.

92 Martin Ringbauer et al. Experimental simulation of closed timelike curves. *Nature Communications* 5. June 19, 2014. https://doi.org/10.1038/ncomms5145.

93 Witch of Endor. Wikimedia Commons. Accessed July 14, 2021. https://commons.wikimedia.org/wiki/Category:Witch_of_Endor_in_paintings#/media/File:Witch_of_Endor_(Nikolay_Ge).jpg.

94 Henry Stuart Liddel et al. *A Greek-English Lexicon*. Clarendon Press, 1961; demon. Merriam-Webster. Accessed July 14, 2021. https://www.merriam-webster.com/dictionary/demon.

95 Plato, *Timaeus*. Perseus/Tufts. Accessed July 14, 2021. http://www.perseus.

tufts.edu/hopper/text?doc=Perseus%3Atext%3A1999.01.0180%3Atext%3D-Tim.%3Apage%3D90.

96 Plato. *The Apology*. CreateSpace Independent Publishing Platform. 2011.

97 Anybody else have haunted toys? Reddit thread. 2019. https://www.reddit.com/r/Parenting/comments/av1cql/anybody_else_have_haunted_toys/.

98 *Ascalapha odorata*. Wikipedia. Accessed July 14, 2021. https://en.wikipedia.org/wiki/Ascalapha_odorata.

99 "List of avian humanoids." Wikipedia. Accessed September 2, 2021. https://en.wikipedia.org/wiki/List_of_avian_humanoids

100 Bird Man Symbol. War Paths 2 Peace Pipes. Accessed July 14, 2021. https://www.warpaths2peacepipes.com/native-american-symbols/bird-man-symbol.htm.

101 "Watcher (angel)." Wikipedia. Accessed September 2, 2021. https://en.wikipedia.org/wiki/Watcher_(angel)

102 Tengu: The Slayer of Vanity. A to Z Photo Dictionary: Japanese Buddhist Statuary. Updated September 2013. http://www.onmarkproductions.com/html/tengu.shtml.

103 Samurai Armor Exhibition to Open at LACMA. The Rafu Shimpo. October 15, 2014. https://www.rafu.com/2014/10/samurai-armor-exhibition-to-open-at-lacma/.

104 Bigfoot. Wikipedia. Accessed July 14, 2021. https://en.wikipedia.org/wiki/Bigfoot.

105 Geoffrey H. Bourne and Maury Cohen. *The Gentle Giants: The Gorilla Story*. Putnam, 1975.

106 Liam Stack. The F.B.I Once Helped in the Hunt for Bigfoot. The *New York Times*. June 6, 2019. https://www.nytimes.com/2019/06/06/us/fbi-bigfoot-file.html.

107 The Dalles. Travel Oregon. Accessed July 14, 2021. https://traveloregon.com/places-to-go/cities/the-dalles/?utm_actcampaign=967294071&gclid=Cj0KCQiA7YyCBhD_ARIsALkj54qBvQeUHTqu0B-GwnXjsaxKjpmwwaY1ghIGk-aCElXmgvxVsutUMAY4aAipsEALw_wcB.

108 Stack. The F.B.I Once Helped in the Hunt for Bigfoot.

109 Francis E. Warren Air Force Base. Wikipedia. Accessed July 14, 2021. https://

en.wikipedia.org/wiki/Francis_E._Warren_Air_Force_Base.

110 "Mather Air Force Base." Wikipedia. Accessed September 2, 2021. https://en.wikipedia.org/wiki/Mather_Air_Force_Base

111 My True Ghost Story. Got Spirits. July 17, 2015. https://www.gotspirits.com/my-true-ghost-story/.

112 Rancho Cordova, California Ghost Sightings. Ghosts Of America. Accessed July 14, 2021. http://www.ghostsofamerica.com/9/California_Rancho_Cordova_ghost_sightings.html.

113 Paula Dale Roberts. Ghostbusters at the Old Historical Cemetery – Sacramento. Your Ghost Stories. April 10, 2007. https://www.yourghoststories.com/real-ghost-story.php?story=656.

114 R. Lewis. Personal communication with the author. June 1, 2019.

115 White Lady. Wikipedia. Accessed July 14, 2021. https://en.wikipedia.org/wiki/White_Lady.

116 James Woods. *The Nuttall Encyclopedia of Universal Information*. Warne, 1909.

117 Michael Bradley. Signs of Demonization. Bible-Knowledge. Updated December 18, 2020. https://www.bible-knowledge.com/signs-of-demonization/; Can Christians Be Demonized? Torch of Christ. March 28, 2018. https://torchofchrist.com/2018/03/can-christians-have-demons.

118 Externals of the Catholic Church – An Unmarried Clergy. CatholicSaints.info. Accessed July 14, 2021. https://catholicsaints.info/externals-of-the-catholic-church-an-unmarried-clergy/.

119 E. Allison Peers, ed./trans. *The Life of Teresa of Jesus: The Autobiography of Ávila*. Harry Platinga, 1995.

120 Wesley Baines. 7 Ways to Fend Off the Devil, From an Experienced Exorcist. Beliefnet. Accessed July 14, 2021. https://www.beliefnet.com/faiths/catholic/7-ways-to-fend-off-the-devil-from-an-experienced-exorcist.aspx.

121 Steve Wood. Paranormal experts can help you give up the ghost. USA Today. October 25, 2013. https://www.usatoday.com/story/news/nation/2013/10/25/ghost-proof-home-halloween/3194693/; Patti Maguire Armstrong. An Exorcist Explains Why the Devil Hates Bells So Much. National Catholic Register. October 1, 2019. https://www.ncregister.com/blog/an-exorcist-explains-why-the-devil-hates-bells-so-much.

122 Jacob Olesen. Crown Chakra Meaning: A Guide to the Seventh Chakra and Its Violet or Purple Color Energy. Color Meanings by Jacob Olesen. https://www.color-meanings.com/crown-chakra-the-seventh-chakra/.

123 File: Battesimo di Cristo" [sic] 1710.jpg. Wikimedia Commons. Accessed July 14, 2021. https://commons.wikimedia.org/wiki/File:Battesimo_di_Cristo%22_1710.jpg.

124 Leslie Kean. *UFOs: Generals, Pilots, and Government Officials Go on the Record.* Three Rivers Press, 2011.

125 U.FO. Secrets Behind You… Accessed July 14, 2021. https://worldstopsecrets.wordpress.com/u-f-o/.

126 Alex Sundby. American Airlines pilot reports "long cylindrical object" zoom by while fying over New Mexico. CBS News. February 26, 2021. https://www.cbsnews.com/news/ufo-american-airlines-pilot-new-mexico-long-cylindrical-object/; Paul Best. American Airlines not denying possible UFO spotting, says: 'Talk to the FBI.' Q13 Fox Seattle. February 24, 2021. https://www.q13fox.com/news/american-airlines-not-denying-possible-ufo-spotting-says-talk-to-the-fbi.

127 Deborah Byrd. Meet Proxima Centauri, Closest Star to the Sun. EarthSky. October 9, 2018. https://earthsky.org/space/proxima-centauri-our-suns-nearest-neighbor/.

128 The Cosmic Distance Scale: The Nearest Neighbor Star. Imagine the Universe! NASA. Accessed July 14, 2021. https://imagine.gsfc.nasa.gov/features/cosmic/nearest_star_info.html.

129 Pluto's Unusual Orbit. Smithsonian National Ait and Space Museum. Accessed July 14, 2021. https://airandspace.si.edu/exhibitions/exploring-the-planets/online/solar-system/pluto/orbit.cfm.

130 Reuben Westmaas. Pluto and Neptune Swap Places Every 248 Years. Discovery. August 1, 2019. https://www.discovery.com/science/pluto-and-neptune-swap-places-every-248-years.

131 Agnes Ullmann. Louis Pasteur. Britannica. Accessed July 14, 2021. https://www.britannica.com/biography/Louis-Pasteur/Research-career; About: Biogenesis. DBpedia. Accessed July 14, 2021. https://dbpedia.org/page/Biogenesis.

132 Reuben Westmaas. 9 Thinks That Make the Earth the Perfect Place for Life. Discovery. August 1, 2019. https://www.discovery.com/science/Earth-Perfect-Place-for-Life; Jerry Bergman. The Earth: Unique in All the Universe. Institute for Creation Research. June 1, 1985. https://www.icr.org/article/earth-unique-all-universe/.

133 Rose Eveleth. The Chance of a Collision in Space Is Practically Zilch. The *Atlantic*. December 16, 2014. https://www.theatlantic.com/technology/archive/2014/12/the-chance-of-a-collision-in-outer-space-is-practically-zilch/383810/.

134 File: HH 901 and HH 902 in the Carin nebula (captured by the Hubble Space Telescope).jpg. Wikimedia Commons. Accessed July 14, 2021. https://commons.wikimedia.org/wiki/File:HH_901_and_HH_902_in_the_Carina_nebula_(captured_by_the_Hubble_Space_Telescope).jpg.

135 Introduction to Chemistry: The Three Laws of Thermodynamics. Lumen. Accessed July 14, 2021. https://courses.lumenlearning.com/introchem/chapter/the-three-laws-of-thermodynamics/.

136 Michael A. Gottlieb and Rudolf Pfeiffer. Conservation of Energy. California Institute of Technology. 2013. https://www.feynmanlectures.caltech.edu/I_04.html.

137 Meyer. *Return of the God Hypothesis*.

138 Hawking: Aliens may pose risks to Earth. NBC News. April 25, 2010. https://www.nbcnews.com/id/wbna36769422.

139 Alan Boyle. 'I'm an Atheist': Stephen Hawking on God and Space Travel. NBC News. Updated September 23, 2014. https://www.nbcnews.com/science/space/im-atheist-stephen-hawking-god-space-travel-n210076.

140 Ian Sample. Stephen Hawking: 'There is no heaven; it's a fairy story.' The *Guardian*. May 15, 2011. https://www.theguardian.com/science/2011/may/15/stephen-hawking-interview-there-is-no-heaven.

141 Kitty Ferguson. *Stephen Hawking: His Life and Work*. Transworld Digital, 2011.

142 Kitty Ferguson. *The Fire in the Equations: Science Religion & Search For God*. Templeton Press, 2004.

143 Jamie Ducharme. Stephen Hawking Was an Atheist. Here's What He Said

About God, Heaven and His Own Death. *TIME*. March 14, 2018. https://time.com/5199149/stephen-hawking-death-god-atheist/.

144 Jeffrey K. Lyons. *Evolution Myths: A Critical View of neo-Darwinism.* Liberty Hill Publishing, 2018.

145 *The Cell: The Spark of Life.* BBC Four. 60 mins.

146 Lyons. *Evolution Myths.*

147 Miller-Urey Experiment. ScienceFacts.net. Accessed July 14, 2021. https://www.sciencefacts.net/miller-urey-experiment.html.

148 Jamie Carter. What is 'Panspermia?' [sic] New Evidence For The Wild Theory That Says We Could All Be Space Aliens. *Forbes*. August 26, 2020. https://www.forbes.com/sites/jamiecartereurope/2020/08/26/what-is-panspermia-new-evidence-for-the-wild-theory-that-says-we-could-all-be-space-aliens/?sh=5e0665bf6543.

149 Queenie H. S. Chan et al. Organic matter in extraterrestrial water-bearing salt crystals. *Science Advances* 4. January 10, 2018. https://www.doi.org/10.1126/sciadv.aao3521.

150 Fred Hoyle. *Intelligent Universe.* Michael Joseph Ltd, 1983.

151 Owen Gingerich. The human brain is by far the most complex physical object known to us in the entire cosmos. AZ Quotes. Accessed July 14, 2021. https://www.azquotes.com/author/29575-Owen_Gingerich.

152 Sharon Begley. Science Finds God. The *Washington Post*/Newsweek. 1998. https://www.washingtonpost.com/wp-srv/newsweek/science_of_god/scienceofgod.htm.

153 Ibid.

154 Called by the Universe: A conversation with Neil deGrasse Tyson. The Science Network. July 23, 2009. http://thesciencenetwork.org/programs/the-science-studio/neil-degrasse-tyson.

155 Rationally Speaking #103 – Neil deGrasse Tyson on Why he Doesn't Call Himself an Atheist. Rationally Speaking podcast. March 9, 2014. https://www.iheart.com/podcast/256-rationally-speaking-31027018/episode/rationally-speaking-103-neil-degrasse-41880611/.

156 Neil deGrasse Tyson and Donald Goldsmith. *Origins: Fourteen Billion Years of Cosmic Evolution.* W. W. Norton, 2005.

157 Newton's laws of motion. Wikipedia. Accessed July 14, 2021. https://en.wikipedia.org/wiki/Newton%27s_laws_of_motion.

158 Causality (physics). Wikipedia. Accessed July 14, 2021. https://en.wikipedia.org/wiki/Causality_(physics).

159 Four causes. Wikipedia. Accessed July 14, 2021. https://en.wikipedia.org/wiki/Four_causes.

160 Tyson and Goldsmith. *Origins.*

161 Ibid.

162 Chelsea Gohd. Scientists Finally Confirm the Milky Way Has a Supermassive Black Hole. Astronomy.com, October 31, 2018. https://astronomy.com/news/2018/10/scientists-confirm-the-milky-way-has-a-supermassive-black-hole.

163 Jeff Parsons. Scientists find proof a supermassive black hole is lurking at the centre of the Mily Way. *Metro*. Wednesday 31. 2018. https://metro.co.uk/2018/10/31/scientists-find-proof-a-supermassive-black-hole-is-lurking-at-the-centre-of-the-milky-way-8092994/.

164 Christoforou, Peter. 10 Interesting Facts about Yellow Dwarf Stars. Astronomy Trek, July 24, 2017. https://www.astronomytrek.com/10-interesting-facts-about-yellow-dwarf-stars/.

165 Melvin Porter. The Size of Our Sun Compared to the Biggest Stars in the Milky Way Galaxy. Owlcation. November 25, 2018. https://owlcation.com/stem/The-Size-of-the-Sun-As-Compare-to-the-Other-Stars.

166 Star Types. Enchanted Learning. Accessed July 14, 2021. https://www.enchantedlearning.com/subjects/astronomy/stars/startypes.shtml.

167 File: NGC 4414 (NASA-med).jpg. Wikipedia. Accessed July 14, 2021. https://en.wikipedia.org/wiki/File:NGC_4414_(NASA-med).jpg.

168 Sarah Chemla. Astronomers were wrong about the number of galaxies in universe – study. The *Jerusalem Post*. January 14, 2021. https://www.jpost.com/health-science/astronomers-were-wrong-about-the-number-of-galaxies-in-universe-655425.

169 Tricia Talbert, ed. NASA's New Horizons Reaches a Rare Space Milestone. NASA. April 15, 2021. https://www.nasa.gov/feature/nasa-s-new-horizons-reaches-a-rare-space-milestone.

170 Elizabeth Howell. How Many Stars Are in The Universe? Space.com. May 17, 2017. https://www.space.com/26078-how-many-stars-are-there.html.

171 Mike Wall. Nearly Every Star Hosts at Least One Alien Planet. Space.com. March 4, 2014. https://www.space.com/24894-exoplanets-habitable-zone-red-dwarfs.html.

172 Nancy Atkinson. 22% Of Sun-like Stars Have Earth-Sized Planets in the Habitable Zone. Universe Today, December 23, 2015. https://www.universetoday.com/106121/22-of-sun-like-stars-have-earth-sized-planets-in-the-habitable-zone/; Scott Neuman. Scientists Estimate 20 Billion Earth-like Planets in Our Galaxy. NPR, November 4, 2013. https://www.npr.org/sections/thetwo-way/2013/11/04/243062655/scientists-estimate-20-billion-earth-like-planets-in-our-galaxy; Seth Borenstein. 8.8 Billion Habitable Earth-Size Planets Exist in Milky Way Alone. NBCUniversal News Group, November 4, 2013. https://www.nbcnews.com/sciencemain/8-8-billion-habitable-earth-size-planets-exist-milky-way-8c11529186; Dennis Overbye. Looking for Another Earth? Here are 300 Million, Maybe. The *New York Times*. November 5, 2020. https://www.nytimes.com/2020/11/05/science/astronomy-exoplanets-kepler.html.

173 Nola Taylor Redd. Earth's Stabilizing Moon May Be Unique Within Universe. Space.com. July 29, 2011. https://www.space.com/12464-earth-moon-unique-solar-system-universe.html.

174 Deborah Byrd. Is It True That Jupiter Protects EARTH?: Space. EarthSky, November 25, 2015. https://earthsky.org/space/is-it-true-that-jupiter-protects-earth/; SmokePatch. Our Giant Guardian Jupiter. Blogger, August 20, 2020. https://www.cubescienceposts.com/2018/04/Jupiter.html; Reporter, Daily Mail. Guardian Planets Jupiter and SATURN Shield the Earth from CATASTROPHIC Comet Collisions. Daily Mail Online. Associated Newspapers, July 31, 2009. https://www.dailymail.co.uk/sciencetech/article-1203405/Guardian-planets-Jupiter-Saturn-shield-Earth-catastrophic-comet-collisions.html; Dennis Overbye. Jupiter: Our Cosmic Protector? The *New York Times*. July 25, 2009. https://www.nytimes.com/2009/07/26/weekinreview/26overbye.html.

175 Arkenstein XII . Are Gas Giants Actually Rare? Astronomy Stack Exchange,

January 1, 1968. https://astronomy.stackexchange.com/questions/33230/are-gas-giants-actually-rare#:~:text=Kepler%20data%20suggests%20that%20the,This%20seems%20suspicious; Stefano Meschiari. Rarity of Jupiter-like planets means planetary systems exactly like ours may be scarce. The Conversation. December 11, 2015. https://theconversation.com/rarity-of-jupiter-like-planets-means-planetary-systems-exactly-like-ours-may-be-scarce-52116.

176 Lewin, Sarah. Life on Earth Can Thank Its Lucky Stars for Jupiter and Saturn. Space.com, January 12, 2016. https://www.space.com/31577-earth-life-jupiter-saturn-giant-impacts.html; Inigo Monzon. How Jupiter and Saturn PROTECT Earth from Killer Asteroids. International Business Times, November 4, 2020. https://www.ibtimes.com/how-jupiter-saturn-protect-earth-killer-asteroids-2882416; Konstantin Batygin, and Greg Laughlin. Jupiter's Decisive Role in the Inner Solar SYSTEM'S Early Evolution. PNAS. National Academy of Sciences, April 7, 2015. https://www.pnas.org/content/112/14/4214; Matt Davis. Why humanity owes a lot to Jupiter. Big Conversation. November 9, 2018. https://bigthink.com/surprising-science/how-jupiter-protects-earth.

177 Rare Earth hypothesis. Wikipedia. Accessed July 14, 2021. https://en.wikipedia.org/wiki/Rare_Earth_hypothesis.

178 John A. Keel. *Operation Trojan Horse*. Anomalist Books, 2013.

179 Gary Bates. Lifting the Veil Ufo Phenomenon. Creation.com. Creation Ministries International, January 23, 2015. https://creation.com/lifting-the-veil-ufo-phenomenon; William Nugent. Alien Abductions Stopped by the Name of Jesus. Ezine Articles, July 7, 2009. https://ezinearticles.com/?Alien-Abductions-Stopped-by-the-Name-of-Jesus&id=2578536; Michael Heiser. Stopping Abductions with Prayer? Dr. Michael Heiser, July 12, 2008. https://drmsh.com/stopping-abductions-with-prayer/; Alien Demons Bow to Jesus' Name. Unleavened Bread Ministry. March 12, 2021. https://www.ubm1.org/?page=aliendemons.

180 Close Encounters of the Fourth Kind. CE4 Research Group. Accessed July 4, 2021. http://www.alienresistance.org/ce4.htm.

181 *Unacknowledged: An Exposé of the World's Greatest Secret*. Michael Mazzola, dir. 2017. 103 mins.

182 Chuck Yeager. Tweet by @GenChuckYeager. June 23, 2015. https://twitter.com/genchuckyeager/status/613566339014266880?lang=en.

183 Chuck Yeager-61 Years of Wearing Rolex. Jake's Rolex World. November 8, 2008. https://www.rolexmagazine.com/2008/11/chuck-yeagerss-rolextheright-stuff.html.

184 John Glenn with Nick Taylor. *John Glenn: A Memoir*. Bantam, 2000; Julie Zauzmer. In Space, John Glenn saw the face of God: 'It just strengthens my faith.'" The *Washington Post*. December 8, 2016. https://www.washingtonpost.com/news/acts-of-faith/wp/2016/12/08/in-outer-space-john-glenn-saw-the-face-of-god/?noredirect=on.

185 Zauzmer. In Space, John Glenn saw...

186 James R. Hansen. *First Man: The Life of Neil A. Armstrong*. Simon & Schuster, 2012.

187 Ibid.

188 Anna Savva. Neil Armstrong 'believed I aliens' after trips to moon says astronauts's son. *Daily Star*. August 5, 2020. https://www.dailystar.co.uk/news/world-news/apollo-astronaut-first-man-moon-22471753.

189 Timothy Good. *Earth: An Alien Enterprise: The Shocking Truth Behind the Greatest Cover-Up in Human History*. Pegasus Books, 2014.

190 Ibid.

191 Buzz Aldrin: AMA. Reddit. 2014. https://www.reddit.com/r/IAmA/comments/2a5vg8/i_am_buzz_aldrin_engineer_american_astronaut_and/.

192 Gary Bates. Lifting the Veil Ufo Phenomenon. Creation.com. Creation Ministries International, January 23, 2015. https://creation.com/lifting-the-veil-ufo-phenomenon; David Morrison. UFOs and Aliens in Space. The Committee for Skeptical Inquiry, February 2009. https://web.archive.org/web/20151023025455/http:/www.csicop.org/si/show/ufos_and_aliens_in_space; Answered Question :: Ask an Astrobiologist :: NASA Astrobiology. Wayback Machine, July 21, 2011. https://web.archive.org/web/20110721050308/http:/astrobiology.nasa.gov/ask-an-astrobiologist/question/?id=1568; Alex Horton. No, Buzz Aldrin didn't see a UFO on his way to the moon. The *Washington Post*. April 10, 2018. https://www.washingtonpost.com/news/retropolis/wp/2018/04/10/buzz-aldrins-ufo-sighting-moon-mis-

Endnotes

sions-mystique-might-have-simple-explanation/.

193 Buzz Aldrin: AMA.

194 Donald N. Michael. *Proposed Studies on the Implications of Peaceful Space Activities for Human Affair.* Brookings Institution, 1961.

195 Ibid.

196 Ibid.

197 Ibid.

198 Ibid.

199 2P171912249EFFAAL4P2425L7M1.JPG. Spirit: All Raw Images. Mars Exploration Rovers. NASA. Accessed July 14, 2021. https://mars.nasa.gov/mer/gallery/all/2/p/513/2P171912249EFFAAL4P2425L7M1.JPG.

200 Sean Potter, ed. NASA to Provide Update on Perseverance 'Firsts' Since Mars Landing. NASA. March 3, 2021. https://www.nasa.gov/press-release/nasa-to-provide-update-on-perseverance-firsts-since-mars-landing.

201 C-SPAN: Buzz Aldrin Reveals Existence of Monolith on Mars Moon. YouTube video. July 22, 2009. https://www.youtube.com/watch?v=bDIXvpjnRws.

202 Astronaut Edwin E. Aldrin, Jr. Wikimedia Commons. Accessed July 14, 2021. https://commons.wikimedia.org/wiki/Category:Buzz_Aldrin#/media/File:Buzz_Aldrin.jpg.

203 Helene Cooper et al. Glowing Auras and 'Black Money': The Pentagon's Mysterious UFO Program. The *New York Times.* December 16, 2017. https://www.nytimes.com/2017/12/16/us/politics/pentagon-program-ufo-harry-reid.html.

204 Ibid.

205 Letter to Steven Aftergood. Defense Intelligence Agency. January 16, 2019. https://fas.org/irp/dia/aatip-list.pdf.

206 Kelsey Atherton. On the Pentagon's wish list: warp drives and invisibility cloaks. C4ISRNET. January 17, 2019. https://www.c4isrnet.com/c2-comms/2019/01/17/pentagon-researched-warp-drives-and-invisibility-cloaking/.

207 Kelly McCarthy. Navy pilot recalls encounter with UFO: 'I think it qas not from this world. ABC News. December 18, 2017. https://abcnews.go.com/US/navy-pilot-recalls-encounter-ufo-unlike/story?id=51856514;

208 Helene Cooper at al. 'Wow, What Is That?' Navy Pilots Report Unexplained

Flying Objects. The *New York Times*. March 26, 2019. https://www.nytimes.com/2019/05/26/us/politics/ufo-sightings-navy-pilots.html.

209 8 News NOW Las Vegas. Unedited Navy Gimbal video.mp4. YouTube video. https://www.youtube.com/watch?v=QKHg-vnTFsM.

210 Defense Department confirms leaked Navy UFO video. WIS News. Updated May 20, 2021. https://www.wistv.com/2021/05/20/defense-department-confirms-leaked-navy-ufo-video/.

211 Denise Chow and Gadi Schwartz. UFOs are about to make their way to the U.S. Senate. Here's whatto know. NBC News. Updated May 24, 2021. https://www.nbcnews.com/science/science-news/ufos-are-make-way-us-senate-know-rcna973.

212 Ibid.

213 Lia De La Cruz. US Pentagon UFO Report Due in June. Earth Sky. May 28, 2021. https://earthsky.org/human-world/us-pentagon-ufo-report-due-june-2021/

214 Amanda Macias. Here's the firepower the Pentagon is asking for in its $715 billion budget. CNBC. Updated May 28, 2021. https://www.cnbc.com/2021/05/28/pentagon-asks-for-715-billion-in-2022-defense-budget.html.

215 9 News NOW Las Vegas. I-Team: A look back at 1989 Bob Lazar interview. YouTube video. May 16, 2019. https://www.youtube.com/watch?v=2GRjgB-Vw9Pk&t=62s.

216 Vinay Menon. Evidence suggests UFO whistleblower Bob Lazar was telling the truth all along. Toronto Star. July 24, 2020. https://www.thestar.com/entertainment/opinion/2020/07/24/evidence-suggests-ufo-whistleblower-bob-lazar-was-telling-the-truth-all-along.html.

217 *Bob Lazar: Area 52 & Flying Saucers*. Jeremy Kenyon, dir. 2021. 96 mins.

218 Erin Blakemore. WWII's atomic bomb program was so secretive that even many of the participants were in the dark. The *Washington Post*. November 2, 2019. https://www.washingtonpost.com/science/wwiis-atomic-bomb-program-was-so-secretive-that-even-many-of-the-participants-were-in-the-dark/2019/10/31/8d92d16c-fb7e-11e9-8906-ab6b60de9124_story.html.

219 The Navy Is Working on Guidelines for Reporting UFOs. *TIME*. Accessed

July 15, 2021. https://time.com/5577853/navy-ufo-reporting-guidelines/.

220 Nola Taylor Redd. What Is Wormhole Theory? Space.com. October 20, 2017. https://www.space.com/20881-wormholes.html.

221 Daniel Clery. For the first time, you can see what a black hole looks like. AAAS. April 10, 2019. https://www.sciencemag.org/news/2019/04/black-hole.

222 Redd. What Is Wormhole Theory?

223 Ibid.

224 Travel through wormholes is possible, but slow. Science Daily. April 15, 2019. https://www.sciencedaily.com/releases/2019/04/190415090853.htm.

225 Bob Al-Greene. Faster than light. Mashable. Accessed July 15, 2021. https://mashable.com/feature/faster-than-light-space-interstellar-travel.

226 Jump drive. Battlestar Galactica Fanon Wiki. Accessed July 15, 2021. https://galacticafanon.fandom.com/wiki/Jump_drive.

227 Andreea Font. Wormholes may be lurking in the universe – and new studies are proposing ways of finding them. The Conversation. January 13, 2021. https://theconversation.com/wormholes-may-be-lurking-in-the-universe-and-new-studies-are-proposing-ways-of-finding-them-153020.

228 K. Steiner. Personal communication with the author. June 1, 2019.

229 Kevin Seeger. "Bubba Exposed" Review of https://www.amazon.com/Gulf-Breeze-Sightings-Ed-Walters/dp/0380708701/ref=cm_cr_srp_d_product_top?ie=UTF8, n.d.

230 "Obituary," *Rose Lawn Funeral Home & Cemetery* (https://www.roselawn-fh.com/mgn/obituary/Garland-PughJr: accessed September 2, 2021), Garland Bland Pugh, Jr., died 15 May 2015.

231 Ibid.

232 Kevin Seeger. "Bubba Exposed" Review of https://www.amazon.com/Gulf-Breeze-Sightings-Ed-Walters/dp/0380708701/ref=cm_cr_srp_d_product_top?ie=UTF8, n.d.

233 "Unidentified Flying Objects and Air Force Project Blue Book." U.S. Air Force, April 25, 2003. https://www.af.mil/About-Us/Fact-Sheets/Display/Article/104590/unidentified-flying-objects-and-air-force-project-blue-book/; "Project Blue Book - Unidentified Flying Objects." National Archives and

Records Administration. National Archives and Records Administration. Accessed September 10, 2021. https://www.archives.gov/research/military/air-force/ufos; Thomas Tulien, ed. "PROCEEDINGS OF THE SIGN HISTORICAL GROUP UFO HISTORY WORKSHOP." Project 1947, February 1949. http://www.project1947.com/shg/proceedings/shgproceed1.pdf; M. J. Banias. 50 Years Ago, the Air Force Tried to Make UFOs Go Away. It Didn't Work. *Popular Mechanics*. December 17, 2019. https://www.popularmechanics.com/military/research/a30257166/project-blue-book-anniversary/.

234 Jerome Clark, The UFO Book: Encyclopedia of the Extraterrestrial (Canton, MI, Visible Ink Press, 1997). Edward J. Ruppelt. *The Report on Unidentified Flying Objects*. CreatSpace Independent Publsihing, 2011; "Project Blue Book - Unidentified Flying Objects." National Archives and Records Administration. Accessed September 10, 2021. https://www.archives.gov/research/military/air-force/ufos.

235 Mark O'Connell. *The Close Encounters Man: How One Man Made the World Believe in UFOs*. Dey Street Books, 2017.

236 Chapter Three: The Classics. NICAP. Accessed July 15, 2021. http://www.nicap.org/rufo/rufo-03.htm.

237 O'Connell. *The Close Encounters Man*.

238 Ibid.

239 Ibid.

240 Greg Daugherty. Meet J. Allen Hynek, the Astronomer Who First Classified UFO 'Close Encounters.' History.com. A&E Television Networks, November 19, 2018. https://www.history.com/news/j-allen-hynek-ufos-project-blue-book; What're Close Encounters of the First, Second, Third, Fourth and Fifth Kind?" The Times of India, March 22, 2003. https://timesofindia.indiatimes.com/whatre-close-encounters-of-the-first-second-third-fourth-and-fifth-kind/articleshow/41097626.cms; Close Encounters of Various Kinds. lpetrich.org. Accessed September 10, 2021. https://lpetrich.org/UFOs/Close%20Encounters.xhtml; David Darling. Close Encounters. In *Encyclopedia of Astrobiology Astronomy and Spaceflight*, n.d. https://web.archive.org/web/20070205105405/http:/daviddarling.info/encyclopedia/C/closeencounters.html; Not Panicking, Ltd. Close Encounters with Extra-Terrestri-

als - Edited Entry. h2g2. Accessed September 10, 2021. https://h2g2.com/edited_entry/A965234; Judith Joyce. *The Weiser Field Guide to the Paranormal: Abductions, Apparitions, ESP, Synchronicity, and More Unexplained Phenomena from Other Realms*. San Francisco, CA: Weiser Books, 2011, 7; Edith Fiore. *Encounters: A Psychologist Reveals Case Studies of Abductions by Extraterrestrials*. New York: Ballantine Books, 1997; William J. Baldwin, Essay. In *Ce-VI: Close Encounters of the Possession Kind*. Terra Alta, WV: Headline Books, 1999, 70; Richard F Haines. *CE-5: Close Encounters of the Fifth Kind: 242 Case Files Exposing Alien Contact*. Naperville, IL: Sourcebooks, 1999; J. Allen Hynek. *The UFO Experience: A Scientific Inquiry*. Ballantine Books, 1972.

241 Dennis Stacy. Close Encounter with Dr. J. Allen Hynek. CUFON. Updated 1991. http://www.cufon.org/cufon/hynekint.htm.

242 Michael D. Swords. Project Sign and the Estimate of the Situation. Bibliotecapleyades. Accessed July 15, 2021. https://www.bibliotecapleyades.net/sociopolitica/sign/sign.htm.

243 Unidentified Flying Objects and Air Force Project Blue Book. USAF. June 1995. https://www.nsa.gov/Portals/70/documents/news-features/declassified-documents/ufo/usaf_fact_sheet_95_03.pdf; Unidentified Flying Objects and Air Force Project Blue Book. U.S. Air Force, April 25, 2003. https://www.af.mil/About-Us/Fact-Sheets/Display/Article/104590/unidentified-flying-objects-and-air-force-project-blue-book/.

244 *Richard Lewis - Air Force at the Last Space Shuttle Launch!.Wmv*. YouTube, 2011. https://www.youtube.com/watch?v=1Kn73spglIA.

245 Best of 2001: Best Ufo Sightings. *San Diego Reader*. December 27, 2001. https://www.sandiegoreader.com/news/2001/dec/27/best-2001-best-ufo-sightings/.

246 Borrego Springs, CA. UFO Hunters. June 9, 2017. https://www.ufo-hunters.com/sightings/search/59744b2d9d2e4cd486f659c3/UFO%20Sighting%20in%20Borrego%20Springs,%20CA%20on%20Tuesday%2006%20June%202017.

247 UFO Sighting in Borrego Springs, California on 2018-02-17. UFOMG. February 19, 2018. https://ufomg.com/2018/02/19/ufo-sighting-in-borrego-springs-california-on-2018-02-17-083000-two-bright-lights-hover-then-fade-

out/.

248 Hynek. *The UFO Experience*

249 Ibid.

250 Ibid.

251 Ibid.

252 Area 51 'Declassified' in U-2 Spy Plane History. BBC News, August 16, 2013. https://www.bbc.com/news/world-us-canada-23731759; Area 51 Fast Facts. Cable News Network, August 2, 2021. https://www.cnn.com/2019/07/31/us/area-51-fast-facts/index.html; Matt Blitz. The Real Story behind the Myth of Area 51, America's Most Famous Top-Secret Military Base. Popular Mechanics, April 30, 2021. https://www.popularmechanics.com/military/research/a24152/area-51-history/; Michael Brice-Saddler. Half a million people signed up to storm Area 51. What happens if they actually show? The *Washington Post*. July 12, 2019. https://www.washingtonpost.com/national-security/2019/07/13/half-million-people-signed-up-storm-area-what-happens-if-they-actually-show-up/; Annie Jacobsen. *Area 51: An Uncensored History of America's Top Secret Military Base*. New York: Back Bay Books, 2012; Ben R. Rich, and Leo Janos. *Skunk Works: A Personal Memoir of My Years at Lockheed*. Boston: Back Bay Books, 1996.

253 Secrets in the Sky: The Untold Story of Skunk Works. History. Accessed July 15, 2021. https://www.history.com/specials/secrets-in-the-sky-the-untold-story-of-skunk-works; Ben R. Rich, and Leo Janos. *Skunk Works: A Personal Memoir of My Years at Lockheed*. Boston: Back Bay Books, 1996; Jay Miller. *Lockheed Martin's Skunk Works*. Leicester: Midland Publishing, 1995.

254 8 News NOW Las Vegas. Bob Lazar describes alien technology housed at secret S-4 base in Nevada -- Part 5. YouTube video. November 8, 2019. https://www.youtube.com/watch?v=4UjqFaQq_7I; "Bob Lazar." Wikipedia. Accessed September 2, 2021. https://en.wikipedia.org/wiki/Bob_Lazar.

255 George C. Wilson. Carter to Support New U.S. Bomber. The *Washington Post*. August 14, 1980. https://www.washingtonpost.com/archive/politics/1980/08/14/carter-to-support-new-us-bomber/d449b8bf-5f2f-4a78-829e-148f5c654c1d/.

256 25th anniversary of B-2 stealth bomber's first flight. The Antelope Valley

Times. July 17, 2014. https://theavtimes.com/2014/07/17/25th-anniversary-of-b-2-stealth-bombers-first-flight/.

257 John T. Correll. Jack Northrop and the Flying Wing. *Air Force* magazine. December 21, 2016. https://www.airforcemag.com/article/jack-northrop-and-the-flying-wing/; Rob V. History of the Flying Wing (from the Early 1900's & Beyond). Aviation History - Century of Flight, December 15, 2020. https://www.century-of-flight.net/history-of-flying-wings/#:~:text=%20History%20of%20the%20Flying%20Wing%20%201,a%20tailless%20craft%2C%20and%20he%20created...%20More%20; Jason C. Engle. Flashback: Back to the Future: The Resurgence of the Flying Wing in the 21st Century. Air Force Materiel Command, December 17, 2019. https://www.afmc.af.mil/News/Article-Display/Article/2041005/flashback-back-to-the-future-the-resurgence-of-the-flying-wing-in-the-21st-cent/.

258 Ibid.

259 "Pin on the Unexplained." Pinterest. Accessed September 10, 2021. https://www.pinterest.com/pin/262827328231073815/.

260 Supersonic Flying Saucers Sighted by Idaho Pilot. *The Chicago Sun*. June 6, 1947, sec. In These United States. Tony Long; June 24, 1947: They Came from ... Outer Space? Wired. Conde Nast, June 24, 2011. https://www.wired.com/2011/06/0624first-flying-saucer-sighting/; Phil Wright. The Sighting. East Oregonian, December 13, 2018. https://www.eastoregonian.com/news/local/the-sighting/article_1dc33f61-868d-5c36-b159-87c8465fb662.html; Walt Crowley. Flying Saucers, February 6, 1999. https://www.historylink.org/File/2067. Charles Apple. UFOs over Washington: The First Report of 'Flying Saucers.' The Spokesman-Review, June 23, 2020. https://www.spokesman.com/stories/2020/jun/23/ufos-over-washington-first-report-flying-saucers/; History.com, ed. "Kenneth Arnold." History.com. A&E Television Networks, February 22, 2010. https://www.history.com/topics/paranormal/kenneth-arnold; Erik Lacitis. 'Flying Saucers' Became a Thing 70 Years Ago Saturday with Sighting near Mount Rainier. The Seattle Times Company, June 24, 2017. https://www.seattletimes.com/seattle-news/northwest/flying-saucers-became-a-thing-70-years-ago-saturday-with-sighting-near-mount-rainier/.

261 Megan Garber. The Man Who Introduced the World to Flying Saucers.

The *Atlantic*. June 15, 2014. https://www.theatlantic.com/technology/archive/2014/06/the-man-who-introduced-the-world-to-flying-saucers/372732/; Guy Aceto. Northrop's Radical Flying Wing Bomber of the 1940s. HistoryNet, July 21, 2020. https://www.historynet.com/northrops-radical-flying-wing-bomber-of-the-1940s.htm#:~:text=In%201940%2C%20while%20Hitler%27s%20legions,featuring%20a%20laminated%20wooden%20wing.

262 File: Edwards Air Force Base – Northrop YB-49 Flying Wing.jpg. Wikimedia Commons. Accessed July 15, 2021. https://commons.wikimedia.org/wiki/File:Edwards_Air_Force_Base_-_Northrop_YB-49_Flying_Wing.jpg.

263 Brandon Hamilton. World UFO Day: Arizona's top 5 UFO sightings. 12 News NBC. July 2, 2018. https://www.12news.com/article/news/local/arizona/world-ufo-day-arizonas-top-5-ufo-sightings/75-570088773; Flying-Saucer-UFO-Evidence. SANTAFEGHOSTANDHISTORYTOURS.com. Accessed September 10, 2021. http://www.santafeghostandhistorytours.com/FLYING-SAUCER-UFO-EVIDENCE.html; K. Randle. Beyond the Rhodes Photographs. Beyond the Rhodes Photographs, January 1, 1970. https://kevinrandle.blogspot.com/2010/10/beyond-rhodes-photographs.html; Patrick Gross. Project Blue Book: Pictures from Project Blue Book. ufologie. Accessed September 10, 2021. http://ufologie.patrickgross.org/htm/bluepics47.htm.

264 The mysterious mister Rhodes. Saturday Night Uforia. Accessed July 15, 2021. https://www.saturdaynightuforia.com/html/articles/articlehtml/mysteriousmrrhodes.html.

265 Ibid.

266 The mysterious mister Rhodes. Saturday Night Uforia. Accessed July 15, 2021. https://www.saturdaynightuforia.com/html/articles/articlehtml/mysteriousmrrhodes.html; Patrick Gross. Project Blue Book: Pictures from Project Blue Book. ufologie. Accessed September 10, 2021. http://ufologie.patrickgross.org/htm/bluepics47.htm.

267 The Rhodes Flying Saucer Photograph. UFO Casebook. August 24, 2011. https://www.ufocasebook.com/2011/rhodesphoto.html.

268 Flying-Saucer-UFO-Evidence. Santa Fe Ghost and History Tours. Accessed July 15, 2021. http://www.santafeghostandhistorytours.com/FLYING-SAU-

CER-UFO-EVIDENCE.html.

269 File: B2 silhouette.JPG. Wikimedia Commons. Accessed July 15, 2021. https://commons.wikimedia.org/wiki/File:B2_silhouette.JPG.

270 Kean, Leslie. *Ufos*. Random House Usa Inc, 2011. *UFO Chased by Belgium F16 Fighter Jets. Dailymotion*. Dailymotion, 2015. https://www.dailymotion.com/video/x3aflsj; Jeva Lange. 30 Years Later, We Still Don't Know What Really Happened during the Belgian UFO Wave. The Week, March 30, 2020. https://theweek.com/articles/905215/30-years-later-still-dont-know-what-really-happened-during-belgian-ufo-wave; The Belgium UFO Wave. UFO Evidence, August 24, 2014. https://web.archive.org/web/20140824010135/http://www.ufoevidence.org/documents/doc404.htm; James Crisp. UFO sightings in Belgium rocket. The *Telegraph*. January 3, 2019. https://www.telegraph.co.uk/news/2019/01/03/ufo-sightings-belgium-rocket/.

271 Belgian hit UFO image was polystyrene, says forger. Reuters July 27, 2011. https://www.reuters.com/article/oukoe-uk-belgium-ufo-idAFTRE76Q2DE20110727.

272 Beth Johnson. "I just stopped to take a picture of this strange site flying over the trees on 150 in Oak Ridge near Union Grove Church. It was large in size. Moving slowly. Not making any sound. Strange." *Facebook*. July 22, 2021. https://www.facebook.com/beth.johnson.5015/posts/10219724390966791.

273 Alex Hollings. Why the F-177 Nighthawk is Such a Badass Plane. *Popular Mechanics*. August 12, 2019. https://www.popularmechanics.com/military/aviation/a28670808/f-117-nighthawk/; The F-117 – Nine Amazing Facts about America's Legendary 'Stealth Fighter.' MilitaryHistoryNow.com, August 19, 2019. https://militaryhistorynow.com/2018/06/03/the-plane-that-wasnt-there-nine-amazing-facts-about-the-f-117-stealth-fighter/; Don Hollway. Stealth Secrets of the F-117 Nighthawk. HistoryNet, January 17, 2021. https://www.historynet.com/stealth-secrets-of-the-f-117-nighthawk-mar-96-aviation-history-feature.htm; F-117A Nighthawk Stealth Fighter. Airforce Technology, 1n.d.. https://www.airforce-technology.com/projects/f117/; F-117 Nighthawk. Lockheed Martin, October 19, 2020. https://www.lockheedmartin.com/en-us/news/features/history/f-117.html.

274 File: F-177 Nighthawk Front.jpg. Wikimedia Commons. Accessed July 15,

2021. https://commons.wikimedia.org/wiki/File:F-117_Nighthawk_Front.jpg.

275 Kyle Mizokami. The F-177 Nighthawk is Allegedly Retired. So Why Is I Secretly Flying Over L.A.? *Popular Mechanics.* February 23, 2021. https://www.popularmechanics.com/military/aviation/a35588664/f-117a-nighthawk-spotted-flying-over-los-angeles-mystery/; Woody, Christopher. The Air Force Retired Its First Stealth Aircraft More than a Decade Ago, but It's Still Lurking in the Skies over the US. Business Insider, July 30, 2018. https://www.businessinsider.com/air-force-f117-nighthawk-stealth-aircraft-still-flies-after-retirement-2018-7; Alex Hollings. The Supposedly-Retired F-117 Nighthawk Spotted in the Skies over LA. Sandboxx, July 15, 2020. https://www.sandboxx.us/blog/the-supposedly-retired-f-117-nighthawk-spotted-in-the-skies-over-la/; Tom Demerly. An F-117, a Stealth Jet That Retired in 2008, Was Spotted Flying over California Again. Business Insider, March 20, 2020. https://www.businessinsider.com/f117-stealth-jet-seen-flying-in-star-wars-canyon-california-2020-3.

276 Rumors of Secret Warplanes Preceded SR-72 Reveal. War is Boring. Medium. November 1, 2013. https://medium.com/war-is-boring/rumors-of-secret-warplanes-preceded-sr-72-reveal-90691e28b42.

277 Ben R. Rich. *Skunk Works.* Back Bay Books, 1996; ("Aurora Myth," Aerospace Daily, 9 October 1990, p. 34;

278 Ben R. Rich. *Skunk Works.* Back Bay Books, 1996; John Pike. Military. Mystery Aircraft - Aurora. Accessed September 11, 2021. https://www.globalsecurity.org/military/systems/aircraft/aurora.htm.

279 James Randerson. Is it a bird? Is it a plane? No It's a secret US spy plane. The *Guardian.* June 24, 2006. https://www.theguardian.com/science/2006/jun/24/freedomofinformation.usnews; Skunk Works Revenues Point to Active Aurora Program, Kemper Says. *Aerospace Daily,* 17 July 1992, p. 102; Sweetman, Bill. The Top-Secret Warplanes of Area 51. Popular Science, October 2006. https://web.archive.org/web/20070706220945/http:/www.popsci.com/popsci/aviationspace/95e16f096bd8d010vgnvcm1000004eecbccdrcrd/6.html; David Cenciotti. B-2 Spirit or New Mysterious Stealth Plane? New Image of Triangular Shaped Plane Emerges. The Aviationist, April 27, 2014. https://

theaviationist.com/2014/04/17/new-image-triangular-mystery/; UFO Files: Secret US Spy Plane Aurora Could Be behind Sightings. The Telegraph Media Group, August 17, 2009. https://www.telegraph.co.uk/news/newstopics/howaboutthat/ufo/6039934/UFO-files-secret-US-spy-plane-Aurora-could-be-behind-sightings.html; Newton, Edmund. Secret Is out on 'Quakes': It's a Spy Plane : Aviation: Analysts Believe That Aurora, a Craft That Can Travel 4,000 M.p.h., Could Be the Cause of Frayed Morning Nerves. Los Angeles Times, April 17, 1992. https://www.latimes.com/archives/la-xpm-1992-04-17-me-607-story.html.

280 Kyle Mizokami. Everything We Know About the Air Force's Secret X-37B Spaceplane. *Popular Mechanics*. July 30, 2019. https://www.popularmechanics.com/military/research/a28543381/x-37b/; Christopher Woody. The Mysterious X-37B Space Plane Is Going Back into Orbit - Here's What It'll Be Doing up There. Business Insider, May 6, 2020. https://www.businessinsider.com/missions-experiments-for-space-force-mysterious-x-37b-space-plane-2020-5; X-37B Orbital Test Vehicle. U.S. Air Force, August 7, 2020. https://www.af.mil/About-Us/Fact-Sheets/Display/Article/104539/x-37b-orbital-test-vehicle/; Valerie Insinna. US Space Force Launches the Mysterious X-37B Space Plane. Defense News, May 18, 2020. https://www.defensenews.com/space/2020/05/17/the-space-force-just-launched-the-mysterious-x-37b-space-plane/; Kiona Smith-Strickland. What's the X-37 Doing up There? Air & Space Magazine, January 20, 2016. https://www.airspacemag.com/space/spaceplane-x-37-180957777/; Sandra Erwin. U.S. Air Force X-37B Spaceplane off to Its Sixth Mission. SpaceNews, August 13, 2020. https://spacenews.com/u-s-air-force-x-37b-spaceplane-off-to-its-sixth-mission/; Mike Wall. X-37B: The Air Force's Mysterious Space Plane. Space, May 15, 2020. https://www.space.com/25275-x37b-space-plane.html.

281 X-37B breaks record, lands after 780 days in orbit. U.S. Air Force. October 27, 2019. https://www.af.mil/News/Article-Display/Article/1999734/x-37b-breaks-record-lands-after-780-days-in-orbit/.

282 Michael E. Salla. *Insiders Reveal Secret Space Programs & Extraterrestrial Alliances*. Exopolitics Institute, 2015.

283 Chandelis Duster. Defense Department confirms leaked video of unidenti-

fied aerial phenomena is real. CNN Politics. April 15, 2021. https://www.cnn.com/2021/04/15/politics/unidentified-aerial-phenomena-defense-department/index.html; Josh K. Elliott. Leaked Footage of 'Pyramid-Shaped' Ufos Is Real, Pentagon Says. Global News. Global News, April 14, 2021. https://globalnews.ca/news/7757069/ufo-pyramid-sphere-leaked-footage-pentagon-uap/; Mia Jankowicz. The Pentagon Confirmed That a Video Showing a Triangular UFO Is Real and Taken by the US Navy. Business Insider. Business Insider, April 16, 2021. https://www.businessinsider.com/pentagon-confirms-ufo-video-real-taken-by-us-navy-cnn-2021-4; Jason Carr. Pentagon Says Leaked UFO Video Is Authentic. WDIV ClickOnDetroit, April 19, 2021. https://www.clickondetroit.com/news/national/2021/04/19/pentagon-says-leaked-ufo-video-is-authentic/; Chandelis Duster. Pentagon Says This Video Taken by Navy Is Indeed a UFO. WXII, July 1, 2021. https://www.wxii12.com/article/pentagon-says-this-video-taken-by-navy-is-indeed-a-ufo/36143765#.

284 File: TriangleBelgium1990.jpg. Wikimedia Commons. Accessed July 15, 2021. https://commons.wikimedia.org/wiki/File:TriangleBelgium1990.jpg.

285 Josh K. Elliott. Leaked footage of 'pyramid-shaped' UFOS is real, Pentagon says. Global News. Updated April 14, 2021. https://globalnews.ca/news/7757069/ufo-pyramid-sphere-leaked-footage-pentagon-uap/.

286 Hilkevitch. In the sky! A bird?

287 Ibid.

288 Hilkevitch. In the sky! A bird?; Richard F. Haines, ed. Report of an Unidentified Aerial Phenomenon and its Safety Implications at O'Hare International Airport on November 7, 2006. Static1, May 14, 2007. https://static1.squarespace.com/static/5cf80ff422b5a90001351e31/t/5d02ec731230e20001528e2c/1560472703346/NARCAP_TR-10.pdf.

289 Chicago O'Hare International Airport UFO Sighting Occurred on November 7, 2006. Digital Research Library of Illinois History Journal. July 11, 2019. https://drloihjournal.blogspot.com/2019/07/chicago-ohare-international-airport-ufo-sighting-occurred-on-november-7-2006.html.

290 Ralph Blumenthal and Leslie Kean. No Longer in Shadows, Pentagon's U.F.O. Unit Will Make Some Findings Public. The *New York Times*. Updated June 3,

2021. https://www.nytimes.com/2020/07/23/us/politics/pentagon-ufo-harry-reid-navy.html; OFFICE OF THE DIRECTOR OF NATIONAL INTELLIGENCE. Preliminary Assessment: Unidentified Aerial Phenomena. Director of National Intelligence. dni.gov, June 25, 2021. https://www.dni.gov/files/ODNI/documents/assessments/Prelimary-Assessment-UAP-20210625.pdf; ODNI Office of Strategic Communications. PRELIMINARY ASSESSMENT: UNIDENTIFIED AERIAL PHENOMENA. Director of National Intelligence, June 25, 2021. https://www.dni.gov/index.php/newsroom/reports-publications/reports-publications-2021/item/2223-preliminary-assessment-unidentified-aerial-phenomena; Julian E. Barnes, and Helene Cooper. U.S. Finds No Evidence of Alien Technology in Flying Objects, but Can't Rule It out, Either. The New York Times, June 3, 2021. https://www.nytimes.com/2021/06/03/us/politics/ufos-sighting-alien-spacecraft-pentagon.html; Julian E. Barnes. U.S. Has No Explanation for Unidentified Objects and Stops Short of Ruling Out ALIENS. The New York Times, June 25, 2021. https://www.nytimes.com/2021/06/25/us/politics/pentagon-ufo-report.html; Matt Stieb, and Chas Danner. Pentagon Releases UFO Report: Here's What We Know. Intelligencer, July 5, 2021. https://nymag.com/intelligencer/article/pentagon-ufo-report-what-we-know.html; Joe Pappalardo. How the PENTAGON Learned to Start Worrying and Investigate UFOs. National Geographic, June 25, 2021. https://www.nationalgeographic.com/science/article/what-the-pentagon-report-says-about-ufos; David Leonard. Up in the Air! US Government's UFO Report Stirs Range of Reactions. Space.com, June 28, 2021. https://www.space.com/pentagon-ufo-report-reactions-uap; Nicole Sganga, David Martin, Olivia Gazis, and Eleanor Watson. Pentagon Task Force's UFO Report Released - Many Cases Remain Unexplained. CBS News, June 25, 2021. https://www.cbsnews.com/news/pentagon-ufo-report-released-many-uap-cases-remain-unexplained/; Helene Cooper, Ralph Blumenthal, and Leslie Kean. Glowing Auras and 'Black MONEY': The Pentagon's Mysterious U.F.O. PROGRAM. The New York Times, December 16, 2017. https://www.nytimes.com/2017/12/16/us/politics/pentagon-program-ufo-harry-reid.html; To the Stars Academy of Arts & Science. TTSA Announces Support for UAP Task Force Inclusion in Intelligence Authorization Act for 2021. PRNewswire, June 24, 2020. https://www.prnewswire.com/news-releases/ttsa-announces-support-for-uap-task-force-inclusion-in-intelligence-authorization-act-for-2021-301083085.html.

291 Julian E. Barnes and Helene Cooper. U.S. Find No Evidence of Alien Technology in Flying Objects, but Can't Rule It Out, Either. The *New York Times*. Updated June 25, 2021. https://www.nytimes.com/2021/06/03/us/politics/ufos-sighting-alien-spacecraft-pentagon.html; Ryan W. Miller, and Matthew Brown. Government Ufo Report Finds No Evidence Flying Objects Are Aliens but Does Not Rule Possibility out, Reports Say. USA Today, June 4, 2021. https://www.usatoday.com/story/news/politics/2021/06/04/pentagon-ufo-report-no-evidence-aliens/7540528002/; US Military UFO REPORT 'Does Not Confirm or Rule out Alien Activity.' BBC News, June 4, 2021. https://www.bbc.com/news/world-us-canada-57355192.

292 Jason Abbruzzese. Obama on UFO videos: 'We don't know exactly what they are.' NBC News. Updated May 26, 2021. https://www.nbcnews.com/science/weird-science/obama-ufo-videos-dont-know-exactly-are-rcna963; Duncan Phenix. Barack Obama Talks about Ufos Again on Late Night Television." WGN, May 19, 2021. https://wgntv.com/news/barack-obama-talks-about-ufos-again-on-late-night-television/; "Obama Admits There Are Objects in the Sky That 'We Can't Explain.'" Yahoo! News, May 20, 2021. https://uk.news.yahoo.com/obama-admits-objects-sky-cant-141257373.html?guce_referrer=aHR0cHM6Ly93d3cuZ29vZ2xlLmNvbS8&guce_referrer_sig=AQAAAJckUMga9b0cON7m_YoK0eDZ5_wWhhwT9kJ2qjh-5VQfNZF-OnEITkmUPNZtlGFpAnT4ALkvI_2-BHdYTZ8amha3JS88vb-pe7xF5IBv7f4j44uvz8i0wNxb0GGTrG68rq3THXZh8HJeQFTX_6vUFm-HPUQmeOsLjf0IF2ipdmJLZRz&guccounter=2.

293 Barnes and Cooper. U.S. Find No Evidence of Alien Technology.

294 Ibid.

295 Cooper et al. Glowing Auras and 'Black Money.'

296 Sébastien Roblin. The Air Force admits the F-35 fighter jet costs too much. So it wants to spend even more. NBC News. March 7, 2021. https://www.nbcnews.com/think/opinion/air-force-admits-f-35-fighter-jet-costs-too-much-ncna1259781; Helene Cooper, Ralph Blumenthal, and Leslie Kean.

Glowing Auras and 'Black Money': The Pentagon's Mysterious U.F.O. Program. The New York Times, December 16, 2017. https://www.nytimes.com/2017/12/16/us/politics/pentagon-program-ufo-harry-reid.html.

297 Brad Howard. Expensive, massive and lethal: The future of the aircraft carrier. CNBC. February 23, 2021. https://www.cnbc.com/2021/02/23/-expensive-massive-and-lethal-the-future-of-the-aircraft-carrier.html#:~:text=The%20latest%20carrier%20in%20the,for%20months%20at%20a%20time.

298 Macias. Here's the firepower the Pentagon is asking for; Jamie, Whitney. Proposed 2022 DOD Budget Would Increase Defense Spending to $715 Billion -- $9.6 Billion over This Year. StackPath, June 3, 2021. https://www.intelligent-aerospace.com/military/article/14204537/proposed-2022-dod-budget-would-increase-defense-spending-to-715-billion-96-billion-over-this-year; The Department of Defense Releases the President's Fiscal Year 2022 Defense Budget. U.S. Department of Defense, May 28, 2021. https://www.defense.gov/Newsroom/Releases/Release/Article/2638711/the-department-of-defense-releases-the-presidents-fiscal-year-2022-defense-budg/.

299 President Dwight Eisenhower Farewell Address. C-SPAN video. Accessed July 15, 2021. https://www.c-span.org/video/?15026-1/president-dwight-eisenhower-farewell-address.

300 William I. Hitchcock. *The Age of Eisenhower: America and the World in the 1950s.* Simon & Schuster, 2018.

301 Preliminary Assessment: Unidentified Aerial Phenomena. dni.gov, June 25, 2021. https://www.dni.gov/files/ODNI/documents/assessments/Prelimary-Assessment-UAP-20210625.pdf.

302 Air Force Instruction 10-206. The Black Vault. October 15, 2008. http://www.theblackvault.com/documents/ufos/AFI10-206.pdf.

303 Lee Speigel. Air Force UFO Rules Vanish After Huffington Post Inquiry. *Huffington Post*. Updated December 6, 2017. https://www.huffpost.com/entry/air-force-deletes-ufo-rep_n_982128.

304 File: PurportedUFO2.jpg. Wikimedia Commons. Accessed July 15, 2021. https://commons.wikimedia.org/wiki/File:PurportedUFO2.jpg.

305 How To Investigate a Flying Saucer. Central Intelligence Agency (CIA). January 21, 2016. https://www.cia.gov/stories/story/how-to-investigate-a-fly-

ing-saucer/; UFO1.jpg. CIA. Accessed July 15, 2021. https://www.cia.gov/static/417812c7f9919ac5f57a2f43cf979686/4a838/UFO1.jpg.

306 *Amateur Photographs of Alleged UFOs. Cia.gov.* Accessed September 11, 2021. https://www.cia.gov/static/417812c7f9919ac5f57a2f43cf979686/4a838/UFO1.jpg.

307 UFO-Sightings = Photos & Data: They are Here! What Do They Want? Santa Fe Ghost and History Tours. Accessed July 15, 2021. http://www.santafeghostandhistorytours.com/UFO-SIGHTINGS.html.

308 David Hatcher Childress, and Bill Clendenon. *Atlantis & the Power System of the Gods: Mercury Vortex Generators & The Power System of Atlantis*, p. 59. Kempton, IL: Adventures Unlimited, 2002.

309 UFO Sighting Photos: 10 Unexplained Pictures From History. *TIME*. Accessed July 15m 2021. https://time.com/4232540/history-ufo-sightings/.

310 New Jersey UFO photos taken during 1952 UFO wave. Open Minds. Accessed July 15, 2021. http://www.openminds.tv/ufo-new-jersey-1952.

311 Bryan Denson. 1997 story: Fifty years of UFO, the truth is still out there. The *Oregonian*. Updated January 9, 2019. https://www.oregonlive.com/history/2015/05/1997_story_fifty_years_of_ufo.html; John Killen. UFO Photos Taken near Mcminnville Still Raise Questions. The Oregonian, May 12, 2015. https://www.oregonlive.com/history/2015/05/past_tense_oregon_ufo_photos_t.html.

312 Edward U. Codon and Daniel S. Gillmor. *Final report of the Scientific Study of Unidentified Flying Objects: Conducted By the University of Colorado Under Contract to the United States Air Force*. E. P. Dutton & Co, 1969.

313 Farmer Trent's Flying Saucer. *LIFE* magazine. June 26, 1950. https://books.google.com/books?id=50oEAAAAMBAJ&pg=PA40#v=onepage&q&f=false.

314 Jerome Clark. *The UFO Book: Encyclopedia of the Extraterrestrial*. Visible Ink Press, 1997.

315 Codon and Gillmore. *Final report of the Scientific Study of Unidentified Flying Objects*.

316 Papers: The McMinnville Photos. Dr. Bruce Maccabee Research Website. Accessed July 15, 2021. http://www.nicap.org/reports/500511_brumac.8k.com_trent2.pdf; Codon and Gillmore. *Final report of the Scientific Study of*

Unidentified Flying Objects.

317 Denson. 1997 story: Fifty years of UFO.

318 Papers: The McMinnville Photos.

319 File: Tren1 600dpi.jpg. Wikimedia Commons. Accessed July 15, 2021. https://commons.wikimedia.org/wiki/File:Trent1_600dpi.jpg.

320 Eric Betz. Aqueducts: How Ancient Rome Brought Water to Its People. *Discover* magazine. October 26, 2020. https://www.discovermagazine.com/planet-earth/aqueducts-how-ancient-rome-brought-water-to-its-people; Aqueducts Move Water in the Past and Today. USGS. Accessed July 15, 2021. https://www.usgs.gov/special-topic/water-science-school/science/aqueducts-move-water-past-and-today?qt-science_center_objects=0#qt-science_center_objects; Christopher McFadden. Uncovering the Secrets of Ancient Roman Aqueducts. Interesting Engineering, March 12, 2018. https://interestingengineering.com/the-rise-and-fall-of-roman-aqueducts; Aqueducts Move Water in the Past and Today. usgs.gov. Accessed September 11, 2021. https://www.usgs.gov/special-topic/water-science-school/science/aqueducts-move-water-past-and-today?qt-science_center_objects=0#qt-science_center_objects; Roman Aqueducts, Aqueducts in Rome. Rome.info. Accessed September 11, 2021. https://www.rome.info/ancient/aqueducts/.

321 Marie D. Jackson et al. Phillipsite and Al-tobermorite mineral cements produced through low-temperature water-rock reactions in Roman marine concrete. *American Mineralogist* 102. https://doi.org/10.2138/am-2017-5993CCBY; Signe Dean. Why 2,000 Year-Old Roman Concrete Is So Much Better Than What We Produce Today. Science Alert. July 4, 2017. https://www.sciencealert.com/why-2-000-year-old-roman-concrete-is-so-much-better-than-what-we-produce-today.

322 Jaclyn Anglis. What Was Greek Fire? Discover The Secret Weapon Of The Byzantine Empire. All That's Interesting. Updated July 2, 2020. https://allthatsinteresting.com/greek-fire#:~:text=Greek%20fire%20was%20created%20in%20the%207th%20century,,his%20concerns%20about%20the%20Arabs%20capturing%20his%20city.

323 Helicopter Hieroglyphs Explained. Rain is Cool. May 23, 2010. http://raincool.blogspot.com/2010/05/helicopter-hieroglyphs-explained.html; File: Hi-

eroglif z Abydos.jpg. Wikimedia Commons. Accessed July 15, 2021. https://commons.wikimedia.org/wiki/File:Hieroglif_z_Abydos.jpg; Thierry. The Abydos Temple Helicopter. fineart.be, July 28, 2008. https://web.archive.org/web/20050728103638/http:/www.finart.be/UfocomHq/usabydos.htm.

324 Helicopter Hieroglyphs Explained; The Abydos Temple Helicopter.

325 Gleason Archer. *A Survey of Old Testament Introduction*. Moody Publishers, 2007; Creation or Evolution. United Church of God and International Association. Accessed July 15, 2021. https://www.ucg.org/bible-study-tools/booklets/creation-or-evolution-does-it-really-matter-what-you-believe/earths-age-does-the-bible.

326 Smithsonian. Scientists discover evidence of early human innovation, pushing back evolutionary timeline. Science Daily. March 15, 2018. https://www.sciencedaily.com/releases/2018/03/180315140733.htm; Stephanie Pappas. Start date for human civilization oved back 20,000 years or so. The *Christian Science Monitor*. July 30, 2012. https://www.csmonitor.com/Science/2012/0730/Start-date-for-human-civilization-moved-back-20-000-years-or-so.

327 Adam Frank. Was There a Civilization on Earth Before Humans? The *Atlantic*. April 13, 2018. https://www.theatlantic.com/science/archive/2018/04/are-we-earths-only-civilization/557180/; Andrew Curry. Gobekli Tepe: The World's First Temple? *Smithsonian* magazine. November 2008. https://www.smithsonianmag.com/history/gobekli-tepe-the-worlds-first-temple-83613665/; Steven Ashley. Could an Industrial Prehuman Civilization Have Existed on Earth before Ours? Scientific American, April 23, 2018. https://www.scientificamerican.com/article/could-an-industrial-prehuman-civilization-have-existed-on-earth-before-ours/; Deborah Byrd. Was Another Civilization on Earth before Humans? EarthSky, April 18, 2018. https://earthsky.org/earth/earlier-human-civilization-silurian-hypothesis/.

328 If we weren't the first industrial civilization on Earth, would we ever know? *MIT Technology Review*. April 20, 2018. https://www.technologyreview.com/2018/04/20/143758/if-we-werent-the-first-industrial-civilization-on-earth-would-we-ever-know/.

329 Elizabeth Zubritsky. Curiosity finds evidence of Mars crust contributing to atmosphere. Phys.org. September 30, 2016. https://phys.org/news/2016-09-cu-

riosity-evidence-mars-crust-contributing.html.

330 Ibid.

331 John Brandenberg. Evidence for a Large, Natural, Paleo-Nuclear, Reactor on Mars. March 2011. https://www.researchgate.net/publication/252946588_Evidence_for_a_Large_Natural_Paleo-Nuclear_Reactor_on_Mars.

332 John Brandon. Was There a Natural Nuclear Blast on Mars? Fox News. Updated June 22, 2015. https://www.foxnews.com/science/was-there-a-natural-nuclear-blast-on-mars.

333 John E. Brandenburg. Evidence of a Massive Thermonuclear Explosion on Mars. *Journal of Cosmology* 25. November 20, 2014. https://archive.org/stream/pdfy-sRmXR7I7gg2jEQFd/Brandenburg_djvu.txt.

334 Morgan McFall-Johnsen and Dave Mosher. Elon Musk says he plans to send 1 million people to Mars by 20150. Business Insider. January 17, 2020. https://www.businessinsider.com/elon-musk-plans-1-million-people-to-mars-by-2050-2020-1; Jamie Carter. NASA Just Left for Mars. Here's How Many Humans Will Be Needed to Populate the Planet. *Forbes*. July 30, 2020. https://www.forbes.com/sites/jamiecartereurope/2020/07/30/nasa-just-left-for-mars-heres-how-many-humans-will-be-needed-to-colonize-the-red-planet/?sh=6f7e70ef29bd.

335 Brandenburg. Evidence of a Massive Thermonuclear Explosion.

336 Handwritten letter by Albert Einstein with famous E=mc2 equation sells for $1.2 million at auction; Elizabeth Howell. Einstein's Theory of Special Relativity. Space.com, March 30, 2017. https://www.space.com/36273-theory-special-relativity.html#:~:text=One%20of%20the%20most%20famous,forms%20of%20the%20same%20thing; Ethan Siegel. Why Does E=Mc^2? Forbes, May 27, 2016. https://www.forbes.com/sites/startswithabang/2016/05/27/why-does-emc2/?sh=3c7d57ca3a70; Nova | Einstein's Big Idea | Library Resource Kit: E = MC2 Explained. PBS. Accessed September 11, 2021. https://www.pbs.org/wgbh/nova/einstein/lrk-hand-emc2expl.html.

337 Handwritten letter by Albert Einstein with famous E=mc2 equation sells for $1.2 million at auction. CBS News. May 22, 2021. https://www.cbsnews.com/news/albert-einstein-emc2-equation-letter-auction-1-2-million/.

338 Adam Eliuahu Berkowitz. Scientists Admit Biblical Account of Destruction

of Sodom is Correct. Breaking Christian News. November 26, 2018. https://www.breakingchristiannews.com/articles/m_display_art.html?ID=26289.
339 Ibid.
340 Evidence of Nuclear War in the distant Past: The destruction of Sodom and Gomorrah. Ancient Code. Accessed July 15, 2021. https://www.ancient-code.com/evidence-of-nuclear-war-in-the-distant-past-the-destruction-of-sodom-and-gomorrah/.
341 Xavier Séguin. The Nuke Bomb of Yahveh. Eden Saga. April 1, 2014. https://www.ancient-code.com/evidence-of-nuclear-war-in-the-distant-past-the-destruction-of-sodom-and-gomorrah/.
342 Ibid.
343 Ibid.
344 Richard A. Lovett. Bible Accounts Supported by Dead Sea Disaster Record? *National Geographic*. December 8, 2011. https://www.nationalgeographic.com/science/article/111208-dead-sea-bible-biblical-salt-dry-science; Amit Malewar. How All Human Civilization Abruptly Ended on the Banks of the Dead Sea? Tech Explorist, November 23, 2018. https://www.techexplorist.com/how-all-human-civilization-abruptly-ended-on-the-banks-of-the-dead-sea/18782/; Owen Jarus. Cosmic Airburst May Have Wiped out Part of the Middle East 3,700 Years Ago. LiveScience, November 28, 2018. https://www.livescience.com/64179-ancient-cosmic-airburst-middle-east.html; Amanda Borschel-Dan. Evidence of Sodom? Meteor Blast Cause of Biblical Destruction, Say Scientists. The Times of Israel, November 22, 2018. https://www.timesofisrael.com/evidence-of-sodom-meteor-blast-cause-of-biblical-destruction-say-scientists/; Eric Mack. New Science Suggests Biblical City of Sodom Was Smote by an Exploding Meteor. Forbes, December 4, 2018. https://www.forbes.com/sites/ericmack/2018/12/04/new-science-suggests-biblical-city-of-sodom-was-smote-by-an-exploding-meteor/?sh=5282574e5c67; Bruce Bower. An Exploding Meteor May Have Wiped out Ancient Dead Sea Communities. Science News, August 8, 2019. https://www.sciencenews.org/article/exploding-meteor-may-have-wiped-out-ancient-dead-sea-communities.
345 File: Raphael – Ezekial's Vision.jpg. Wikimedia Commons. Accessed July 15, 2021. https://commons.wikimedia.org/wiki/File:Raphael_-_Ezekiel%27s_Vi-

sion.jpg.

346 File: Madonna Col Bambino e San Giovannio – 1400s.png. Wikimedia Commons. Accessed July 15, 2021. https://commons.wikimedia.org/wiki/File:Madonna_Col_Bambino_e_San_Giovannino_-_1400s.png.

347 Thomas Horn and Cris Putnam. *Exo-Vaticana*. Crane, MO: Defender, 2013.

348 Keel. *Operation Trojan Horse.*

349 Greg Daugherty. George Adamski Got Famous Sharing His UFO Photos and Alien 'Encounters.' History. January 9, 2020. https://www.history.com/news/george-adamski-ufo-alien-photos; The truth is out there? Billy Meier's UFO images. BBC News. December 3, 2019. https://www.bbc.com/news/in-pictures-50634120; The Zeta Reticuli (or Ridiculi) Incident. Astronomy.com. Accessed September 11, 2021. https://astronomy.com/bonus/zeta; 10 Reasons Why Aliens Are Actually Fallen Angels or Demons. Alien UFO Sightings, August 14, 2017. https://alien-ufo-sightings.com/2016/04/10-reasons-aliens-actually-fallen-angels-demons/.

350 Archbishop Chrysostomos of Etna. Alien Abductions and the Orthodox Christian. Orthodox Christian Information Center. Accessed July 15, 2021. http://orthodoxinfo.com/praxis/alien_abduct.aspx.

351 Juju Chang and Jim Dubreuil. Man Claims Aliens Send Him Messages. ABC News. August 18, 2009. https://abcnews.go.com/Primetime/story?id=8347902.

352 J. Allen Hynek and Jacques Vallee. *The Edge of Reality: A Progress Report on Unidentified Flying Objects*. CreateSpace Independent Publishing, 1975.

353 Ibid.

354 An Orthodox Christian Understanding of Unidentified Flying Objects (UFOs). Transfiguration of the Lord. Accessed July 15, 2021. http://www.holy-transfiguration.org/library_en/sc_ufo4.html.

355 Hynek and Jacques Vallee. *The Edge of Reality*; Seraphim Rose. *Orthodoxy and the Religion of the Future*. Platina, CA: Saint Herman of Alaska Brotherhood, 2013.

356 Debbora Battaglia. *E.T. Culture: Anthropology in Outerspaces*. Duke University Press Books, 2006; C. D. B. Bryan. *Close Encounters of the Fourth Kind: Alien Abduction, UFOs, and The Conference at M.I.T.* Knopf, 1995; Christine Aprile.

Nordic Aliens: Mystery of Nordic Extraterrestrials. Gaia, November 28, 2018. https://www.gaia.com/article/nordic-aliens.

357 Mark O'Connel. *The Close Encounters Man*. Dey Street Books, 2017, p. 102.

358 Matthew Shaer. A Secret Tunnel Found in Mexico May Finally Solve the Mysteries of Teotihuacán. *Smithsonian* magazine. June 2016. https://www.smithsonianmag.com/history/discovery-secret-tunnel-mexico-solve-mysteries-teotihuacan-180959070/; Temple of Quetzalcóatl. Britannica. Accessed July 15, 2021. https://www.britannica.com/place/Temple-of-Quetzalcoatl; Return of Pahana – the Lost White Brother of the Hopi and the Sacred Tablet. Ancient Pages, June 5, 2021. https://www.ancientpages.com/2018/03/05/return-of-pahana-the-lost-white-brother-of-the-hopi-and-the-sacred-tablets/.

359 5175. Nachash. Bible Hub. Accessed July 15, 2021; The Shining One – The Old Serent. Harrison Woodward. March 6, 2014. https://harrisonwoodard.com/2014/03/the-shining-one-the-old-serpent/; Genesis 3:1 - 'Serpent' or 'Shining One'? Biblical Hermeneutics Stack Exchange, September 1, 1968. https://hermeneutics.stackexchange.com/questions/47317/genesis-31-serpent-or-shining-one; David Curtis. Spiritual Warfare Pt 3: Serpent or Shiny One? Ephesians 6:10-12 - Spiritual Warfare Pt 3: Serpent or Shiny One?: Berean Bible Church, February 1, 2015. https://www.bereanbiblechurch.org/transcripts/ephesians/eph-06_10-12_spiritual-warfare-pt03.htm; Bnonn Tennant. Who Is the Serpent in Genesis, and Is It an Actual Snake? Bnonn Tennant (the B Is Silent). bnonn.com, April 5, 2019. https://bnonn.com/who-is-the-serpent-in-genesis/.

360 Arthur C. Clarke: Biography. The Arthur C. Clarke Foundation. Accessed July 15, 2021. https://www.clarkefoundation.org/arthur-c-clarke-biography/.

361 Antonia Blumberg. Pope Francis Say He Would Baptize Martians, Asks 'Who Are We To Close Doors? *Huffington Post*. May 12, 2014. https://www.huffpost.com/entry/pope-francis-aliens_n_5310935; Pope Francis Offers Martians Baptism. ABC News, May 13, 2014. https://www.abc.net.au/news/2014-05-13/pope-offers-baptism-to-martians/5448548; Elizabeth Dias. Pope Francis: It's about More than Martians. Time, May 14, 2014. https://time.com/99616/for-pope-francis-its-about-more-than-martians/; Stoyan Zaimov. Pope Francis

Talks about Aliens; Says He Would Welcome Martians to Receive Baptism. The Christian Post, May 13, 2013. https://www.christianpost.com/news/pope-francis-talks-about-aliens-says-he-would-welcome-martians-to-receive-baptism-119630; Pope at Mass: The Holy Spirit Makes the Unthinkable Possible. Vatican Radio, May 12, 2014. http://www.archivioradiovaticana.va/storico/2014/05/12/pope_at_mass_the_holy_spirit_makes_the_unthinkable_possible/en1-798509.

362 2889. Kosmos. Bible Hub. Accessed July 15, 2021. https://biblehub.com/greek/2889.htm.

363 Michael Thomas. UFO's with Boyd Bushman and his last interview. YouTube video. October 24, 2014. https://www.youtube.com/watch?v=VA3HV_gfq80.

364 David Mikkelson. Did Boyd Bushman Provide Evidence of Alien Contact? Snopes. October 31, 2014. https://www.snopes.com/fact-check/boyd-bushman-aliens/.

365 Boyd Bushman. Rational Wiki. Accessed July 15, 2021. https://rationalwiki.org/wiki/Boyd_Bushman.

366 Cosmic Disclosure: Inside the Secret Space Program. Gaia. Accessed July 15, 2021. https://www.gaia.com/series/cosmic-disclosure.

367 Representative Dennis Kucinich UFO. YouTube video. October 31, 2007. https://www.youtube.com/watch?v=gSRWRbuMqyc.

368 Michael M. Phillips. What Kuncinich Saw: Witnesses Describe His Close Encounter. The *Wall Street Journal*. January 2, 2008. https://www.wsj.com/articles/SB119923872081461417.

369 "In Celebration of the Honorable Paul Hellyer," *Turner & Porter Funeral Directors* (https://turnerporter.permavita.com/site/TheHonorablePaulHellyer.html?s=40: accessed September 2, 2021), Paul Hellyer, died 08 August 2021.

370 Andrew Siddons. Visitors From Outer Space, Real or Not, Are Focus of Discussion in Washington. The *New York Times*. May 3, 2013. https://www.nytimes.com/2013/05/04/us/politics/panel-convenes-in-washington-to-discuss-aliens.html.

371 R. Siva Kumar. 'Aliens exist', confirms govt official. Headlines and Global News (HNGN). November 15, 2016. https://www.hngn.com/articles/217156/20161115/aliens-exist-confirms-former-govt-official.htm.

372 Paul Hellyer, Ex Defence Minister, Believes In Aliens. *Huffington Post*. Updated February 9, 2014. https://www.huffingtonpost.ca/2013/06/05/paul-hellyer-aliens-ufos-video_n_3390295.html; Kashmira Gander. Former Canadian defence secretary Paul Hellyer calls on governments to reveal UFO information. The *Independent*. April 20, 2015. https://www.independent.co.uk/news/world/americas/former-canadian-defence-secretary-paul-hellyer-calls-governments-reveal-ufo-information-10190024.html; "Paul Hellyer." Wikipedia. Accessed September 2, 2021. https://en.wikipedia.org/wiki/Paul_Hellyer; Jim Coyle. Cabal Keeping UFO Secrets to Blame for World's Woes, Says Former Cabinet Minister Paul Hellyer. thestar.com, April 11, 2015. https://www.thestar.com/news/gta/2015/04/11/cabal-keeping-ufo-secrets-to-blame-for-worlds-woes-says-former-cabinet-minister-paul-hellyer.html?rf; Chris Matyszczyk. Canada's Ex-Defense Minister: Aliens Would Give Us More Tech If We'd Stop Wars. CNET, January 5, 2014. https://www.cnet.com/news/canadas-ex-defense-minister-aliens-would-give-us-more-tech-if-wed-stop-wars/; Peter Rakobowchuk. Paul Hellyer Defends Aliens after Stephen Hawking's Warning. thestar.com, May 3, 2010. https://www.thestar.com/news/canada/2010/05/03/paul_hellyer_defends_aliens_after_stephen_hawkings_warning.html; Matthew Coutts. Former Canadian Defence Minister Paul Hellyer Says Aliens Will Help Humans If We Stop Wars. Yahoo! News, January 7, 2014. https://ca.news.yahoo.com/blogs/dailybrew/former-canadian-defence-minister-paul-hellyer-says-aliens-205829262.html.

373 Chris Lackner. Alien technology the best hope to 'save our planet:' [sic] ex-defence boss. Ottawa Citizen. February 28, 2007. https://web.archive.org/web/20080430213154/http://www.canada.com/ottawacitizen/news/story.html?id=3e57926c-bfeb-4ff3-acf6-50c575ee996c.

374 Chris Matyszczyk. Canada's Ex-Defense Minister: Aliens Would Give Us More Tech If We'd Stop Wars.

375 James Bartley. "Grand Strategy of the Reptilians." Bibliotecaplayades.com. Accessed September 11, 2021. https://www.bibliotecapleyades.net/sumer_anunnaki/reptiles/reptiles50a.htm.

376 VFTB 034: Joe Jordan – Stopping Alien Abductions. PID Radio. iHeart radio. February 7, 2010. https://www.iheart.com/podcast/966-pid-radio-29260505/

episode/vftb-034-joe-jordan-stopping-50522468/; Joe Jordan. Mystic-Skeptic Radio Show/Podcast with David Daniel Gonzalez. Other. *BuzzSprout*, August 9, 2017. https://www.buzzsprout.com/84561/475962; 27 Of Joe Jordan Podcasts Interviews: Updated Daily. OwlTail. Accessed September 11, 2021. https://www.owltail.com/people/NdzjL-joe-jordan/appearances; STOP Alien Abductions, Is It Possible? YES. CE4 Research Group . Accessed September 11, 2021. http://www.alienresistance.org/ce4.htm; *Alien Intrusion: Unmasking a Deception*. Accessed September 11, 2021. https://alienintrusion.com/cast.

377 Close Encounters of the Fourth Kind. CE4 Research Group.

378 Stanton T. Friedman and Kathleen Marden. *Captured! The Betty and Barney Hill UFO Experience: The True Story of the World's First Documented Alien Abduction*. Weiser, 2007; John G. Fuller. *The Interrupted Journey*. New York, NY: Dell Publishing, 1967; Walter N. Webb. A Dramatic UFO Encounter in the White Mountains, NH, Confidential Report to NICAP. NICAP.com, September 19, 1961. http://www.nicap.org/reports/610919hill_report2.pdf.

379 Brian Dunning. Betty and Barney Hill: The Original UFO Abduction. Skeptoid podcast. October 21, 2008. https://skeptoid.com/episodes/4124.

380 Ibid.

381 Higher, Faster, Stronger: 1950s Experimental Aircraft. *Wired*. August 23, 2008. https://www.wired.com/2008/08/gallery-experimental-50s-aircraft/.

382 Robert Sheaffer. *The UFO Verdict: Examining the Evidence*. Amherst, NY: Prometheus Books, 1986.

383 Clark. *The UFO Book*.

384 Chang and J Dubreuil. Man Claims Aliens Send Him Messages.

385 Chrysostomos of Etna. Alien Abductions and the Orthodox Christian.

386 Directory of Exorcists, Deliverance Counselors, and Investigators. Camelot Warfare Library. Accessed July 15, 2021. https://web.archive.org/web/20180630104937/http:/saint-mike.org/warfare/library/directory-exorcists-deliverance/.

387 Gabriele Amorth; Nicoletta V. MacKenzie, trans. *An Exorcist Tells His Story*. Ignatius Press, 1990.

388 Ibid.

389 Ibid.

390 Seraphim Rose. *Orthodoxy and the Religion of the Future*. St. Herman Press, 1997.
391 Ibid.
392 Brad Steiger. *Project Blue Book*. Ballantine Books, 1987.
393 John Ankerberg and John Weldon. *The Fact on UFO's and Other Supernatural Phenomena*. Harvest House Pub, 1992.
394 Keel. *Operation Trojan Horse*.
395 Clifford Wilson. *Close Encounters: A Better Explanation*. Master books, 1978.
396 An Orthodox Christian Understanding of Unidentified Flying Objects (UFOs).
397 *How To Summon A Pleiadian. YouTube*, 2017. https://www.youtube.com/watch?v=LKhrSuZ2oTk.
398 *How to Summon a Pleiadian Lightship. YouTube*, 2017. https://www.youtube.com/watch?v=AVJJ--3XQtk.
399 Project Blue Book (UFO) part 1 of 1. FBI Records: The Vault. Accessed July 15, 2021. https://vault.fbi.gov/Project%20Blue%20Book%20%28UFO%29%20/Project%20Blue%20Book%20%28UFO%29%20part%201%20of%201/view.

www.ingramcontent.com/pod-product-compliance
Lightning Source LLC
Chambersburg PA
CBHW072141100526
44589CB00015B/2033